RHETORIC, TECHNOLOGY,
AND THE VIRTUES

RHETORIC, TECHNOLOGY, AND THE VIRTUES

JARED S. COLTON
STEVE HOLMES

UTAH STATE UNIVERSITY PRESS
Logan

© 2018 by University Press of Colorado

Published by Utah State University Press
An imprint of University Press of Colorado
245 Century Circle, Suite 202
Louisville, Colorado 80027

 The University Press of Colorado is a proud member of the Association of University Presses.

The University Press of Colorado is a cooperative publishing enterprise supported, in part, by Adams State University, Colorado State University, Fort Lewis College, Metropolitan State University of Denver, Regis University, University of Colorado, University of Northern Colorado, Utah State University, and Western State Colorado University.

∞ This paper meets the requirements of the ANSI/NISO Z39.48-1992 (Permanence of Paper)

ISBN: 978-1-60732-805-6 (pbk.)
ISBN: 978-1-60732-806-3 (ebook)
DOI: https://doi.org/10.7330/9781607328063

Library of Congress Cataloging-in-Publication Data

Names: Colton, Jared S., author. | Holmes, Steve, 1983– author.
Title: Rhetoric, technology, and the virtues / Jared S. Colton, Steve Holmes.
Description: Logan : Utah State University Press, [2018] | Includes bibliographical references and index.
Identifiers: LCCN 2018021462| ISBN 9781607328056 (pbk.) | ISBN 9781607328063 (ebook)
Subjects: LCSH: Social media—Moral and ethical aspects. | Virtue. | Rhetoric—Moral and ethical aspects. | Technology—Moral and ethical aspects.
Classification: LCC HM741 .C634 2018 | DDC 302.23/1—dc23
LC record available at https://lccn.loc.gov/2018021462

Cover illustrations: © Naruchad (top left), © Xelbr/Shutterstock (bottom right)

CONTENTS

ACKNOWLEDGMENTS

All book projects are invariably the end product of a process that draws upon the generosity and kindness of large network of collaborators and conversations. In terms of direct input on the book, we are grateful to each of the anonymous reviewers of our manuscript. Each offered generous critical feedback that was instrumental in helping us develop and refine the scope of this book. We also extend our thanks to the editorial team at the University Press of Colorado and Utah State University Press. In particular, series editor Michael Spooner expertly helped us navigate our reviewers' feedback on the way toward publication. We also thank Rachael Lussos for her exacting copyediting and feedback on the final revision stages of this manuscript. Alongside direct input, countless individuals were instrumental in encouraging us to move forward with this project, but we would like to name a few: James J. Brown Jr., John Gallagher, Scot Barnett, John Duffy, Caddie Alford, Patricia Fancher, and Jonathan W. Stone.

Portions of chapter 1 appeared in earlier versions in "Ethos, Hexis, and the Case for Persuasive Technology," *enculturation* 23 (2016); an early version of chapter 3 appeared in "A Social Justice Theory of Active Equality for Technical Communication," *Journal of Technical Writing and Communication* (forthcoming); an early version of chapter 4 appeared in "Revisiting Digital Sampling Rhetorics with an Ethics of Care," *Computers and Composition: An International Journal* 40, (2016); and portions of chapter 5 appeared in earlier forms in "'Can We Name The Tools?' Ontologies of Code, Speculative Techné and Rhetorical Concealment," *Computational Culture* 5 (2015). We thank those publications for permission to reproduce this material in revised form.

Finally, both of us owe a tremendous debt to the faculty at our respective institutions, Utah State University and George Mason University, for their encouragement, as well as those at our doctoral program at Clemson University. Victor J. Vitanza chaired each of our dissertations in the RCID program, which was to our good fortune. His theoretical (anti)foundations undeniably impacted our views of rhetoric and ethics. We both had the benefit of learning from great scholars such as Steven B. Katz, Victor Villanueva, Patricia Ericsson, and many others. Perhaps

most influential to our project were the work of and discussions we had
with Todd May, whose thought on Rancière, Foucault, and Cavarero
heavily shaped our understanding of ethics.

JARED

Of course, I want to thank Steve for being such a dependable, driven,
and kind coauthor. I look forward to many more years of discussion and
collaboration. I also want to thank my girls, Olivia, Lucy, and Greta, for
bringing so much joy to my life and reminding me it's often the day-to-
day things that count the most. Finally, I give thanks to my wife, Ashley,
who knows this book as well as I do and has supported me throughout
this project and others with generosity, care, and patience. She is my life
partner, and I dedicate this book to her.

STEVE

While it seems obvious, I do wish to thank in print my coauthor Jared
for being an outstanding coauthor and collaborator the past few years. I
look forward to many more years of conversations and writing with him.
I also thank my parents (John and Pat) and my siblings (Nate, Chris,
and Emily). It was difficult enough finishing one—let alone two—book
projects during the same period of time, and I cannot begin to express
my thanks for their patience.

RHETORIC, TECHNOLOGY, AND THE VIRTUES

1
INTRODUCTION

About ten years ago, the social media company Viki (2007) launched a new interface with a novel purpose. Viki, a name that combines the words *wiki* and *video*, offers international audiences the ability to watch and subtitle global television programming and films in over two hundred languages. In one notable illustration of their aims, according to Tammy Nam in a post to *The Viki Blog*, April 24, 2014, marked the beginning of Viki's Billion Words March: "a year-long campaign to champion access to online TV shows and movies for 360 million people worldwide with deafness and hearing loss." To support this effort, Viki users engage in three main activities: segmenting (dividing videos into sections so textual content can be added), subtitling (primarily for translation), and captioning (service for deaf and hard-of-hearing audiences). Any available television show or film has a volunteer channel team. Each channel team is composed of segmenters, subtitlers, language moderators, and a channel manager. In addition to enabling content access for the deaf community, Viki lists the cross-cultural sharing of video content as another exigency, with Korean-to-English and Japanese-to-English translation (and vice versa) representing some of the most popular captioning practices. Viki has enjoyed a considerable degree of success, as the company's running tally counter on October 21, 2015, listed over 137,626 contributors who have captioned over 1,008,399,825 words.

In *Rhetoric, Technology, and the Virtues*, we seek to answer a basic question about this type of rhetorical situation: how and in what way should digital rhetoricians consider forms of networked collaboration such as Viki's and other digital practices to be ethical goods? For many readers, such a question may seem unnecessary to ask in the context of Viki captioners, as few would consider the captioners' practices as anything but an ethical good and a positive social contribution. But why? What working definition of ethics enables us to identify such a practice as an ethical good? Do we locate ethics within the individual moral motive of the captioners? Is it that a Viki user follows a correct a priori moral principle that is universal and unchanging for all time? Is it the greater

DOI: 10.7330/9781607328063.c001

good that makes these practices ethical? Is it care for the deaf and hard-of-hearing communities, the Other?

Furthermore, Viki is a complex ethical situation because not all its users are supporting a single ethical good, such as helping to create access for the deaf or hard-of-hearing community. A quick survey of Viki's community forum conversations reveals a wide range of value-driven rhetorical motives and purposes:

1. global university or high-school students who enjoy practicing translation into a nonnative language;

2. fans who enjoy sharing cultural programs across cultures (indeed, despite their Billion Words March campaign, Viki strongly appeals to television fan culture: "All subtitles are created by fans like you!") ("Join Viki's Subtitling Community" 2016);

3. individuals who simply enjoy being part of this particular community (i.e., they derive value out of the community interactions and not necessarily the specific practices of the community);

4. deaf and able-bodied users seeking to increase accessibility for the deaf community;

5. users incentivized to receive premium content in exchange for their actions, including access to georestricted video content (because Viki employs gamification,[1] some users may be motivated by a spirit of competition);

6. users taking part in numerous discussion forums devoted to a wide range of often heated criticism and debate about the quality of different programs' genres (drama versus comedy), which programs are more important to caption, and certain actors (we particularly recommend "The Pervert's Club" thread for a humorous discussion of male Korean television stars); and

7. users making ethical decisions entirely unrelated to captioning about how to respond to one another during live chats and timed comments in communal viewing sessions of a particular television program.

This list is hardly exhaustive. Any discussion of ethical practices in digital platforms such as Viki also now must consider James J. Brown's claim in his book *Ethical Programs* that not all ethical decisions in a networked space are even made by humans. He provocatively suggests that software carries its own forms of ethical decision making (Brown 2015). Continuing our example of Viki, this decision making would include the particular gamified algorithms that offer positive reinforcement in response to Viki users' activities, as well as the proprietary sharing of and restrictions to the invisible realms of packet sharing, cookies, and aggregating user data. As a case in point, many users have complained that the Viki app can be installed on some smart televisions and not others (such as Samsung), which represents an ethical decision at the level of protocol, inclusivity, and capitalistic competition.

Viki is hardly unique in this regard. Indeed, most if not all social media and networked interfaces play host to a wide range of ethical motives and practices that may not be attributable to a single or limited set of overarching purposes. Our concern is that the research fields related to rhetoric and composition have yet to develop specific frameworks that can better enable us to describe and evaluate these multiple distinct ethical motives. In *Rhetoric, Technology, and the Virtues*, we suggest that a neglected ethical paradigm, Aristotelian virtue ethics, offers important resources for addressing ethics in a networked age. In general, virtue ethics avoids rational principles, universal maxims, or means-ends thinking. Instead, virtue ethics is grounded in the dispositions individuals develop through their daily living practices—practices in the present that increasingly involve social media and digital technologies. Virtue ethics is historically interested in the cultivation of habitual dispositions, specifically those that guide ethical actions in particular and contingent rhetorical situations. As a result, we believe virtue ethics offers digital rhetoricians across a wide variety of institutional contexts—academic or industry—a set of important critical resources for helping to understand how we can distinguish ethical from unethical actions within networked spaces without having to impose the types of universal standards of morality decades of rhetorical scholarship and critical theory have decried.

BEYOND POSTMODERN ETHICAL CONCERNS

In chapter 2, we introduce virtue ethics in detail through an overview of some of the major ethical frameworks philosophers and rhetoricians have engaged with over the past few decades. Some of these ethical frameworks are familiar to those working in the rhetorical tradition, but other frameworks may be comparatively unfamiliar to established scholars and readers who are new to conversations about ethics. These frameworks include ethical paradigms such as deontology, utilitarianism, and postmodernism. Of these and other ethical paradigms, it is arguably postmodernism that continues to exercise a considerable influence in digital rhetoric scholarship. Thus, in the introduction to this book, we identify some of the common ethical characteristics of this postmodern ethical thought in order to highlight our thesis that virtue ethics offers a necessary point of support and extension for digital rhetoric.

For readers who are new even to the idea of digital rhetoric, let alone ethics in philosophy and rhetoric, we offer a few definitions up front. If you are reading a book on the subject of digital rhetoric, you are likely already familiar with the idea of rhetoric, as well as its variety of definitions over time, but we give a brief introduction to the term, just in case. Rhetoric as a concept stems back to the writings or records of a variety of ancient Greek thinkers such as Plato and the sophists. Plato's most famous student, Aristotle, gave us the definition of rhetoric most readers who have sat through a college-level writing or rhetoric class at some point have encountered: "an ability, in each particular case, to see the available means of persuasion" (Aristotle 2006, I.2.1355a). While the Greeks were thinking primarily about oral forms of persuasion, twentieth- and twenty-first-century rhetoric scholars have sought to apply, extend, or reconfigure ancient rhetoric concepts (e.g., *ethos, pathos, logos, techne, kairos,* the canons [of memory, arrangement, style, delivery, and invention], *topoi, chora*) to encompass digitally mediated communication.[2] At a very basic level, Douglas A. Eyman's purposefully general definition of digital rhetoric is quite accurate to this reconfiguration: "The term 'digital rhetoric' is perhaps most simply defined as the application of rhetorical theory (as an analytic method or heuristic for production) to digital texts and performances" (Eyman 2015, 44). Indeed, for readers interested in a complete and comprehensive treatment of digital rhetoric research, we highly recommend Eyman's book, *Digital Rhetoric: Theory, Method, Practice* (Eyman 2015). Following from this general definition, digital rhetoricians—our intended audience for this book—include a wide variety of academic and nonacademic audiences: university students and teachers of digital rhetoric and writing, web designers, corporate managers, technical and professional communicators (practitioners and teachers), social media content creators, and others who use or study digital-communication genres, to name a few.

Broadly considered, ethics is a common area of inquiry within digital rhetoric research, stemming from its foundations in a broader field often called *rhetoric and composition* or *rhetorical studies.* Nevertheless, it is possible to spot certain trends and oversights within past and current scholarly conversations. In their introduction to their book *Foregrounding Ethical Awareness in Composition and English Studies,* Sheryl I. Fontaine and Susan M. Hunter argue that well into the mid-1990s, rhetoric and composition scholarship approached ethics through two dominant approaches (Fontaine and Hunter 1998). First, ethics was a classroom-based practice wherein writing teachers created assignments to make students think about ethics in various rhetorical situations (without teaching specific ethical frameworks). To be clear, this first approach amounts to the avoidance of teaching specific ethical frameworks, such as virtue ethics or utilitarianism, at all. The goal of teaching critical awareness is not to teach students specific theories of ethical reasoning; rather, this approach functions as a generalized appeal for students to think about moral action in their writing absent a particular recommendation about how to act. In the second approach, ethics was simply adherence to established codes, such as laws against jaywalking or speeding (e.g., deontological) (Fontaine and Hunter (1998).

With regard to John Duffy's critically neglected essay "Ethical Dispositions: A Discourse for Rhetoric and Composition,"[3] another trend within rhetoric and composition studies' approach to ethics has been a clear shift away from the Enlightenment or Platonic language of universals, metanarratives, and rationality we often see in the language of other ethical systems such as utilitarianism and deontology (as we discuss in chapter 2) (Duffy 2014). As a direct consequence of the rise of cultural studies, poststructuralism, and postmodern theoretical approaches—terms we define momentarily—Duffy (2014) notes, "The term 'ethics' lost ground to the terminology of 'power,' 'politics,' and 'ideology'" (216). To be sure, postmodernism is hardly a coherent or unified body of thought. What Duffy illustrates is simply the more generalized way in which scholars over the past few decades have to a great extent accepted a postmodernist challenge to rationality or universal axioms. Gary A. Olson (1999) acknowledges a similar consequence of this theoretical shift. Summarizing (and not supporting entirely) the perspective of some postmodern theorists, Olson comments, "Ethics is dead. . . . No system or code of moral values can universally regulate human behavior" (71). Still, one can easily infer that many postmodern theorists' primary goal is less to abandon ethical thinking and more to reorient its purpose. A good number of postmodern (and poststructuralist) approaches take the form of examining systems of meaning with the goal of identifying how universal or naturalized truths, goods, or belief systems have only ever supported particular and frequently inegalitarian ideological systems such as patriarchy, capitalism, eurocentrism, racism, ableism, homophobia, and transphobia. These approaches are obviously motivated by ethical concerns, even if they are not framed in such language.

As we demonstrate in the chapters that follow, a great deal of ethical scholarship in digital rhetoric has repurposed and refashioned these approaches. For example, we can draw on any number of postmodern ethical frameworks to offer a justification for an ethical motive for Viki's project, such as the critique of the presumption of able-bodied users among other social media content hosts. Popularized by rhetorical theorists who have drawn upon critical theory and cultural studies methodologies, critique in general refers to the critical demystification or unveiling of a hidden logic disguised by a given prevailing cultural ideology (patriarchy, capitalism, etc.) that enables cultural and rhetorical practices.[4] As we discuss in chapter 3, social media interfaces such as YouTube unwittingly privilege the norm of able-bodied users as universal viewers or content creators—a form of privileging that can also be found in other broad aspects of US culture and media. A common ethical move grounded in postmodern ethics would seek to reveal this tacit able-bodied ideology at play in this assumption as, for example, not a self-evident truth but as a contingently privileged half of an abled/disabled body binary.[5] In other words, the goal of a postmodern rhetorician might be to establish the lack of a foundation for presupposing nondisabled bodies as a universal or naturalized state of being (see Dolmage 2014). Postmodern ethics thereby would help digital rhetoricians challenge naturalized metanarratives, which support practices that cater primarily to able-bodied users. Postmodern ethics would then work to reveal this problem as not natural or inherent to the human condition and then advocate with or on behalf of the marginalized community of deaf users for inclusion as part of how social media designers imagine their audiences.

While work on feminism (Ballif 1998; Powell and Takayoshi 2003), digital writing (Pandey 2007), and discourse analysis (Barton 2008), as well as on Emmanuel Levinas (Bernard-Donals and Drake 2008; Davis 2010; Gehrke 2010), Mikhail Bakhtin (Bernard-Donals and Capdevielle 2008; Juzwik 2004), and Jacques Derrida (Brown 2015; Davis 2010), have complicated some of these postmodern positions, Duffy (2014) concludes that many scholars continue to view ethics as "a process of inquiry" (Fontaine and Hunter 1998, 8; see also Porter 1993, 1998) in which ideas about the good and the moral are located not in moral codes or specific values but in "local narratives and shifting identities" (Micciche 2005, 162, in reference to Kirsch 1999). In response to our opening question in this introduction (how do we classify digital rhetoric practices as ethical?), we suspect a good number of academic readers who are versed in these scholarly conversations would be inclined to answer through postmodern frameworks or related sets of theoretical or cultural studies topoi along the lines of the ableist critique we mention in the previous paragraph.

However, as many commentators from a variety of humanities backgrounds have noted, a lingering issue is that postmodern ethics tends to function primarily as an "ethic" (if you will) of critique. Postmodern theorists frequently do not seek to offer an alternative way to retheorize normative or affirmative ethical values because such thinkers invariably criticize such values as products of a contingent ideology framed through rational or foundational thought. By *normative*, we mean a term common to philosophical treatments of ethics that informs us how we *should* act in response to a given set of ethical guidelines. In other words, postmodern ethics' goal of destabilizing the means to establish ethical values does not in itself offer straightforward ways to theorize affirmative ethical practices beyond the call to include marginalized ideas and to create or recognize the spaces from which nonnormative voices speak.

This point is memorably highlighted by the French sociologist Bruno Latour (2004b), whose work is being drawn upon by a growing number of digital rhetoricians (Brown 2015; Gries 2015; Holmes 2014a; Rivers 2014). In his essay "Why Has Critique Run Out of Steam?," the problem Latour (2004b) highlights is that both global-warming deniers (conspiracy theorists) and postmodern relativists similarly use the contingency of meaning to challenge truth claims. As a result, academics and nonacademics alike have become skeptical of any appeals to "matters of fact"—what the mind can or cannot logically derive from immanent rational processes *and* what invariable truths of nature science can empirically describe. The consequence of this practice of challenging all truth claims is that any appeals to facts become "eaten up by the same debunking apparatus" (Latour 2004b, 231).

While in the political service of progressive causes at times (see Latour 2004a), Latour observes that the postmodernists who claim the relativism of facts do not acknowledge that the view of matters of fact they are challenging was never realizable in the first place. As Latour (1993) highlights in *We Have Never Been Modern*, this perspective views human culture and nonhuman nature as existing in separate spheres to the point that the philosopher or scientist can represent an objective reality (nonhuman nature) without any contamination from culture. In response to this viewpoint, postmodernists often simply deny that interpretation is neutral or objective, thereby making all human cultural and rhetorical practices attributable to a still separate but contingent sphere of human culture. Latour calls this nature/culture split the "modern Constitution" (Latour 1993).

To be clear, Latour's point should not be confused with the claim that negative political and economic forces do not exist in the world.

While we offer more treatment of Latour's thought in chapters 6 and 7, a quick gloss on his point here is that our purely social explanations and human-centered critiques of these phenomena only tell part of the story. By contrast, he argues that the sphere of human culture has always been composed through the, at times, unpredictable influence of non-humans. Hence, ethico-political interests for Latour shift from a critique of "matters of fact" toward an analysis of how humans and nonhumans have always comingled in shared "matters of concern": symmetrical actor-networks that compose the space of concrete and material reality. According to Latour, "asymmetrical" accounts of how rhetorical agency functions fail to consider the agency and influence of both human and nonhuman actors. By contrast, "symmetrical" accounts do not privilege one form of agency over the other in producing explanations for how rhetorical activities emerge and circulate in the world. As a basic example, rather than examining how one human motive attempts to influence an audience, Latour's work helps us consider how nonhuman agents, such as the lighting of a room, may exercise some subtle influence on how an audience is persuaded or how a digital rhetorician sets rhetoric into motion. Latour therefore posits that an ethic emerges from the careful tracing of each unique actor-network that composes a matter of concern rather than assuming each actor-network is reducible to a human motive from a predetermined ideological or methodological lens (historical dialectics, Marxism, capitalism, semiotics, knowledge/power, etc.) (Latour 1993).

Latour's thinking has come to function as a rallying cry for a growing number of critical theorists from different disciplinary backgrounds, including rhetoric (Gries 2015; Lynch and Rice 2014; Rickert 2013; Rivers 2015), who seek to rethink ethical concerns in rhetoric from an alternative perspective to postmodern critique. Latour (2004b) argues for a new kind of critic, one whose work can be applied to constructing new paradigms, practices, and communities multiple types of people (not just scholars) can use and be a part of. Latour declares that the role of this new kind of critic

> is not the one who debunks, but the one who assembles. The critic is not the one who lifts the rugs from under the feet of the naïve believers, but the one who offers the participants arenas in which to gather. The critic is . . . the one for whom, if something is constructed, then it means it is fragile and thus in great need of care and caution. (Latour 2004b, 246)

Literary theorist Rita Felski's notion of "postcriticism" makes a similar appeal for critical theorists to attend to ethical and political "re-construction" after (Derridean) "de-construction," or reconfiguration after demythification (Felski 2015, 17). Indeed, there seems to be a growing interest among certain critical theorists not to avoid or move away from critique but to categorize it as but one (ethical) tool among many others in a researcher's analytic and compositional arsenal. Yet, with Duffy's observations about the pervasive influence of postmodernism as a case in point (Duffy 2014), not enough researchers in the humanities or, we argue, rhetoric and composition are beginning to make this turn, especially with regard to ethics in digital contexts.[6]

REHABILITATING VIRTUE ETHICS IN DIGITAL RHETORIC

Running parallel to our interest in virtue ethics, Latour is well aware of the need to articulate some new positive moral values to examine matters of concern, stating, "The practical problem we face, if we try to go that new route, is to associate the word criticism with a whole set of new positive metaphors, gestures, attitudes, knee-jerk reactions, habits of thoughts" and that addressing this ethical system would require "new habit form[ation]" (Latour 2004b, 247). Latour's use of the term "habit" is important for our effort to revitalize a virtue ethics framework because the Greek root of *habit* is *hexis*—a key term for Aristotle. Indeed, Ellen Quandahl (2003) connects virtue ethics to rhetoric in an essay on emotion's role in writing. She states that the virtues are "characteristics of habits (*hexeis*) of feeling and action that develop through activities. Thus the name for moral virtue (*ethike*), is related to *ethos*" (Quandahl 2003,15). Yet, the translation of *hexis* (singular) into *habit* requires qualification, as contemporary notions of habit lose some of the complexity of the ancient Greek treatment. In Aristotle's *Nicomachean Ethics, hexis* is a term often translated as bodily comportment, state, or disposition. It is a genus of moral virtue in the sense that the disposition arises from both conscious and nonconscious forms of habituation (ethos) achieved through repeated activity (*energeia*) and thus is something that cannot come about by nature but only through repeated practice (Gross and Walzer 2008; Hawhee 2004).

In fact, as we discuss in chapter 2, this connection between virtue ethics and ethos as habituation rather than artistic proof represents a strong point of overlap and extension within an area in which digital rhetoricians have already started to work (Fleckenstein 2005; Miller 2001). However, hexis is a unique and particular form of habituation. Hexis is derived from the Greek verb *echein*, which means "to have or possess," in the sense of an *active having*. A hexis is what produces a virtuous action to guide wisdom (*phronesis*), but it is not commensurate with the completed action. Rather, the *hexeis* (plural) are the cultivated bases for orienting oneself toward virtuous activity in varied circumstances. To paraphrase Socrates's example in Plato's *The Republic*, a good ethical habit is to return an item one has borrowed from a neighbor, but this does not necessarily mean a virtuous person should return a borrowed weapon to a "madman" (Plato 1992, 331b–332a). Hexis is the disposition, the orientation or comportment, that guides decision making across multiple and contingent rhetorical situations. For Aristotle, the hexeis include intellectual virtues and vices along with ethical ones. Notably, ethical virtue is a "*hexis proaretike* or 'a state disposed to choosing' (1106b36), but art or *techne* is *hexis poietike* or 'a state disposed to producing' (1140a7–8), and practical wisdom a *hexis praktike* ('a state disposed to acting') (1140b4–5)" (Lockwood 2013, 24). In this regard, virtue ethics' attention to the embodied and the material contexts and habits of dispositional formation also meets up with rhetoricians' contemporary interests in materiality, such as Rickert's notion of "ambient rhetorics" (Rickert 2013), Hawhee's notion of "physiopoiesis" or "arts of becoming" (Hawhee 2004), and many others with whom we engage throughout the book.

As evidence of the applicability of virtue ethics to digital technologies and networks, consider the opinion of one of the few contemporary social media virtue ethicists, Shannon Vallor (2010), who declares,

> Virtue ethics is, arguably, the best and perhaps the only solution to this quandary [of ethical decision making in dynamic systems], for while it does reject the use of *a priori* criteria for ethical decisions, that is, criteria that transcend the concrete conditions of human flourishing, it still allows us to speak of sound ethical choices within such contexts, choices that reflect shared normative principles of broader significance and application. (160)

It is important to note that in her description, virtue ethics is positioned as a supplementary framework rather than a complete or total replacement for other ethical systems. In fact, one primary benefit of turning to virtue ethics and the language of ethical dispositions is that we can see how postmodern and cultural studies paradigms often seek to create ethical dispositions even if they do not explicitly use this language. Revisiting Duffy's article once more (Duffy 2014), we can see he offers a useful example from two different schools of composition pedagogy, a body of research that examines effective theories and practices for the teaching of writing. On the one hand, expressivists (Elbow 1998) believe writing is a very personal and apolitical process of self-discovery. On the other hand, critical theory pedagogy views a political motive—intentional or unintentional—as inherent in all aspects of the writing process. Yet, while expressivist and critical theory pedagogies in rhetoric and composition studies may have dramatically different interpretations of how we approach the political nature of writing in the classroom, Duffy demonstrates that both groups nevertheless presuppose positive (normative) values in cultivating ethical dispositions in their students, such as impartiality in evaluating others' claims, intellectual courage in stating controversial beliefs, diligence in problem solving, and accountability in representing others' arguments fairly and accurately (Duffy 2014).

In addition, Duffy describes dispositions of ethical teaching practices both camps support, including cultivating a disposition of respect for student writers and humility in the sense of avoiding the top-down "banking model" of pedagogy (Duffy 2014, 226). (In the "banking model," criticized famously by critical theorist Paulo Freire (2000), an educator makes a "deposit" of knowledge into an empty student or audience who sits in the classroom and passively receives this deposit.) Beyond Duffy's observations, we also might think of the various shared ethical commitments in the fields of rhetoric, including the advocacy of inclusivity, respect for difference, and critique of injustice. To sum up, even postmodern arguments to decenter meaning in language and question assumptions must contend with the ways in which the hexeis form ethical dispositions specific to our communicative interactions with one another as well as how the environments and technologies through which we communicate also participate as dynamic players and not passive backdrops.

OVERVIEW OF RHETORIC, TECHNOLOGY, AND THE VIRTUES

Despite the flexibility and power of virtue ethics, it is not a common approach to digital rhetoric, even among digital rhetoricians who have argued for the enduring relevance of classical thought for a digital age. Beyond Quandahl (2003) and Duffy (2014, 2017), virtue ethics enjoys little popularity in digital rhetoric, rhetoric and composition, technical communication,[7] or communication fields writ large (unless we include the ethics of care as connected to virtue ethics, a connection some outside the field of rhetoric have made and that we reinforce in chapter 4). Indeed, searching through the past decades of research in *Rhetoric Society Quarterly, Philosophy and Rhetoric, College Composition and Communication, Technical Communication Quarterly,* and other major periodicals aligned with rhetorical studies encounters few references to the virtues or hexis as virtuous bodily comportment. Indeed, even researchers who have gone back to reclaim early Greek thinkers for digital technologies, such as Michelle Ballif (1998) (the sophists) and Kathleen Welch (1999) (Isocrates), have dismissed the importance of Aristotle's virtue ethics for digital rhetoric (and rhetorical thinking more broadly). In a related criticism, and with unintentional irony, Patricia Bizzell (1992) writes, "We postmodern skeptical academics are *habitually* fearful that any talk of teaching virtue will tend to introduce exclusions, as socially privileged groups in our diverse nation arrogate to themselves the right to define what virtue is taught" (6; our emphasis). Yet, as a close reading of Aristotle confirms, virtue ethics does not commit us to the type of false universal axioms Bizzell (1992) and a great number of postmodernist thinkers rightly seek to avoid. Instead, what emerges in virtue ethics is a critically neglected means of differentiating ethical from unethical forms of digital rhetoric practices that are grounded in dispositions and repeated activities. It is important to note that virtue ethics is able to make such differentiations without relying on notions of the rational subject criticized by decades of postmodern and poststructuralist thought.

In the chapters that follow, we revisit the enduring relevance of the Aristotelian framework that undergirds contemporary virtue ethics, providing clear points of overlap with and departure from existing research on digital rhetoric and ethics as well as rhetoric and technology in general. *Rhetoric, Technology, and the Virtues* offers a key contribution by extending Aristotle's framework through two groups of thinkers: (1) contemporary virtue ethicists (e.g., Anscombe 1958; Hughes 2011; MacIntyre 2007; Nussbaum 2015; Vallor 2010; 2011; Williams 1985) and (2) political theorists who do not self-identify as virtue ethicists but whose work either stems from dispositional ethics or elaborates on contemporary virtue ethics frameworks. While there are several good reasons for drawing on political theorists outside digital rhetoric scholarship and rhetorical studies, our primary reason for this methodology lies in the following distinction: unlike many political theories, which tend to focus on restructuring governments, institutions, and systems, the theorists we draw upon view politics as a set of ongoing practices and specific actions (a focus on doing, one might say) individuals and communities can engage with in a variety of contexts. It is this emphasis on doing that we believe creates a number of important overlaps with the goals of digital rhetoricians who are similarly invested in rhetoric as both a practice of education and an active political practice.

After chapter 2, our theoretical overview of virtue ethics, each remaining chapter employs at least one such political theorist to update one of

Aristotle's hexeis for digital rhetoric, including Jacques Rancière (1992; 1995; 1999) (on justice), Adriana Cavarero (2011) (on care/reciprocity), Martha Nussbaum (2015) (on generosity), Jane Bennett (2010) (on patience), and Bruno Latour (2004b) (on fairness). Each chapter also illustrates its specific hexis through a related case study of relevant contemporary rhetoric and writing practices in digital networks.

Chapter 2 offers a more detailed explanation of classical and contemporary virtue ethics thought in contrast to, but alongside, other prevailing ethical systems employed by digital rhetoricians, particularly postmodernism, utilitarianism, and deontology. Our purpose in charting these conversations is to emphasize the various motives that led to virtue ethics falling out of favor with contemporary rhetoricians, despite the existence of numerous twentieth-century advocates such as Elisabeth Anscombe, Hannah Arendt, Bernard Williams, Alasdair MacIntyre, and Paul Ricoeur. After establishing this context, we put forth several exigencies for employing a virtue ethics framework in digital rhetoric, including responses to rhetoricians (Ballif 1998; Welch 1999) who have questioned the usefulness of Aristotle's thinking for digital rhetoric. In closing this chapter, we highlight how the language of virtue ethics is already present in a variety of contemporary rhetorical paradigms, including Rickert's ambient rhetoric (Rickert 2013).

In chapter 3, our first case study, we consider the hexis of justice through a discussion of closed captioning in social media videos. We foreground the political philosophy of Jacques Rancière (1992; 1995; 1999), whose work, as Ethan Stoneman (2011) highlights, is in tacit dialogue with rhetoric's prevailing interests in aesthetics and politics (e.g., Vitanza 1997; Vivian 2000). We argue that Rancière's unique definition of politics, which exists in dissensual activities that make visible hierarchies—or "partitions of the sensible"—offers a way to rethink justice as a habit, or hexis, of verifying another individual's political equality. At length, we compare Rancière's political thought with digital rhetoricians' interests in video production, (Arroyo 2013; Blakesley 2007; Halbritter 2012), activism (Gurak 1997; Sheridan, Ridolfo, and Michel 2012), and technical communication with rhetoric researchers' (Agboka 2013, 2014; Frey et al. 1996) attempts to theorize social justice through frameworks that rely on passive equality (such as liberalism). The latter are included in no small part because technical communication and rhetoric scholars such as Sean Zdenek (2011; 2015) are some of the few in rhetorical studies who have engaged rhetorics of closed captioning. How digital rhetoricians can enact active forms of social justice with and on behalf of the deaf community and other affected communities with regard to closed captioning technologies is a concern for technical communicators. Thus, we argue that a Rancièreian hexis of active equality as justice helps digital rhetoricians in industry and educational contexts that use YouTube screencasts (e.g., instructions, how-to videos, promotional video games, advertisements) make visible this partition of the sensible by actively producing accurate closed captions—not as an add-ons in postproduction processes but as a significant element of video production. For Rancière, such a hexis also suggests that this ethical practice of the verification of political equality is never finished. Thus, once captions have been produced, we engage the prevailing presence of racist partitions of the sensible within closed captions in the television shows *Breaking Bad* and *The Wire*. This example confirms that digital rhetoricians can benefit from viewing justice as the cultivation of an ongoing hexis of active equality for multiple communities whose equality goes unrecognized.

We document in chapter 4 how, among digital rhetoricians, an ethic of remix (Palmeri 2012) and cultural appropriation has become part of the logic of the digital, notably encapsulated by Alex Reid (2007) ("ripping," "mixing," "burning"), Jeff Rice's (2007) idea of a "rhetoric of cool," and more broadly, through digital rhetoricians' use of Gregory Ulmer's (1994) electracy theory (Arroyo 2013; Holmevik 2012). We argue that the logic of remix—not unlike closed captioning—can benefit from the cultivation of a specific hexis of care. We develop this claim by drawing upon a feminist ethics of care, in particular the recent work of the Italian political philosopher Adriana Cavarero. By designating vulnerability as an ontological category, Cavarero highlights that a significant part of what constitutes being human is that, throughout life, "the singular body is irremediably open" to two responses: "wounding and caring" (Cavarero 2011, 20). Not only are no two persons' lifetimes of vulnerable exposures to others identical, but the degree to which a person is vulnerable to others also changes depending upon life circumstances. In other words, though we are always vulnerable, context governs the degree to which we can be wounded and the degree to which we require care. Thus, as an ethical disposition, a hexis of care would include the constant and practiced awareness and consideration that no relation to others is neutral because all are vulnerable to one degree or another, even in digital spaces, and one's decision making to remix or sample must always take into account this relational vulnerability. When a digital rhetorician samples from a community or culture or individual, she is not merely "taking whatever she can find and using it" to compose freely, as Rice (2003) puts it; rather, she is also taking part in acts of caring and wounding for any individual or community connected to the content and forms from which she samples.

In chapter 5, we take up the hexis of generosity in Aristotle's work, updated through the philosopher Martha Nussbaum (2015), to examine "slacktivism" as a potential ethical practice. While debates over slacktivism are almost exclusively couched in what we identify as a utilitarian ethics (means-ends effectiveness), we suggest slacktivism can also signal the development of a disposition of generosity—a disposition that can find its expression in repeated cases of charitable and civic activism, online and offline. We look at the social media slacktivism in phenomena such as KONY 2012, the Ice Bucket Challenge, and *Humans of New York* as cases that, on the surface, may seem to be ineffective or effective forms of slacktivism in terms of the overall ends they achieve. KONY 2012 and the Ice Bucket Challenge, for example, do not appear to have used different rhetorical methods, but one seems to have achieved better ends than the other when discussed in terms of utility. We counter that supplementing such evaluations of slacktivism with the language of virtue ethics enables us to more deeply consider how each site produces the conditions for developing dispositions of generosity, thus reframing how we look at successful cases of slacktivism, rather than simply looking at the ends the slacktivism achieves.

In chapter 6, we concede that a limitation of Aristotle's virtue ethics (along with Rancière's, Cavarero's, and other thinkers' we previously consider) is anthropocentrism (the view that human beings are the center of the universe). Anthropocentrism is a clear problem in an era in which digital rhetoricians are increasingly forced to contend with the environmental impact of the production and use of digital technologies (Weisser and Dobrin 2002). This chapter asks, how might digital rhetoricians develop an ethic of patience (*proares*), or slowness to anger, for taking ethical actions on behalf of the environment? In dialogue with contemporary rhetorical interests in new materialism (Gries 2015; Rickert 2013; Rivers 2014), Jane Bennett's political philosophy of new materialism (the vibrancy and aleatory agency of matter), for example, extends Rancière's politics of dissensus to partitions of the sensible created by human/nonhuman (or nature/culture) divisions. Bennett advocates for what we see as a hexis of patience in terms of forming rhetorical responses to environmental damage to avoid outrage and scapegoating as primary reactions to environmental disasters. For our case study, we examine how outrage functions in social media related to environmental issues, focused specifically on the #DroughtShaming movement in 2014 that employed social media to shame wealthy Los

Angeles homeowners who refused to curb their water usage in response
to the ongoing California drought. While outrage in this case was useful in stimulating national awareness (and, by some accounts, even
local legislative action), a hexis of patience recommends that we do not
allow these forms of viral shaming to abstract users' own participation
from within complex environmental systems. Cultivating this ethical
disposition makes sure humans do not mistake their outrage at the
participation of certain human actors as constituting the entirety of the
appropriate ethical response, thereby missing how their own hexeis are
always already shaped by these diverse assemblages.

Finally, chapter 7 concludes the book by looking ahead to some of
the ways in which digital rhetoricians can use virtue ethics to engage
with emergent forms of digital technologies. We look at examples such
as GPS and behavioral tracking, algorithmic regulation, and even the
ethics of hospitality in software development, as Brown has documented
in *Ethical Programs* (Brown 2015). We also call on rhetoricians to see
the virtues as overlapping. Teachers of rhetoric in particular should not
teach our framework as a rigid heuristic. By contrast, it is much more
productive for students to go through the process of tracing users'
behaviors in digital networks and trying to have a dialogue about what
types of virtues are necessary and important to cultivate (and how we
might help cultivate them). Following from this claim, we close by tracing what we believe is one of the most important hexeis for the present
moment: Latour's (2004b) hexis of fairness. Fairness signals above any
other disposition the need to look squarely at concrete ethical behaviors
in formation in localized networks while resisting the desire to attribute
their motivation solely to some hidden totalizing political system.

At the outset, we want to clarify the audience for this book. Our goal
in writing this book was to offer a text that could be taught in advanced
undergraduate and graduate classrooms. Indeed, creating such a text
was no easy task. We found ourselves balancing wanting to produce
the type of critical rigor that would appeal to professional researchers
while nevertheless remaining able to narrate some of these ideas to an
audience who may never have heard of virtue ethics or other ethical
frameworks beyond clichés in pop culture or proverbial phrases such as
patience is a virtue. We do believe the current book performs this balancing act, and we hope it gives enough of a primer for rhetoric's interests in virtue ethics for other scholars to take up the mantle in either
direction: performing more theoretical research into the relationship
between virtue ethics and rhetoric or using these frameworks to teach
rhetorical ethics in the university classroom.

Finally, although we try to stress this point throughout the manuscript, we want to be very clear in emphatically stating that *we do not believe virtue ethics is the only ethical framework that should be employed* in digital rhetorics. Different ethical frameworks can help us achieve different ethical ends. While many criticize utilitarianism's ability to justify charity over social justice, the philosopher Peter Singer, for example, argues that utilitarianism can in fact be used to ethically promote charitable acts people would otherwise not perform. Our belief is not that virtue ethics is superior to every other ethical form. Nevertheless, we do believe virtue ethics offers some advantages, particularly for examining digital rhetoric in an age in which new technologies enable us to perform acts past civilizations could not imagine. Ironically, it is a 2000+-year-old ethical theory that we demonstrate offers several ways to theorize and articulate ethics within these networked spaces. In an era of #fakenews and #altfacts, who would not agree that the hexis of honesty, for example, could use revisiting and updating? The language of virtue ethics and dispositions shows us ethics is not only about correct principles and how we rationalize those principles but also about how our various digital assemblages and technologies actually take part in producing habitually ethical beings.

In sum, our aims in *Rhetoric, Technology, and the Virtues* are quite simple: we want to reclaim a role for dispositional (virtue) ethics in an attempt to overcome certain limitations of postmodern relativism and rational universality alike by grounding digital rhetoric ethics in users' habits and practices.

2

TOWARD A VIRTUE ETHICS
IN DIGITAL RHETORIC

This chapter offers an introduction to classical and contemporary approaches to virtue ethics. The most straightforward route is to establish how virtue ethics differs from other ethical approaches and why virtue ethics fell out of favor among rhetoric and writing scholars as well as philosophers and ethicists more broadly. As a result, this chapter is not intended as a comprehensive summary of ethics in the rhetorical tradition. Rather, our more modest goal is to identify a few major paradigms of ethics researchers in rhetorical studies have responded to and endorsed and, in turn, to demonstrate how virtue ethics can refine and extend some of these interests for readers already familiar with this body of work, as well as those who are brand new to ethics and rhetoric conversations.

In the first section of this chapter, we discuss some of the common ethical frameworks that might be used to apply to our example of Viki, the social networking closed-captioning community we mention in the introduction. We feature brief discussions of deontology and utilitarianism, but our primary focus is on certain features of the ways in which postmodern ethical frameworks have been taken up in rhetorical scholarship. Our goal is not to dismiss the entirety of postmodern thought, let alone summarize all of what is already a complex—and by no means coherent—group of artistic, capitalist, cultural, or theoretical practices. Instead, we seek to identify one of the central limitations of these postmodern frameworks (or, more accurately, limitations inherent in the ways in which these frameworks are often employed by past and present rhetorical scholarship) when it comes to the desire to avoid attributing normative values. To sum up, postmodernism's well-established aversion to normativity is the critical impasse we believe virtue ethics is ideally suited to supplement.

In the second section, we offer a more detailed overview of classical accounts of virtue ethics from Aristotle's (2002) *Nicomachean Ethics* and other relevant texts. We demonstrate how this framework enables us to respect postmodernism's rejection of a universal ethical system while

DOI: 10.7330/9781607328063.c002

nevertheless retaining the ability to discuss life-affirming normative ethical values grounded in individuals' particular behaviors and practices. In the third section, we start to turn toward contemporary applications and extensions of Aristotle's virtue ethics by explaining some of the reasons this ethical system was set aside by rhetoricians. While there are certainly good justifications for some of these criticisms, the more accurate claim is that virtue ethics was not abandoned or rejected as much as it was never explicitly taken up by rhetoricians. By comparison, we note how the reemergence of philosophical interest in virtue ethics in philosophical tradition actually coincides with the advent of postmodernism. Rather than seeing virtue ethics as explicitly opposed to postmodernism, the work of contemporary ethicists in philosophy such as Elisabeth Anscombe, Alasdair MacIntyre, and others indicates that their turn to virtue ethics shares many of the same rhetorical exigencies that brought about rhetoricians' interest in postmodernism. The historical context of the twentieth-century reemergence of virtue ethics, then, offers us an importance exigency for examining virtue ethics as a supplemental ethical framework to further and extend some of the interests of postmodern frameworks.

In the fourth section, we move from these philosophical conversations toward the work of contemporary theorists whose works engage digital technology and networked communication practices through the virtues. We focus in particular on the work of the contemporary philosopher of technology Shannon Vallor. In her pivotal essay, "Social Networking Technologies and the Virtues," Vallor (2010) maps out three key exigencies for taking up virtue ethics in the digital age. In sum, these exigencies include the following: (1) if technologies influence our ethical habits, we need an ethical framework that acknowledges and tries to understand this habit formation; (2) alongside well-known theorists such as Michel Foucault, a virtue ethics framework never assumes technological progress equates to moral progress and instead asks us to examine the hexeis, or ethical dispositions (virtues and vices), being developed in relation to the development of new technologies; and (3) because a virtue ethics framework acknowledges that our ethical dispositions are difficult to change, and we cannot discuss ethics apart from the material and social environments we find ourselves in, it follows that ethicists can no longer responsibly separate discussions of morality from those of technological development and the multiplicity of ethical (or unethical) behaviors such new technologies are capable of supporting.

Vallor's thought helps motivate and enable us to productively connect these exigencies to digital rhetoric scholarship. In the final section of this chapter, we suggest our field does have a number of more recent researchers who are engaged with similar ethical concerns and whose work has a considerable degree of overlap with a virtue ethics framework. We find a number of productive overlaps with rhetorical scholarship steeped in the language of bodily and material dispositions as well as habits, such as Kristie S. Fleckenstein's discussion of cyberethos (Fleckenstein 2005) and Thomas Rickert's ambient rhetoric (Rickert 2013). Rather than call for a complete about-face in rhetorical studies, then, we believe virtue ethics can help provide a better language for many of the values we in the field of rhetoric and composition already endorse without using these specific terms.

REVIEW OF MAJOR ETHICAL FRAMEWORKS

In order to understand the need to look to virtue ethics, it is first necessary to take account of some of the features of past and current ethical frameworks. While we rely on Aristotle's basic framework, we believe virtue ethics thought (including those theories tacitly invested in virtue ethics) can and has moved beyond Aristotle in interesting and productive ways. To help readers map these frameworks against one another, in this section we refer back to our opening illustration of the Viki community in an examination of the three ethical frameworks rhetoricians have alternatively criticized or employed in the past: utilitarianism, deontology, and postmodernism. Utilitarianism and deontology are two of the dominant rationalist (e.g., reliant upon reason and logic) lenses that have influenced how ethical goods can be manifested in contemporary political systems (seen most prominently in the political frameworks of libertarianism and liberalism, as we highlight in chapter 3) and are implicitly present in many rhetoric and composition arguments, while postmodernism has historically offered an alternative and nonrational approach to ethics.

Utilitarianism

Utilitarianism is a branch of normative ethical thought sometimes called *consequentialism,* and it stems from eighteenth- and nineteenth-century British philosophers Jeremy Bentham (2007) and John Stuart Mill (1998), respectively. While subsequent articulations of consequentialism differ over time, one consistent thesis of utilitarianism is that an action can be considered good or right only if the consequence is beneficial or useful to a majority. Rather than look at the character of a rhetorical agent, the ethical principle that motivates their actions, or the value of an act in and of itself, utilitarianism instead seeks to assess the outcomes and effects of a given action in order to determine ethical values. For example, a utilitarian may justify an act of lying if that act benefits the greater good. In fact, many readers are already acquainted with utilitarianism even if they have never heard the term before. The philosophical foundation of capitalism is utilitarian in spirit, presupposing that individuals are best at defining their own needs, desires, or goals and that granting individuals the freedom to make their own choices (even if selfish) results in the greatest possible satisfaction for the majority of people. One can also observe utilitarianism in cost/benefit-analysis business models, in which the costs of a given action are weighed against the benefits it may achieve.

In brief, utilitarianism is also known as a philosophy of pragmatism and common sense, most often framed simply as the ends justify the means, in which the means are justified if the end is deemed the greater good. While it is true that one can read a great deal of past and contemporary rhetoric and ethics scholarship and never encounter this specific term, it is important to observe that many researchers' ethical stances have been most often implicitly discussed in resistance to utilitarian frameworks, though the promotion of utilitarian perspectives does occur. Consider a tacit version of utilitarianism that can be found within a paradigm called *current-traditional rhetoric* (CTR). In contrast to many contemporary approaches that strive to understand writing as a *process* of brainstorming, drafting, revising, receiving feedback from other writers, and revising again, CTR focuses only on the final product. Common examples include the universal five-paragraph-format essay taught in many composition or AP English courses in high schools around the United States. Adjusting style or tone of writing to different audiences is not a concern. Instead, rhetoric is reduced to correct grammar, syntax, style, spelling, and logical development. As Sharon Crowley (1990) notably complained, CTR historically abstracts rhetoric from political-economic relations through a reduction of writing to an objective, formalist, transparent, and instrumental vehicle for the transmission of rational/logical thinking (see also Moon 2003). Such a positioning of rhetoric as only a means to an ethical end stems from utilitarian thinking.

To sum up, we can locate the influence of and response to utilitarianism in a number of cultural practices of interest to teachers, students, and professional researchers in rhetoric. However, as Crowley's criticism about CTR makes clear, there are some issues with utilitarian approaches to rhetoric and ethics that must be noted. To offer an example specific to digital rhetoric, trying to apply only a utilitarian framework to the Viki captioning example runs into immediate difficulty. In terms of theorizing ethical goods, contemporary utilitarian ethicists, such as the philosopher Peter Singer (2011), have argued that utilitarianism can theoretically redistribute resources to people with disabilities when they would benefit more from those resources than nondisabled people. Yet, another philosopher, Amartya Sen (2004), (and other critics) rightly complains that there are too many circumstances under which utilitarianism would unfairly distribute fewer resources to people with disabilities than to nondisabled people on the grounds that people with disabilities would derive less benefit from those resources or that the good of the majority would outweigh the needs of the seemingly smaller population of people with disabilities. In partial confirmation of this trend, MIT and Harvard recently received public criticism and lawsuits for failing to caption videos on their educational modules.

As a hypothetical example, imagine a provost at a large public research university reads Tamar Lewin's February 12, 2015, article in the *New York Times* on MIT and Harvard's legal difficulties and decides to be proactive. Within a short period of time, this provost convinces the faculty senate to pass a recommendation for professors to make sure any online video content presented in any university classroom has appropriate captions. One does not need much imagination to predict the response of likely well-intentioned but already overburdened professors or to question how underpaid adjunct professors without university-issued technology and offices are even supposed to engage in the sort of captioning practices the Viki community manifests. In other words, to fulfill this mandate may require universities to invest substantially in IT departments (e.g., offering faculty training or technological resources), thereby begging the question of utility given the relatively small or nonexistent percentages of deaf or hard-of-hearing students in any given classroom.

In addition, it is not clear a utilitarian framework can account for the ways in which Viki users voluntarily contribute unpaid labor in their leisure time to cultivate this particular habit of captioning, nor is it clear utilitarianism would describe the cost as worthy of the ends it achieves for a variety of audiences. At most, a utilitarian might argue that Viki's closed-captioning initiative is ethical because of the global effect achieved (which would be difficult to measure), but a utilitarian framework cannot adequately explain all the various motives and rhetorical aims of Viki users, of whom many may have no greater good in mind when they caption.

To clarify one potential source of confusion, while we are obviously leading readers toward the thesis that the use of virtue ethics is more effective than utilitarianism for digital rhetoric practices and more in line with ethical commitments in rhetoric and composition, this new emphasis does not mean utilitarianism should be dismissed out of hand. Utilitarian thinking can often be one's only recourse when a desired outcome can only occur by an action that is the lesser of two evils, so to speak. In this way, utilitarianism is often thought of as an ethical framework built upon pragmatism and common sense, when one can only justify one's actions by the ends they produce. Our more limited observation is simply that utilitarian ethical concerns are not able to explain *all* the ethical behaviors that form in complex networked interfaces such as Viki.

Deontology

Similar to utilitarianism, our second paradigm, deontology, is likely unfamiliar to many readers. While this particular term is not widely employed, we nevertheless demonstrate that it exercises an influence across a wide variety of rhetorical practices. A deontological approach to ethics measures ethical behavior by how closely one adheres to a given ethical rule, such as the eighteenth-century German idealist philosopher Immanuel Kant's categorical imperative, which is typically a rationally derived principle that can be applied universally regardless of the specific contexts or particular individuals involved. Kant produces multiple formulations of the categorical imperative to guide such maxim making, the first being to act in such a way that your actions could be universal law. His second formulation, which stems from the first, is quite well known and contrasts utilitarianism: "Act so that you treat humanity, whether in your own person or in that of another, always as an end and never as a means only" (Kant 1969, 429). Here Kant, in effect, is arguing that humans should never be treated solely as instruments to another's ends. From deontological thinking come our ideas of human rights and creating laws, duties, and obligations to govern behavior in response to those rights. Indeed, Kant's prohibition against lying even instructs us not to lie to a would-be murderer who asks us to reveal the hiding place of their intended victim. Common axioms, such as the ways in which most university professors invariably include a bit of verbiage akin to "thou shalt not plagiarize" on their syllabi each semester, stem from a deontological ethics approach. In fact, Sheryl I. Fontaine and Susan M. Hunter suggest that composition studies up until the mid-1990s engaged ethics primarily through a de facto deontological approach, such as the prescription against plagiarism (i.e., a system of legal or informal codes designed to regulate behavior) (Fontaine and Hunter 1998).

With regard to the Viki captioning project, deontology certainly can and does play a role. While most users probably never have any reason to click on this link, Viki does have a publically available legal page, which includes its terms of service for elements such as intellectual property and copyrights, which enforce ethical conduct in relationship to both US and international standards for streaming copyrighted content. Viki's legal page also lists prohibited conduct, such as impersonating another individual or business entity (Viki 2007). However, it is important to highlight the fact that deontology does not encompass all forms of ethical behaviors related to Viki. As a notable illustration, there are no laws in the United States that state "thou shalt caption everything." There are currently no laws that require videos on social media and popular video hosting sites like YouTube and Vimeo to contain captions. FCC captioning laws apply to television, and—with YouTube as a case in point—such laws have yet to be extended to online video broadcasting. Perhaps as an indirect result, calls to engage captioning are few and far between alongside digital rhetoricians' otherwise commendable calls to engage video production and literacy (see chapter 3).

Even if the United States were to begin passing deontological captioning laws for social media, these laws would likely help the US deaf community but not necessarily Viki's global audience. It is very unlikely that an unapologetically ethnocentric and monolingual culture such as the United States (expressed in ideas of American exceptionalism) would require captioning in 240 languages, let alone beyond the commonly translated major language groups such as Spanish, French, Japanese, Chinese, French, Italian, Hindi, Arabic, and so on. Furthermore, while recent work by Tom Wheeler and the Federal Communications Commission (FCC) has made captioned programming on services such as Netflix and Hulu more comprehensible for the deaf and hard of hearing (Washeck 2016), how do we ethically analyze and produce quality captions? Just because a law or policy has been created does not mean that as a result people are being treated equally in all circumstances—an issue we also discuss in chapter 3 by examining racism in closed captioning. YouTube's autocaptioning algorithm, for example, is so inaccurate that entire social media video channels exist to satirize its poor captioning results. A related issue also arises: is the creation of the law itself the only way to encourage individuals to enact ethical goods? Even most legal ethicists do not equate law and ethical norms; in other words, law and ethics are not coextensive, though many laws are derived from ethical principles, such as the value in honesty and fairness. For example, we might consider lying to family or friends as generally unethical, but such an act most often is not prohibited by law (unlike, of course, lying in a courtroom under oath). Our larger point, simply, is that turning solely to law or deontology as an ethical recourse does not readily help us explain all rhetorical motives for ethical behaviors in a networked age.

Virtue ethics, as we highlight below, is neither a framework for deciding action solely to achieve desired consequences, as we see in utilitarianism, nor is it built on doing one's duty as derived from reasoned foundational principles, as we see in deontology. While morality as adherence to the law is useful for forcing television companies and, hopefully in the future, social media video providers to caption their materials, it is clear other frameworks are required to describe Viki users' voluntary acts of captioning.

Postmodernism

Perhaps the most influential "ethical" paradigm of the past few decades for researchers in rhetorical studies and other humanities disciplines has been postmodern ethics. We place "ethical" in scare quotes because we readily acknowledge that postmodernism has never functioned as a unified ethical framework (or even body of thought) since the pivotal French theorist Jean-Francois Lyotard's pioneering use of the term "postmodern" in his 1979 publication of *The Postmodern Condition* (Lyotard 1984). Many canonical theorists associated with this movement (Derrida, Jameson, Haraway, Hutcheon, Foucault, Levinas, etc.) offer dramatically different theories, emphasizing Marxism, Heidegger, postcolonialism, Foucauldian archaeology, Lacanian psychoanalysis, poststructuralism, indebtedness to the Other, and other theoretical and philosophical approaches. Nevertheless, it is not an overgeneralization to state that advocates affiliated with postmodernism share a commitment to vocabularies of respect for cultural difference and multiplicity, specifically advocating the value of creating or recognizing the spaces, discourses, and identities that have been historically marginalized or negated by dominant metanarratives such as capitalism, patriarchy, racism, religion, and homo- and transphobia, among others.

As a result, we can find postmodern approaches in the cultural studies and critical theory branches of rhetoric and composition studies, including notable work in the past by James Berlin, Malea Powell, Sharon Crowley, Victor Villanueva Jr., and countless others. In his article "Poststructuralism, Cultural Studies, and the Composition Classroom," for example, Berlin (1988, 1990) applies a fairly generalized but accurate postmodern framework to explain teaching practices in the rhetoric classroom. According to Berlin, there are no neutral aspects of rhetorical interaction; all parts of the writing process, from the genres or forms we use to the individual word choices we make, are influenced by social ideologies. Just the basic idea, for example, of teaching a business memo form as opposed to a sonnet in a technical writing classroom may privilege or mirror the forms of writing desired by the business and managerial classes of capitalism. In a great deal of postmodern thought, there are no absolute principles or universal truths, no natural laws to employ in descriptions of reality, ethics, and potentiality. Across his corpus of writing, Berlin argues that there is a great deal of power in demonstrating knowledge is contingent rather than universal. If knowledge is contingent, no particular type of person or group has privileged access to answering these types of questions; instead, marginalized groups and voices can argue for alternative forms of meaning to be considered (Berlin 1990, 489–90). Theorists such as Jacques Derrida (1978) make similar criticisms when discussing the notion of the enlightenment liberal subject. Employing the work of Derrida, Berlin draws our attention to the instability of the idea of a subject who can autonomously think, write, and act when and where they choose as a product of a "unified, coherent, autonomous, transcendent subject of liberal humanism" (Berlin 1992, 20). In other words, poststructuralists and many postmodern thinkers view liberal human subjectivity as a constructed entity that relies upon historically contingent social and institutional structures to form meaning and create arguments.

What Berlin and many in rhetoric and composition studies have particularly appreciated about many postmodern theorists is the idea that humans cannot escape language, that humans are bound to it, even with language's many internal contradictions—thus the need for rhetoric. Furthermore, the lack of a "center," or a stable source of meaning, allows for limitless politically progressive revisions. While Berlin is talking about nondigital texts, we can find numerous examples of this criticism of discourse and ideology within digital rhetoric (e.g., Selfe and Selfe 1994). James E. Porter notably theorized a postmodern ethics for digital rhetoric, tacitly and at times explicitly working to build ethical frameworks without developing specific rules or principles but by drawing on cultural studies topoi. Indeed, Porter declares, "Ethics is decision making—but it is decision making that involves question and critique" (Porter 1993, 223). While this term can mean different things to differ thinkers, critique, as Berlin helpfully describes, is the process of identifying the enabling ideological conditions of discourse (Berlin 1992, 22).

In other words, as Porter notes, rather than describing an intact or standardized system of ethical values, postmodern rhetorical ethics is "*a process of inquiry* by which we determine what is right, just, or desirable in any given case" (Porter 1998, 29; emphasis in original). This shift from normative values to a process of inquiry means ethics and rhetoric can no longer be thought of as separate fields of inquiry; rhetoric can no longer be seen as solely a means for ethical aims, as one might see in the history of philosophy, and such a rhetorical ethics can never be based upon a universal truth but is always committed to contingent values of particular situations. This commitment to contingency arguably holds more sway in postmodern discussions of ethics than does any other commitment, as postmodern ethics specifically has wished to distance itself from deontology and reason-based ethics such as utilitarianism, each of which can be seen as invested in "the possibility of a 'disinterested and detached standpoint' that has universal standing" (Porter 1998, 50).

While it is difficult to list any truly representative examples of postmodern ethics as a process of inquiry, consider three examples from well-established digital rhetoricians: Johndan Johnson-Eiola, Kathleen Welch, and Cynthia L. Selfe and Richard L. Selfe Jr. Johnson-Eilola comments that "any object, collection of objects, or contexts can be 'read' by tracing and retracing the slipping, contradictory network of connections, disconnections, presences, absences, and assemblages that occupy problematic spaces" (Johnson-Eilola 2010, 33). In other words, rhetorical meaning in digital texts is seen not as neutral or self-evident but instead as a reflection of contingent or particular ideological backgrounds and positions. A webtext for a corporation that promotes its products for a first-world audience might be disguising or ignoring the exploited labor in its (so-called) third-world factories. Here, rather than accept the corporation's self-representation as neutral or unproblematic, much in postmodern theory asks us to look for what contingent ideological interests a given credible appeal masks. In *Electric Rhetoric*, Welch (1999) similarly turns to Isocrates as a figure who anticipates a great deal of postmodern rhetoric in that the word *logos* (speech) for Isocrates was not universal or fixed but instead represented a "flux of language, thought, and action" (Welch 1999, 45). Where meanings appear to be naturalized or fixed, postmodernists invariably attempt to locate what sort of nonuniversal and contingent logics undergird these structures. As a final example, Selfe and Selfe's canonical essay, "The Politics of the Interface," describes how using a computer's primary graphical user interface (the "desktop") conditions the user as a capitalist laborer. Selfe and Selfe redescribe writing and rhetoric in digital spaces not as a neutral vehicle for the transmissions of thought but as an "electronic contact zone" (via Marie Louise Pratt 1992) in which established meanings are only temporary settlements of various ideological forces competing for dominance (Selfe and Selfe 1994).

As we gesture toward in the introduction, digital rhetoricians' interest in postmodernism makes a great deal of sense. Postmodernism provides critical ways for marginalized groups and their entities to contest and challenge how naturalized assumptions about sexuality, femininity, and race, for example, have been used to create and maintain systems of oppression, from broad-based state institutions and laws (e.g., segregation) to the everyday words we use to speak and write with that maintain certain individuals as a generalized and often excluded Others. Duffy argues that in many ways the various research fields associated with rhetoric and composition have "become a postmodern discipline" (Duffy 2014, 212), thereby indicating the extent to which many of us are postmodern ethicists whether we self-identify as such or not.

The Problems of Postmodern Ethics

The problem, however, as numerous commentators have observed, is that decentering the ground or foundation for ethical values makes it very difficult to recoup any semblance of a normative (i.e., value-driven) commitment. In recognition of this challenge, consider Porter's commendable effort in his book *Rhetorical Ethics and Internetworked Writing* to try to reexpress some of the normative or affirmative values of postmodern ethics (Porter 1998). As an aside for readers who are new to rhetoric and composition studies, *Rhetorical Ethics and Internetworked Writing* (Porter 1998) is by far one of the most comprehensive efforts to address rhetoric and ethics for digital rhetoric (at least up until the more recent publication of Brown's *Ethical Programs* (Brown 2015). Porter rightly notes that there are some clear moral commitments in postmodern thought as rhetorical studies has taken it up, even if the language of ethical discourse—with terms such as *morality, ethics, right and wrong*—is avoided. In postmodern ethics' seemingly first and foremost commitment to a contingent process of inquiry, postmodern thinkers do seem to hold some pretty clear moral values—such as a commitment to difference and an obligation to include, liberate, and care for particular communities and individuals in specific and local situations, particularly those excluded by language and political systems by race, gender, and sexuality.

One of the values of postmodernism, then, is an investment in radical inclusivity, in which even contradicting values have a place next to each other and ignored or forgotten values are brought to the forefront of discussion. For example, postmodern scholarship is often quick to point to the reliance on linguistic binaries in politics, scholarly critique, and even everyday language, such as men/women, white/black, straight/gay. The postmodern scholar asks a reader not only to recognize the privileging of certain categories over others (men over women, white over black, etc.) but also to look to forgotten "middle terms," "third spaces," or forgotten "others," as Victor J. Vitanza has notably insisted (Vitanza 1991). Regarding the straight/gay binary, for example, a postmodern critique would demonstrate that yes, the category of straight in this instance has been historically privileged in many societies by law, cultural values, and traditions; however, this same postmodern critique would also ask the reader to look to the forgotten categories, such as transgender, bisexual, and asexual, and push the reader to question the stability of the categories and the binaries in the first place. The goal of highlighting these marginalized categories is generally what is meant by a commitment to radical inclusivity. Nevertheless, most postmodern thought by design does not explicitly say what it advocates or what it is committed to, as the potential for unintentionally perpetuating a binary, which then excludes some value or group, is too great.

Porter (1998) rightly admits that commitment to such values is a kind of moral positioning, even if influential rhetoricians such as Berlin and Vitanza attempted to distance themselves from the language of ethics. For example, Vitanza advocates a "counterethic" of "resistance and disruption" in criticism of traditional ethics, which he deems "irresponsible" because of their "penchant for 'totality'" and punishment (Vitanza 1990, 241). Postmodern thinkers such as Berlin and Vitanza clearly have an ethic (similar though not identical), but a significant part of that postmodern ethic is to avoid any kind of foundational principle or methodology by which ethical behavior should be informed. This avoidance is what makes Porter's attempt to name the specific ethics to which he is committed (and in turn critiques, such as Vitanza's, of such positioning) a challenge. If one is "true" to a postmodern ethical sensibility as a process of inquiry, eventually such commitments will be undercut as only contingent and partial values.

INTRODUCING ARISTOTLE'S VIRTUE ETHICS

To this point, we have offered a brief summary of some of the traditional ethical frameworks of utilitarianism and deontology, as well as certain features of the ethics of postmodernism, which we have developed in direct contrast to the first two. Once more, our goal in this chapter is not to provide an entire overview or dismissal of postmodern ethics.[1] Rather, in examining the difficulty common uses of postmodern frameworks have in addressing the affirmation of ethical values, we hope to provide a point of contrast to highlight the enduring relevance of virtue ethics. In this section, we offer a basic outline of virtue ethics as a framework that maintains postmodernism's commitment to contingency but at the same time is able to articulate particular ethical and unethical dispositions and behaviors in digital spaces.

Since most if not all contemporary virtue ethics start in dialogue with Aristotle, it is necessary to begin with an overview of his view of hexis, which he discusses primarily in the *Nicomachean Ethics* (Aristotle 2002). For Aristotle, ethical virtues are character or agent based and focus on the concept of hexis, or the disposition, state, or bodily comportment of a person brought about by the development of habits (1105b25). Unlike Plato, who insists ethics is the epistemic knowledge of the good, Aristotle posits that virtuous hexeis—such as patience, courage, temperance, and liberality—are developed not solely through reason or by learning rules but through practice of the emotional and social skills that enable us to work toward *eudaimonia*—human flourishing and general well-being within a community (often (mis)translated as happiness)—in various situations. Notably, the hexeis emerge from the body and the social/material environment rather than purely through reason or rationality. Therefore, Aristotle does not follow Plato in viewing ethics as only *theoria* (i.e., theoretical knowledge in science or metaphysics). Aristotle also would not seek to develop universal axioms as normative frameworks as later enlightenment philosophers of rationality such as Kant did. Far from presupposing a disembodied individual rational actor who can make ethical decisions separate from lived experience, ethics as virtuous hexeis exists only in forms of embodied action in support of eudaimonia (human flourishing), which can only have itself and not another goal (such as wealth acquisition or utilitarian ends) as its aim. This aim of eudaimonia is accomplished both in the ethical practice itself and in the end achieved by that practice, as we explain below.

Hexeis can also be unethical—what Aristotle calls "vices"—and what determines a hexis as a virtue rather than a vice is the mean "between excess and deficiency" (Aristotle 2002, 1106a25–b28). If a virtue has too much of a hexis or is deficient in that hexis, the virtue becomes a vice. For example, an individual with a virtuous hexis of indignation (as well as justice) expresses anger when they recognize people are being treated unfairly. Excess indignation would amount to misconstruing one's envy of others as injustice, and someone with a deficiency in indignation would find joy in the unfair treatment of others. Significantly there is no mathematical formula or perfect line of reasoning for determining this mean. One must take into account the specific circumstances of an event and the place of the individual within that event (Aristotle 2002, 1106a36-b4). The idea of a mean or middle term does not mean we should not feel passionate about a subject or a cause but only that our degree of passion, anger, patience, graciousness, and so forth should be determined by the particular situation; too much or not enough expression of a particular hexis can result in harm to others or oneself. Aristotle (2002) is careful to hedge on the flexibility of the virtuous mean.

> This much, then, is clear: the middle characteristic [the mean] in all cases is praiseworthy, but one ought to incline sometimes toward the excess, sometimes toward the deficiency, for in this way we will most easily hit on the middle term and what is well done. (1109b24–27)

Someone with a hexis of patience (which we discuss in chapter 6) has a sense of how long to wait before actively responding to a given situation. Depending on the context, they are slow to rush to judgment but not too slow. Such a hexis is a vice if that person either is so outraged they impatiently hurt or force harmful actions on others or they wait so long the moment to produce positive action goes unrecognized. However, embodying the hexis of patience does not equate to identical behavior in different circumstances. A person most likely would wait longer to ask for professional medical attention with regard to a one-day-old cold than they would regarding a broken leg, but a person who has developed a hexis of patience will have a sense of when to rush to treatment and when to wait. Notably, this hexis cannot simply be taught or learned through reasoning. Rather, a hexis of patience, or any other hexis, must be learned through repeated practice and requires the kinds of material conditions that enable this repetition. Developing such a hexis requires witnessing and then recognizing such virtuous expressions in others, and no expression of one ethical hexis will ever look identical to another expression of that same hexis from the same individual.

Other key elements of Aristotle's virtue ethics that are important to expound upon include the ideas that ethics (1) is a branch of politics and therefore must be able to be practiced; (2) is imprecise, unfixed, and nonprincipled; and (3) has internal and external goals or is self-reinforcing in its goal of eudaimonia. In the next few paragraphs, we explain each of these elements.

In contrast to many ethical positions that can be considered postmodern (though again, as we note above, we understand these cannot be generalized easily), Aristotle (2002) considers ethics a branch of politics. As a contrasting example, in Diane Davis's rhetorical scholarship on the philosopher Emmanuel Levinas, she locates a presymbolic ethico-rhetorical relation as always preceding and at work in any rhetorical act—whether we are conscious of it or not. She rightly acknowledges that we cannot derive a political system such as liberalism or libertarianism from such a notion of ethics as rhetorical "response-ability" (Davis 2010,120). This acknowledgment does not make her work on presymbolic ethico-rhetorical relations unimportant, though by design it does make applying such an ethics to practice difficult.[2] In contrast to such a position, Aristotle (2002) argues that ethics must be practicable, or applicable to practices. In fact, the audience for his *Nicomachean Ethics* is statesmen. If the goals of politics are centered around creating a system that produces the best possible conditions for communal flourishing, the goal of ethics is for individuals and groups to create hexeis that enable them to enable and contribute to that communal flourishing. For Aristotle (2002), then, ethics is concerned very little with creating an untouchable abstract theory of ethics or an appropriately fixed action in all circumstances; instead, he is much more interested in the development of hexeis that lead to practical and ethical decision making in real social situations.

Alongside the practical element of virtue ethics is an element we cannot reinforce enough. Unlike the two dominant modes of ethical thought we discuss in the first section of this chapter, utilitarianism and Kantian deontology, but similar to postmodern ethics, the study of ethics for Aristotle is imprecise, unfixed, and nonprincipled, at least in the sense of a fixed principle guiding one's actions. Virtue ethics claims no single principle, such as "never lie" or "the needs of the many outweigh the needs of the few," or even a set of principles (such as the ten commandments) that assist a person in deciding on an ethical action in all situations. One of the most oft-quoted passages from Aristotle's *Nicomachean Ethics* demonstrates this point: "It is a mark of the educated man and a proof of his culture that in every subject he looks for only so much precision as its nature permits" (Aristotle 2002, 1094b23–25). Ethics does not engender the kind of precision and exactness we might find in mathematics. This acknowledgment also helps explain why Aristotle feels ethics should focus on the character and habits of the agent rather than on specific actions based upon a principle. Instead of teaching people correct principles or rules—which do not take into account all the various emotions, personalities, and affective capabilities we might find in humanity and beyond—one should help people develop the kind of hexeis that best enable them to be ethical in varying situations.

This recognition of the multiple dimensions of moral decision making means virtue ethics, like postmodern ethics, is not built upon foundational principles established solely by reason, and, thus, virtue ethics is never fixed. We cannot reiterate enough that far from offering a list of maxims to memorize, such as the catechism in the Christian tradition or a series of predetermined rules or regulations to follow, Aristotle's virtue ethics only applies to our modes of conduct with respect to our contingent and embodied situations. As Aristotle (2002) puts it, matters of ethics

> have as little fixity about them as questions of what is healthful; and if this is true of the general rule, it is still more true that its application to particular problems admits of no precision. . . . Agents are compelled at every step to think out for themselves what the circumstances demand. (1104a3–7)

We overemphasize this point because, as we explain below, some rhetoricians have misidentified virtue ethics as fixed, inflexible, and privileging only those in power. This view could not be further from the truth.

Finally, as regards key elements of virtue ethics, each virtue has internal and external goals and is thus self-reinforcing. In *Confronting Aristotle's Ethics*, classicist Eugene Garver nicely sums up this characteristic of virtue ethics.

> Among the modes of action that we choose in the first place because of [good outcomes], we choose and do some of them for their own sake. We admire, praise, and try to emulate courage, liberality, and justice not only because we think their practices are usually beneficial but also because we want to *be* courageous, liberal, and just. Therefore . . . we call these things virtues. (Garver 2006, 4; emphasis in original)

Thus, considering justice as a virtue, for example (see chapter 3), takes into account that being just is a reward unto itself—one feels good about being just and wants to be identified as just; however, being just also achieves good ends—the equal and fair treatment of others. Answering this question is one way to identify a hexis as virtue rather than vice: is a particular hexis something to be admired in and of itself and also a practice that leads to productive ends for oneself and others?

It is this self-reinforcing feature of virtue ethics that allows us to advocate for certain values while respecting contingency, which we believe constitutes a step beyond the main problems of postmodern thought. Two key elements of virtue ethics enable us to make this claim. First, virtue ethics offers us a resource for making normative claims without binding us to universal ethical axioms. For example, MIT media studies theorist Sherry Turkle (2011) has consistently (and not uncritically) argued that our online relationships are damaging our offline forms of face-to-face conversation. The title of her most recent book, *Alone Together*, supports her thesis that increasing our amount of online togetherness has actually made us more socially isolated. If teens only break up with their boyfriends or girlfriends via text messages or Facebook updates, then, Turkle's logic goes, they are missing the opportunity to cultivate face-to-face interpersonal abilities, such as how to act with grace and empathy in delivering difficult news (Turkle 2011). By contrast, within a virtue ethics framework, there are no a priori grounds for making these sorts of totalizing or even—in Turkle's case—heavily qualified claims about digital technology's relationship to behavior. Virtue ethics is quite comfortable with the claim that some individuals may use social media and flourish in both online and offline relationships while others may not.

If we were to find evidence that unequivocally supports Turkle's assertions (which have been challenged by numerous researchers), virtue ethics allows us to argue a hypothetical claim, such as developing virtues of commitment is more difficult in online social environments given that anonymity allows for low exit and entry barriers for friendship. This claim might in fact accurately describe how certain users form dispositions in online spaces that can also impact their offline relationships. However, virtue ethics argues that these conclusions are not invariable or fixed for all time, especially as technology-human relationships change and evolve. Nevertheless, virtue ethics does allow us to identify certain good and bad features within regularized habits that emerge in particular spaces. A virtue ethics framework would not seek to offer totalizing or universal axioms such as "social media is good (or bad) for establishing enduring social relationships" and instead would inquire into the particular conditions that contribute to users developing various possible ethical dispositions (virtue and/or vice). For this reason, we like to think of Aristotle's virtue ethics as producing not universal but *emergent* normative values. In other words, these normative values are not determined through reason outside our engagement with others and the material world. Rather, these values emerge, and will continue to emerge and change, within and alongside our local and global interactions with our families, our neighborhoods, social media, and so forth.

These ethical values that result from the cultivation of semipermanent dispositions (i.e., our "second nature") depend upon the particular habits of individuals involved, as well as the particular digital systems and communities each individual is caught up within. Above any other

principle, Aristotle's ethics deal with the pragmatic and the concrete—
phronesis rather than Plato's *episteme*. You are ethical because of how
you repeatedly act and not simply because of what you know. These virtues may be emergent, but they are *actual*.[3] These are actual dispositions
that influence how actual actors behave in digital networks.

Second, we can find a framework for describing normative values
within Aristotle's notion of eudaimonia (happiness; flourishing), which
is the ultimate ethical aim of cultivating virtuous hexeis (Aristotle 2002).
Notably, unlike postmodern thought, virtue ethics is willing to name
its ethical goal, that of eudaimonia. Aristotle urges us to form habits
that bring human flourishing and a general sense of well-being in and
of themselves. For example, he discusses how individuals motivated by
greed (a vice) will continually seek happiness through a feeling of ongoing lack (*pleonexia*), no matter how much wealth they attain, whereas
someone who has developed a hexis of generosity will begin to find joy
in the expression of that disposition (1129a32–3; see chapter 5). This
provides a loose but normative and practicable framework.

To offer another example, Aristotle is infamous for supporting slavery. He claims slaves should not bother trying to cultivate hexeis that
lead toward eudaimonia simply because so many of their daily practices
are nothing but a means to someone else's (e.g., their master's) end.
However, reading against the grain of Aristotle's own thought, this argument simultaneously suggests slavery is an immoral social arrangement
because it means some individuals will never be able to flourish within
this economic system. As we discuss in chapter 6, contemporary environmental virtue ethicists have similarly found in Aristotle's thinking a
normative commitment to flourishing beyond solely humanist concerns:
eudaimonia "presupposes a harmonious integration with the rest of
nature, and represents an objective condition of doing well in one's
environment, rather than subjective satisfaction with one's condition"
(Bina and Vaz 2011, 173). Therefore, even if eudaimonia does not give
us a concrete list of systematic behaviors or step-by-step instructions to
follow to achieve happiness, it nevertheless offers digital rhetoricians
some important identifiable dispositions to support the achievement
of eudaimonic ends (or, conversely, to locate situations in which eudaimonia cannot be achieved).

THE NEGLECT OF VIRTUE ETHICS IN RHETORIC

Arguably, virtue ethics has never really fallen out of favor in rhetoric
and composition studies (let alone digital rhetoric studies); rather, it is

more accurate to state that virtue ethics has never really been popular in the twentieth and twenty-first centuries as a viable framework for engaging with rhetorical and ethical problems. To say virtue ethics has been completely neglected in rhetoric and composition scholarship would be inaccurate—see Fleckenstein (2005), Candace Spigelman (2001), and Sandra Stotsky (1992) for examples; however, Porter rightly implies this general neglect of the virtues in his discussion of the influence of postmodernism on rhetorical ethics. Porter (1998) argues that many postmodern rhetoric commentators invested in ethical concerns (as most are) have conflated or confused all ethical systems with deontological and reason-based Enlightenment ethics (27). He points in particular to the prominent influence of rhetoricians such as Berlin and Vitanza, each of whom we briefly mention above. Berlin (1990), for example, saw any discussion of ethics as counterintuitive to postmodern politics. Ethics for Berlin was something that privileges the elite and abstract universal reasoning of an autonomous, free-willing self in contrast to the values acquired through material, embodied, and community-specific experiences.

> The consideration of any topic under the heading of "ethics," however, creates an immediate stumbling block. . . . To dwell on ethics is to risk elevating an historically specific mode of thought to a universal standard. A central feature of this gesture today is the assertion of the bourgeois individual of liberal humanism, the autonomous self who freely adjudicates competing moral claims. This self is then situated in opposition to suspect, self-threatening material conditions and the dangers of communal encounters. Recent discussions of ethics thus tend to fall comfortably into the privileging of the subjective and the personal, relying on an individuous distinction between the individual and the social, the private and the public, the solitary and the communal. (quoted in Porter 1998, 27).

While this critique finds some footing in its evaluation of utilitarianism and deontology (though some neo-Kantians and utilitarians may disagree with the totality of these statements), as our summary above indicates, most if not all of these claims are not true with regard to a virtue ethics framework, which explicitly acknowledges the *inability* to be ethical solely through abstract reasoning. Virtue ethics also does not privilege the individual over the community or vice versa. Even if we choose to locate virtuous hexeis in the individual, a virtue ethics framework acknowledges that one develops such hexeis in the context of communal values and the repetition of embodied and situated practice. Finally, virtuous hexeis are never fixed but emerge and change through the different situations people find themselves in.[4]

As Fleckenstein points out in her essay "Cybernetics, *Ethos*, and Ethics," this trend of dismissing or conflating virtue ethics alongside other ethical frameworks has continued in contemporary digital rhetoric scholarship (Fleckenstein 2005). Many have been quick to dismiss Aristotelian methods and values for theorizing ethical rhetoric in the digital era. In a footnote, Fleckenstein (2005) comments that some of the most prominent critics have been Barbara Warnick, Michelle Ballif, and Kathleen Welch (and each advocates a different alternative to Aristotle) (Fleckenstein 2005, 343). Warnick (2001) explores digital ethics through postmodern critical theory, commenting that neoclassical rhetoric in general and Aristotle's rhetoric in particular are anachronistic with respect to new information technologies and digital rhetoric. Ballif and Welch, in contrast, have each argued for neoclassical approaches to digital rhetoric: Ballif (1998) turns to sophistic rhetoric, and Welch (1999) turns to Isocrates, but they remain united in a dismissal of the relevance of Aristotelian ethics (see Fleckenstein 2005, 343).

Though his topic is not virtue ethics, poststructuralist philosopher and political activist Todd May (2008) makes an argument that might help explain this aversion to explicitly turning to any ethical framework or the tendency to conflate all ethical frameworks as something to be avoided. He notes that the problem of moral language in postmodern thought is mainly a political problem (and Porter draws similar conclusions; see Porter 1998, 26–31). May notes that in US politics in particular, the politics of the conservative Right has laid claim to the language of morality. In contrast, the politics of the Left (with which most postmodern thought is identified, including May's own thought) has criticized these moral stances because the Right's views of morality are opposed to the equal rights of various marginalized groups, such as those of the LGBTQ community. Because of the Right's claim to morality, the Left (and May includes progressive academics and political activists) sees the term "morality" as containing "dictatorial and provincial" connotations: "The argument runs roughly like this: since there are no universal moral values, no set of values can claim ultimate superiority over any other; therefore, people should be exposed to a diversity of moral views" (May 2008, 102). May (2008) explains how for some progressive activists, this political stance is connected to continental postmodern thought, in particular the works of Michel Foucault, Gilles Deleuze, Jacques Derrida, and Emmanuel Levinas—all thinkers upon whom rhetorical studies has drawn extensively.

May (2008) argues that none of the above thinkers is against morality itself; rather, each is against transcendent moral values and the history of moral discourse, a history that attempts to draw upon transcendent values, often through religious or other foundational texts, to establish fixed and oppressive rules of behavior. Not only do these postmodern thinkers agree that transcendent moral values do not inherently exist, they argue that the enforcement of such values is intolerable (103). Note how such a stance of intolerability is itself the advocacy of a value and is related to standards or norms (if flexible ones) that would determine such intolerableness—such as commitments to difference, equality, or inclusivity. Thus, for May, "At issue here is not the term morality. We may call these matters what we like. However, we are inescapably entrenched in an arena of [ethically] normative judgment, of judgments of the better and the worse that are supposed, in one way or another, either to bind people to or discourage them from something" (May 2008, 104).[5] A more thorough examination of why rhetorical studies has historically turned to postmodern and poststructuralist thought for ethical treatments would take up more time and is not the purpose of this book. Nevertheless, we feel it is safe to say rhetoric and composition's historical neglect of virtue ethics is perhaps (at least in part) a result of this reliance on postmodern and poststructuralist discourse.

The Twentieth-Century Reemergence of Virtue Ethics outside Rhetoric

Just as a few rhetoricians have been careful not to dismiss virtue ethics out of hand with the advent of postmodern thinking (e.g., Duffy 2014, 2017; Fleckenstein 2005; Quandahl 2003), a few philosophers in the twentieth century also see its value. Intriguingly, these scholars' turn to virtue ethics parallels the emergence of postmodern thought, and arguably because of similar exigencies. The main figures responsible for the reemergence and survival of contemporary virtue ethics are Elisabeth Anscombe (1958), Bernard Williams (1985), and Alasdair MacIntyre (2007). Other subsequent prominent philosophers, such as Phillipa Foot (2001), Paul Ricoeur (1992),[6] and Martha Nussbaum (1993, 2015), have made a significant impact on the subject as well, if sometimes indirectly.

Contemporary virtue ethics emerged in the late 1950s due in no small part to Elisabeth Anscombe (1958). In her now-famous (among philosophers) article "Modern Moral Philosophy," she is critical of conceptions of ethics that are law or rule based. While such law-based frameworks are mostly indebted to Kantian deontologies, Anscombe also sees utilitarianism as too heavily bound to claims that certain means-ends rules could be applied universally to any ethical problem. This latter point is readily seen in a pop-culture example. In the film and television series *Star Trek*, the character Spock justifies many different actions with one seemingly simple utilitarian rule: "The needs of the many outweigh the needs of the few." In response to this kind of rule-based moral philosophy, Anscombe calls for a return to Aristotle's concept of virtue and its related key terms of *character, disposition,* and *flourishing* and for understanding ethics as always situational, never bound to a fixed principle or rule (Anscombe 1958).

Bernard Williams (1985) similarly rejects rule-based ethics. He does so in part because of how easy it is to (1) create a scapegoat based upon those who do not follow a particular rule in totality when something goes wrong and (2) vindicate those who did follow the rule, even if harmful actions were the result of that rule following. Williams finds rule-based ethics too restrictive to be applicable to how people actually live. To counter this restrictiveness, Williams pushes to expand our concept of ethics as Aristotle did by considering ethics broadly and moral outcomes specifically to be comprised of nonrational factors such as emotions, luck, community and family relationships, and societal ideals, most prominently social justice (Williams 1985).

The person who has done perhaps the most for the revitalization of virtue ethics in the twentieth century is Alasdair MacIntyre (2007). MacIntyre's criticism of contemporary ethics is equally as damning as Anscombe's and Williams's. However, rather than solely argue for a revitalization and reframing of virtue ethics, MacIntyre historicizes virtue in his book *After Virtue: A Study in Moral Theory.* His argument is that any understanding of virtue is something that is always going to be determined by history and culture. For example, various cultures throughout history privileged certain hexeis in relation to excellence as more important than others, or at least as more prized in the pursuit of excellence. MacIntyre claims that this privileging could be seen in the ideal of the disposition of the warrior found in Homer's writings, the gentleman politician in classical Athens, and the saint in early Christianity. Each disposition privileged a different set of virtues. Most prominent in MacIntyre's history is his critique of modern capitalist societies, which he argues understand virtue in terms of effectiveness (cf. Katz 1992) rather than in terms of Aristotle's emphasis on excellence toward eudaimonia. This shift in emphasis has resulted, MacIntyre argues, in a culture that values the pursuit of wealth over virtues of honesty, courage, and justice. Significantly, MacIntyre emphasizes that no one set of virtues is universal, that a productive understanding of virtues is always an understanding of virtues as "dispositions which will not only sustain practices and enable us to achieve [ethical] goods internal to practices, but which will also sustain us in the relevant kind of quest for the good" (MacIntyre 2007, 219). Therefore, unlike rule-based ethical frameworks, an understanding of ethics as dispositions seeks virtues that sustain political communities and motivate continual inquiry into the character of the good—and thus continually question that character—rather than presuppose reason could somehow discover universal moral principles or obligations that will always serve all people in all instances.

While these examples may offer a positive response to virtue ethics, not all philosophers have accepted this call to reconsider virtue ethics. A common criticism among various philosophers is that virtue ethics does not produce systematic principles for guiding ethical action. This is true. However, Anscombe (1958) and others (notably Rosalind Hursthouse 1999) show that focusing on ethical dispositions rather than systematized principles can guide moral action. Also, many rhetorical theorists argue that the problems of systematized or codified values can be highly problematic (see Hawk 2007; Vitanza 1997), so most in rhetoric would be wary of any call for systematized ethics. In fact, this is arguably one of the main reasons to take issue with Aristotle's particular version of virtue ethics. His impulse to taxonomize the virtues and to hierarchize certain virtues over others is problematic for various reasons, including that such practices tend to reify our understanding of virtues rather than retain their flexibility. Other philosophers have criticized virtue ethics as too reliant on communal values, making moral practices difficult to change. As we have noted, this is a strength of virtue ethics, at least with regards to understanding how rhetoric works on people, because the emphasis of virtue ethics on the role of habit in developing ethical dispositions shows that people do not just change their behaviors because of new knowledge: moral habits are difficult to change, and this change may include questioning communal values, advocating for changing communal practices, and even adjusting the environment in which people develop certain hexeis. Finally, critics of virtue ethics say virtues are culturally relative; however, one can make the argument that cultural relativism is a challenge to any ethical problem. For rhetoricians, especially those who have tended to lean toward postmodern conceptualizations of language and morality, this critique of relativism is not a problem but a call for the importance of rhetoric in all ethical inquiry. Indeed, for centuries, rhetoric has dealt quite comfortably with probable proofs, *doxa*, and phronesis rather than objectivity, episteme, and truth.

THREE EXIGENCIES FOR VIRTUE ETHICS IN DIGITAL TECHNOLOGY

So far in this chapter, we have developed a brief history as to why virtue ethics has not been taken up in rhetorical studies. We have also provided an introduction to virtue ethics through the thought of Aristotle and shown how, similar to postmodernism, virtue ethics saw its reemergence in the twentieth century in response to rule-based, universal, and foundationalist ethical frameworks. Before we argue the final piece of our framework, we must demonstrate why virtue ethics should be taken up in rhetorical studies, particularly digital rhetoric studies.

Among scholarship on ethics of technology outside rhetoric, there has been a recent turn to virtue ethics. For example, Andrew Feenberg and Maria Bakardjieva discuss the "virtues of community" in questioning the role of consumerism and citizenship in online communities (Feenberg and Bakardjieva 2004); Stephen Bolsin, Thomas Faunce, and Justin Oakley discuss the virtues of transparency and sincerity when using portable digital technologies as vital to achieving quality and safe healthcare (Bolsin, Faunce, and Oakley 2005); Cynthia Townley and Mitch Parsell discuss student plagiarism through a virtue ethics lens (Townley and Parsell 2004); and Miguel Sicart (2005) applies a virtue ethics framework to computer gaming ethics. Most prominent, and most convincing in our opinion, is the work of Shannon Vallor (2010; 2011; 2016). Though her area of study is not rhetoric and composition, she, perhaps more than any of the above thinkers, provides three important exigencies for turning to virtue ethics in digital technologies and thus digital rhetoric.

Vallor (2010) rightly notes that discussing ethics in the digital age is tricky. Technologies are constantly changing and evolving to our needs and desires and, in turn, changing those needs and desires. Because of this ever-changing situation, if we are to discuss ethics and technology, the framework we use must be flexible and able to adapt to those particular technological changes, and it must be general enough to appeal to common normative interest. In other words, such an ethical framework must be able to speak to specifics (of technological engagement in gaming, social media, social justice, etc.) while carrying broad enough appeals (to honesty and justice, for example) that people can find such a framework applicable to a wide variety of life experiences and situations. Vallor believes "virtue ethics provides just such a framework" (Vallor 2010, 158), and we agree.

Vallor goes on to list specific reasons a virtue ethics framework is so useful in the digital era. First, if people are not born with virtues but must develop them through repeated practice so as to make these practices habits, or hexeis, we cannot evaluate morality simply by the arguments, policies, or rules people institute or argue for. Even if someone says they believe in equality or argues that we should live by a principle of inclusivity, such a claim is not the end of virtue ethics; rather, that person must also look at the habits they have developed, asking, "Do my repeated actions reinforce and express my moral beliefs?" If this is true of ethics, and if "a given technology significantly alters the nature and patterns of the activities that people regularly perform, it directly impacts the moral development of persons so affected, a long-term effect that is distinct from its immediate social consequences, but certainly no less important" (Vallor 2010, 158). Briefly put, if technologies affect the development of our ethical habits, we need to be using an ethical framework that takes habit forming into consideration.

Vallor's second reason is of more communal, even global concern. Namely, as communicative practices across different cultures have changed greatly over time, these practices have each engendered virtues for maintaining *impersonal* communication lines with disparate groups of people, ties that enable cooperation and commerce, if not always friendship and community building. A virtue ethics framework (not unlike a Foucauldian lens) would look at the advent of more recent, much faster communication technologies—many of which were developed for purposes of monetary gain, such as social media, screencasting, and text and video chatting—and rather than assume social progress is occurring, would ask if the hexeis being developed were still conducive to the kinds of social cooperation necessary for maintaining important and ethical *impersonal* relationships (Vallor 2010, 159).

Vallor's third reason to turn to a virtue ethics framework for discussions of technology is perhaps the most crucial and broadest exigence (Vallor 2010). A virtue ethics framework recognizes that virtues and vices are neither easily developed nor easily changed. As we mention above, this aspect of virtue ethics is considered a weakness by some ethicists, though we believe it is merely more realistic and therefore a strength of the framework. Such an acknowledgment perpetually creates new exigencies for those interested in the development and proliferation of digital technologies. Related to the first exigence, and keeping the larger history of technology in mind, digital technologies are relatively new, but habits are hard to break. Thus, if technologies play a key role in the kinds of ethical hexeis we develop, considering the human-technology relationship in rhetorical studies is now more vital than ever. Rhetoricians claiming to be interested in ethics or politics in any capacity who also have claimed to be able to separate such concerns from technological rhetorics can no longer make this claim, at least not from a virtue ethics perspective. In a virtue ethics framework, such a claim would be irresponsible and inaccurate, and those who make such a claim only have themselves to blame when technologies influence undesirable institutional reform and the development of unethical behaviors in individuals. Now is the time (especially for those of us working in technical communication, usability, and technology design) to engage in discussions of technological engagement and ethics so we can have *some* influence over the kinds of virtues or vices our technologies take part in producing in us.

SYMPATHETIC OR OVERLAPPING WORK IN THE RHETORICAL TRADITION

One of our reasons for featuring Vallor's position in detail is that we believe her three exigencies point to strong overlaps within related works in digital rhetoric, rhetorical studies, and technical communication studies that do not specifically employ the language of virtue ethics. Earlier, we mention Fleckenstein's cyberethos (Fleckenstein 2005), which is certainly a sympathetic framework. While she focuses on ethos rather than hexis per se, she specifically urges us to resist discussing ethics independent from material contexts and lived experience in keeping with a virtue ethics approach. Other examples include Ellen Quandahl's exploration of the relationship of *thumos* and hexis in order to challenge the privilege of the rational *cogito* of the student writer (Quandahl 2003), and Godwin Agboka's call for researchers in technical communication "to actively and progressively change a few habits" (Agboka 2014, 299) to better enact social justice certainly is consistent with virtue ethics thought. Collin Brooke, in *Lingua Fracta*, similarly argues that we must study new media rhetoric in terms of users' actual "ecologies of practice" rather than just assume the way a designer intends an interface device to work will tell us all we need to know about it (Brooke 2009, 45–46). By extension, we argue (along with ethicists such as Vallor) that virtue ethics is the ethical system that best corresponds to considering the evaluation and development of these user practices as opposed to inferring the presence (or absence) of particular ethics without looking at the behaviors being developed.

Indeed, the language of virtue ethics, relying on terms such as *disposition, orientation, comportment,* and *habit,* rather than *rule* or *duty,* also shares concerns within the material and nonhuman turn in rhetoric studies. Acknowledging that nonhumans—including animals, technologies, and objects—have agency, multiple scholars of nonhuman rhetoric have made the claim that it is ethically irresponsible for rhetoricians to ignore the rhetorical capacities of our material environment (Barnett 2010; Brown 2015; Rivers 2014). Thomas Rickert (2013), for example, argues that there is an ambient rhetoricity in the materiality that surrounds us. This materiality affects us, even persuades us, often on a level of which we are not conscious. If Davis, through Levinas, locates rhetoric as a pre-symbol relation to the unknowability of the human Other, then Rickert, through Heidegger, suggests it is the connection to the material world (*Welt*) that is also a source of this presymbolic relation. When he turns to ethics, Rickert turns to notions of ethos, arguing that our understanding of ethos should exceed conscious subjectivity and that we should understand ethos as "pertain[ing] to how we live, how we dwell" (Rickert 2013, 222). He writes,

> When we broaden the word [*ethos*], in accordance with the ancient Greek conception, we see that character and credibility themselves emerge from a way of life that is itself already embedded within locations, communities, societies, and environments and hence "spoken" by them even as we create and transform them. (Rickert 2013, 222)

Thus, rather than turn to the language of deontology and Enlightenment-reasoned ethics, in which the development of universal ethical values is somehow performed solely through reason, separate from lived experience, Rickert (2013) argues that "our ethics are not something exterior we bring in and deploy but rather a set of *comportments* that emerge from life as it is lived, from what we do, say, and make" (223; our emphasis). While by no means do we argue Rickert is a tacit virtue ethicist, it is no doubt not an accident that he, in drawing extensively on Martin Heidegger, uses a term such as "comportment" to discuss ethics. In *Bodily Arts*, Debra Hawhee, in a short and tantalizingly brief discussion of hexis (Hawhee 2004, 40–41), offers "bodily comportment" as one way to translate this term. While developing this connection further is beyond the scope of this chapter and book, it is worth noting Heidegger works through Aristotle's notion of hexis as an existential structure of *DaSein* in his *Basic Concepts of Aristotelian Philosophy* lectures (Heidegger 1996).[7]

In chapter 6 we offer another example of a tacit call for "dispositional ethics" from Jenny Rice's *Distant Publics* (Rice 2014). She offers what we see as a call to form some new habits to create social change rather than rely on simply exposing people to problematic ideological world-views (i.e., critique). Drawing on affect theory and space and place scholarship, she notes it is difficult for politically minded writing teachers to change students' political ideas in a single college class since world-views form throughout the course of students' lives and, especially, through their repeated practices outside the classroom. Here, Rice (2014) says we cannot change minds, but we can try to create "new discursive habits" of thinking of ourselves as beings produced by political and environmental relations who can therefore intervene (if we choose) in these assemblages, rather than merely seeing our emotional outrage as sufficient proof of political participation (98). Her work, along with Sid Dobrin and Christian Weisser's (Weisser and Dobrin 2002) work on ecocomposition, tacitly calls for the adoption of certain dispositional attitudes toward attending to writers' entanglements with the environment.

One other area of research within digital rhetoric and rhetorical scholarship more broadly that has points of overlap with virtue ethics lies in the concept of ethos. Many readers are no doubt familiar with Aristotle's discussion of ethos (alongside pathos and logos) as a persuasive appeal (Aristotle 2006, I.2.2 1356a4). Digital rhetoricians also know this concept quite well. In *Virtual Politik*, Elizabeth Losh discusses how a web designer maintains the ethos—"the character or image of rhetorical credibility"—of a legislator's website (Losh 2009, 24; see also Miller 2001). By contrast, other rhetorical scholars have sought to offer a more complex notion of ethos as an ongoing mode of habituation that cultivates a rhetor's mind and body over time. For example, Michael J. Hyde suggests Aristotle's ethos extends beyond the ordinary credibility or moral character of the speaker and also encompasses the ways in which rhetorical selves fluidly emerge through an ongoing process of social and discursive habituation (Hyde 2004, xiii). While Hyde does not make the connection, it is worth noting that this notion of ethos as habituation shares a link to hexis. As the philosopher Claire Carlisle observes, most post-Aristotelian approaches to the concept of habit or habituation "simply elaborate the Aristotelian thesis that moral virtue is 'the child of habit [ethos],' which 'ends up as our [second] nature [*physis*]'" (Aristotle 2002; Carlisle 2014, 103; see also Holmes 2016, 2017). According to Carlisle and other philosophers, hexis is a specific form of ethos and differs only in the extent that it refers primarily to a semistable—which is not to say rigid or inflexible—disposition specific to ethical conduct, whereas ethos—in Hyde's sense—characterizes a much broader and more diverse range of material, spatial, and affective inputs.[8]

TOWARD A VIRTUE ETHICS IN DIGITAL RHETORIC AND TECHNOLOGY

In featuring these examples, we hope to demonstrate that there are already a good number of tacit appeals for a dispositional ethics in rhetorical thought. We also see a great deal of work in grounding ethics within material, ecological, and embodied rhetoric and writing practices. Thus, we believe a virtue ethics perspective would endorse this trend in thinking about our environment and how it influences the development of our ethical habits. More specifically with regard to technology, a virtue ethics framework would argue that one way in which we can evaluate the ethics in object-oriented and material rhetorics is to analyze how the given technology alters the characters and habits of the people who use it or are affected by it, consciously or nonconsciously. At the most, the argument could be made that virtue ethics demystifies the kinds of comportments, habits, or dispositions such scholarship is calling for, scholarship that (in the tradition of Berlin) has potentially conflated all ethical frameworks as deontological and therefore avoids giving a more specific name to such a framework, which we believe is a tacit virtue ethics framework. At the least, we argue that virtue ethics supplements such scholarship.

If the most popular technologies in use today—from social media to wearable technologies—are undeniably taking part in the kinds of habits each of us is developing, it seems virtue ethics is just the framework for looking at the ethics of technology-human relationships. In addition to Rice (2014), we also argue in later chapters (via an engagement with Jane Bennett's new materialism and a hexis of patience [Bennett 2010] and Bruno Latour's call for what we see as a hexis of fairness [Latour 2004b]) that there is a great deal of tacit interest in cultivating some new ethical dispositions for rhetoric and writing teachers' interests in the nonhuman.

While Vallor tends to stick with a quite literal Aristotelian framework, and we rely on it as well to some extent, we also want to argue for some contemporary thought that is virtue ethics in all but name, which we believe can move Aristotle to more interesting places he did not necessarily get to. Indeed, our case studies that follow largely begin to both retain and extend some of Aristotle's conceptions in order to think through how virtue ethics can help us comprehend the rhetorical ethics in various social media systems and digital technologies.

3

THE PRACTICE OF EQUALITY
AS A VIRTUE

In chapters 1 and 2, we reiterate the need to theorize ethics in digital rhetoric without falling back on the Enlightenment rationality of utilitarianism and deontology or ignoring the insights of postmodern critique.[1] Our contention is that Aristotle's basic virtue ethics framework enables a normative (value-driven) ethical activity that can respect postmodern relativism and situatedness without reinscribing a universal or rationalist framework. To develop this idea, our remaining chapters investigate how to expand the notion of virtue ethics to encompass specific rhetorical situations in digital and networked spaces.

In this chapter, we start with one of the most fundamental concerns for digital rhetoricians who are interested in politics and ethical matters: social justice. The overwhelming literature on this subject both within and outside rhetoric and composition studies testifies to its importance, with David Sheridan, Jim Ridolfo, and Anthony J. Michel's recent book, *The Available Means of Persuasion: Mapping a Theory and Pedagogy of Multimodal Public Rhetoric* (Sheridan, Ridolfo, and Michel 2012), offering an excellent contribution in this area. However, as we contend in this chapter, calls for individuals to participate in digital activism far outstrip the development of normative ethical frameworks to guide or explain these practices beyond various iterations of postmodern ethics. As we argue below, virtue ethics offers an important way to advocate for specific ethical values within activist public rhetorics.

One such hexis that speaks directly to digital rhetoricians' interests in activism is Aristotle's hexis of justice. *Justice*, a term usually reserved for politics, is unique and perhaps even radical in Aristotle's sense, for it is also an ethical disposition—not how one should be treated but how one should act and behave. In commonsense understanding, at least in the US context, we usually view justice not in terms of how individuals are treated by each other but rather in terms of how the state treats its citizens. For example, in recent protests over police brutality toward African American males, the cries of "justice for Freddy Gray" or "Tamir Rice" are designed

DOI: 10.7330/9781607328063.c003

to change institutional mechanisms to ensure better treatment (i.e., achieve justice). These appeals—not unimportant ones by any means—distill to a basic claim: "treat us better." While not incommensurate with the latter, Aristotle's justice as a hexis differs in that justice is something individuals strive to enact with one another regardless (though not exclusive) of institutional treatment, and—as we demonstrate below—this requirement presupposes institutions must preserve nonutilitarian conditions under which individuals can realize eudaimonia.

While Aristotle's early articulation of justice is compelling, we agree fully with Fleckenstein (2005) that certain elements of his thinking require careful elaboration to be useful for digital rhetoric. To this assertion, we also add that it is necessary to qualify some of the contradictory or unegalitarian elements of his framework. For example, Aristotle does not offer a definitive thesis about justice. Numerous researchers have observed that Aristotle ties ethics and political laws together—"Justice is complete virtue toward another person" (Aristotle 2002, 1.1129b27)—but he also writes "everything that is lawful is in a way just" (1.1129b12). It is not clear in the latter passage how Aristotle would support civil disobedience to secure the conditions under which justice can be practiced. In a different but related vein, while Aristotle is undeniably concerned with equality of a certain type, it is true he argued slaves were largely incapable of realizing eudaimonia. The latter simply had few opportunities to develop hexeis that were not in service of means-ends directives of their owners, whereas the hexeis that lead toward eudaimonia can only exist for their own ends. Obviously, we disagree with Aristotle's conclusions on this matter.

Simply put, our efforts to update this particular hexis of justice will retain Aristotle's general conception of a hexis—this active having (*echein*) that must be cultivated akin to a second nature to guide ethical action—but update his understanding of justice through scholarship more directly related to the concerns of contemporary theorists and digital rhetoric.[2] One such framework lies in the writing of the French political philosopher Jacques Rancière (1992; 1995; 1999), which usefully supplements current political frameworks that influence conceptions of social justice in digital rhetoric. Rancière's thought offers digital rhetoricians a language for verifying equality via practices within institutional and noninstitutional contexts, where change can be slow and inequality can be pervasive. His notion of politics is unique. Politics exists in acts that disturb what he calls "partitions of the sensible" or the "police order." These partitions of the sensible are cultural practices or structures that actively participate in inequality by perpetuating hierarchy and the control of even one human being over another. Political acts, then, are not solely parliamentary deliberation or campaigning for votes but are any active verification of another's equality that disturbs such a partition of the sensible. In contrast to liberalism's political goal of forming consensus, Rancière's philosophy offers a politics of dissensus. Because Rancière is interested in cultivating politics as an ongoing process of self and collective verifications of equality, hexis captures perfectly Rancière's call for individuals and collectives to engage in habituated practices of the verification of equality as part of the articulation of social justice in research, teaching, and industry.

In what follows, we introduce Rancière's political theory of active equality (a hexis of justice) as a supplement to the dominance of liberal passive equality frameworks. While it is true many postmodern theorists, especially in the case of public sphere theorists (Fraser 1997; Squires 2000; Warner 2005), have challenged liberal democratic rationality and consensus as, in reality, exclusionary and contingent, we nevertheless find these same postmodern thinkers often pressing their critique back into the mechanisms of liberal democratic political philosophy by recommending activist practices such as lobbying and campaigning, with Laura J. Gurak's examination of "copyleft" as a clear case in point (Gurak 1997). Our concern is simply that the intentional or unintentional default to liberal democratic political mechanisms (or, conversely, the failure to elaborate in detail how one moves from critique of mechanisms to active political production) leaves digital rhetoricians in a position in which we identify social justice as enacting a form of passive equality in which social justice exists only when the prevailing legal or dominant institution enables the redress. By contrast, Rancière offers a way to cultivate a disposition of social justice as a form of active equality in which individuals and collectives can enact social justice as the active verification of their own and others' political equality both within and independent from the institutional redistribution of justice.

We illustrate this hexis by applying Rancière's thought to a study of closed captioning in two ways: (1) by examining ableism and lack of accessibility in the absence of legal requirements for YouTube videos to require closed captioning, and (2) by examining implicit racism in audio-to-text transcriptions in general. On the one hand, because closed captioning is not required by YouTube, a partition of the sensible presently exists for deaf users and global non-English-speaking audiences. In more basic terms, producing closed captions for viewers is not considered part of the common sense of a video producer or sharer. In this context, passive forms of institutional social justice might include requesting a company-policy change to include captions in all online videos and then waiting for the policy to take effect. By contrast, the value in Rancière's framework is that social justice is not dependent upon any individual digital rhetor's ability (or desire) to produce change through institutional mechanisms of the redistribution of justice. At the same time, the rhetor's communicative practices can nevertheless make visible unegalitarian partitions of the sensible in a tangible manner for multiple audiences and actors. To illustrate the distinction between active and passive forms of politics, we consider the scenario of a digital rhetorician who works for a company that posts videos to YouTube and who comes to see the complex rhetorical practice of producing captions as an enactment of social justice. However, simply composing captions as a vital part of video production is not sufficient, as Sean Zdenek (2011, 2015) has argued. For example, one readily finds ineffective and racist captions in television shows as popular as *Breaking Bad* that highlight the "negative" discursive patterns of African American or Mexican American characters. Cultivating a Rancièreian hexis, a digital rhetorician who is producing videos can redress these forms of inequality by verifying the equality of those they are about to represent in terms of the language choices used to communicate to the deaf and hard-of-hearing communities.

PASSIVE MODELS OF ENACTING SOCIAL JUSTICE

Calls for social justice or digital activism abound, both inside rhetorical studies and outside it. Yet, beyond many references to Paulo Freire (2000) and Henry Giroux (1983) (postmodern critiques), these appeals broadly stop short of recommending *how* social justice can be enacted as an individual and communal ethical practice. For example, copyright has been a consistent concern for digital rhetoricians (DeVoss and Webb n.d.). Laura J. Gurak has particularly called for "the need for more activism and attention on the part of communication teachers and researchers in regard to copyright and fair use—toward what Andrea Lunsford called 'copyleft' and away from the corporate paradigm that threatens to reshape copyright law (especially in regard to communication technologies) for the next century" (Gurak 1997, 342). It is clear Gurak is working through a loose postmodern ethical framework that questions capitalism's belief in the "free market" as universal or naturalized human law or good and instead locates contingent and selfish profit motives as lurking behind copyright. Yet, her specific notion of justice stems from a recognizably liberal democratic framework. While this term *liberal democratic* can mean a variety of things, here we simply mean activism often consists of signaling the presence of an injustice to an institutional body—by voting or contacting your local congressman or senator—and then waiting for that institutional body to make a change to law or policies, which will ideally rectify the injustice.

While Gurak certainly does not exclude alternative forms of activism, her de facto list of recommended activist practices includes working through national organizations (NCTE, CCCC, MLA, NCA) to use the "power of their numbers to speak against legislation that is harmful to the public domain" and using digital tools to create "lobby-matics" that enable members to easily cut and paste various appeals "into a simple letter to their representatives in Washington" (Gurak 1997, 337). She also supports the independent formation of new lobbying bodies, such as the Digital Freedom Coalition (DFC). Finally, Gurak makes a strong appeal for digital rhetoric teachers to include the complex and political nature of copyright on syllabi and to teach students about these elements directly as part of course content. Clearly, the activist nature includes—and, again, our remarks are in no way intended as critical of these engagements—lobbying for legislation, universities passing their own policies, and teachers working with these themes in the classroom (Gurak 1997).[3]

To examine this turn to social justice, and before turning to Rancière, we briefly compare two models of social justice: liberal and libertarian political philosophies, the most dominant social justice frameworks at work in the United States and Europe. Each framework arguably stems from the Enlightenment philosopher John Locke (1988, 1996), who grounded politics in natural rights. Following Locke, Robert Nozick (1974) notably articulated the basis for contemporary libertarian frameworks. In brief, libertarian systems of thought hold that the state's primary goal is to maximize and protect an individual's rights, often by attempting to minimize the state's interference in citizens' lives as much as possible. In this system, equality is a secondary concern and social injustice occurs when states or organizations fail to ensure people's ability to exercise their liberty. At best, any concerns for equality in libertarianism reflect this commitment to minimal governance, such as the sense of the equal opportunity of private companies and consumers to purchase or sell products. By extension, a libertarian digital rhetorician (perhaps a technical communicator) interested in social justice might work to avoid infringing upon citizens' liberties by making sure clients or customers know exactly what they are purchasing or exactly how a product functions. In this framework, the stereotypical tasks of a digital rhetorician—making sure the language is clear, precise, simple, and honest (as seen in technical communication manuals)—is the primary activity they can practice *to prevent injustice*. It is critical to note that they *cannot actively create justice* in the eyes of a libertarian framework, for ensuring the distribution of justice remains the responsibility of the state through laws and policies ensuring free-market exchange. In addition, a libertarian digital rhetorician may not seek to develop a habit of viewing inequalities of gender, race, class, ability, and sexuality as social injustices unless they infringe upon such free-market exchange. As a result, even when they do not use this term, a great number of rhetoric and writing scholars have implicitly sought to challenge a libertarian approach to social justice.

By contrast, liberalism represents a great number of social justice theories currently practiced. Similar to libertarianism, liberalism views social justice as enacted by the state and its institutions. However, unlike libertarianism, which is most invested in free-market exchange, liberalism is interested in equality and views this equality as something distributed by a governing body. The liberal philosopher John Rawls prominently argued this position. He maintained that the social and economic inequalities of a social system should only exist to "the greatest benefit of the least-advantaged members of society" (Rawls 1971, 5–6). In contrast to the libertarian, then, the liberal digital rhetorician may recognize the unequal treatment of people by class, gender, race, ability, and sexuality as injustices; nevertheless, according to the framework of liberalism, *the digital rhetorician is not enacting social justice* even in trying to persuade those in power to change laws and policies. It is liberalism's view that *social justice only occurs when the end goal is reached* and new laws or policies are institutionalized and enforced to correct the injustice. Under this framework, the digital rhetorician might take part passively—and positively—to change a system of social justice by calling to include marginalized groups and adhering to laws of affirmative action or accessibility in document design practices, but only the system can actively create social justice through a change in law, policy, or protocol.

In current research, the implied theoretical model of social justice—liberalism—places the locus on the institution (often the state) to ensure enactments of justice. This research significantly foregrounds the dimension of liberalism that—even beyond postmodern criticism—makes it difficult to enact social justice. To explain this difficulty, we refer to a notion of "passive equality" (May 2008, 5). In brief, passive equality describes systems of political organization wherein humans are viewed as receivers of equality distributed by an organization or a state rather than as active enactors of equality. While passive equality is undeniably useful for achieving certain aspects of social justice, and is by all means preferable to any political system not interested in equality, we contend that understanding social justice solely in terms of passive equality nevertheless poses at least two obstacles in enabling digital rhetoricians to practice social justice. First, passive-equality frameworks do not inevitably encourage researchers to explore how an individual digital rhetorician can enact social justice on their own, independent of institutional mechanisms; instead, they focus on signaling an injustice and waiting for institutional or state correction. Second, this institutional distance often makes it difficult to cultivate the desire in an individual digital rhetorician to engage in social justice when the system may seem so broad and removed from the effects of their own individual agency.[4]

To reiterate, in identifying liberalism as a form of passive equality, we still believe liberalism is in many ways a more desirable framework than is a libertarian or other perspective that prioritizes other values over equality. However, the significant point for determining active and passive frameworks of social justice lies in which entities—individuals or organizations/the state—are able to enact social justice. To be clear, under a liberal paradigm, the only entity that can "grant" the digital rhetorician power (in terms of justice) is the equitable method of distribution found in the enforcement of a system's protocols, an organization's policies, a state's laws, or—at best—those who are empowered to employ those methods. It is not a form of equality any individual can practice outside legitimate institutional channels.

To be sure, digital rhetoricians are familiar with similar criticisms of liberal democracy. Sheridan, Ridolfo, and Michel, for example, specifically theorize a multimodal public sphere without "reinscribing a naive liberal ideal of equal access for all participants" (Sheridan, Ridolfo, and Michel 2012, 17). They retain the term "public sphere" minus the Habermasian meaning of "formally elegant, inherently rational, self-completing and self-regulating entities" (see Habermas 4, quoted in Brouwer and Asen 2010, 4). Indeed, their version of kairos, taken from Eric Charles White (1987), teaches students different mediums to "create the conditions within which students—as members of various and overlapping publics and counterpublics—can theorize their own situated decisions about public participation" (Brouwer and Asen 2010, 17) in ways that may be "unpredictable" and that range from small-scale tactical interventions to interacting with broader publics. Similarly, as we argue below, work that sees justice as a virtue is interested in blurring any division between actions on a smaller scale and those concerned with broader public and institutional work. In this way, Sheridan, Ridolfo, and Michel offer a definition of public spheres as a "a set of contested and complementary, affective and desire-laden imaginary social phenomena brought into being through multiple acts of rhetorical poesis, addressed to strangers and occurring over time and in spaces that are simultaneously discursive, cultural, and material" (Sheridan, Ridolfo, and Michel 2012, 21). This definition echoes mostly postmodern criticisms by Michael Warner (2005), for whom publics are produced through creative "world making" rather than being static things that exist. Simply put, these sorts of public sphere frameworks offer us the conditions through which we can teach students without specifically requiring that they participate in a particular type of public interaction.

While it is impossible to offer a representative summary of digital rhetoric and activism scholarship due to the large amount of scholarship published in this area, a number of digital rhetoricians follow Sheridan, Ridolfo, and Michel's (2012) lead in calling for shifts in scholarly paradigms to acknowledge the role of digital tools in creating conditions of possibility for activism. As an example of digital rhetoricians who employ liberal democratic frameworks, or the language of counterpublics, Laurie Goodling's webtext essay in *Kairos*, "MOAR Activism, Please," argues that "digital activism allows for vastly creative forms of rhetoric (both visual and sonic) that could not be accomplished simultaneously in print media or underground radio prior to the existence of Web 2.0" (Goodling 2015; see also Jones 2009). While work by media studies theorists such as Alexander R. Galloway's (Foucauldian-Deleuzian) treatment of protocol (Galloway 2006), as well as the rise of surveillance and "big-data" tracking, may cause us to temper these generalizations, the more significant point is that Goodling's conception of activism represents one trend within digital rhetoric, namely, an argument justifying digital tools as a serious or legitimate method of activism. Goodling argues, "This shift in dynamic puts the power in the hands of the user as one who transmits and circulates at her will, on her timeframe, and to the extent she desires. It levels the playing field to some degree, and it provides opportunity for voices to be heard that might otherwise be ignored by those holding the reigns in politics and media" (Goodling 2015). Goodling's emphasis lies primarily in identifying the conditions of possibility for individual digital activists to become effective digital public sphere participants rather than identifying which types of public spheres or institutions are good or ethical to support. On this note, digital rhetoricians also must be careful in asserting or even implying that digital counterpublics presuppose inherent ethical goods. As noted public sphere theorist Warner ably documents in his discussion of counterpublics, arguments to merely create the conditions of possibility for digital activism decoupled from specific forms of ethical advocacy can simultaneously open the door for trolling, hate groups (the KKK, in Warner's discussion), anti-LGBTQ groups, and many other marginalized ideological orientations (Warner 2005).

THE LIMITATIONS OF PASSIVE EQUALITY
FOR PRACTICING SOCIAL JUSTICE

Echoing Sheridan, Ridolfo, and Michel (2012), we do not wish to dismiss the importance of using passive-equality frameworks or to reduce the necessity for a wide variety of critique-driven and productive scholarship that calls for social justice on behalf of the marginalized in any way. The current era requires a wide variety of especially multimodal kairotic responses. In calling attention to passive forms of social justice, it is important to acknowledge again that active and passive forms of equality are neither opposed nor mutually exclusive, nor do they signify effective or ineffective forms of social justice. Our goal is to observe that passive frameworks have built-in limitations in terms of recognizing the variety of active forms of social justice that can also enable digital rhetoricians to work toward political equality. For example, one problem with passive equality is that it tends to legitimate the abilities of those in power (administrators, politicians, elites, policy writers) to maintain the allegedly naturalized channels they have established to enact social justice. Numerous critics of liberalism and public discourse have established the existence of this problem (Fraser 1997; Harvey 2007; Young 1990).

By contrast, a far greater problem is that there exists a particular form of elitism even in many ostensibly democratic forms of justice. This larger issue revolves around the ways in which equality is discussed. In many liberal theories, equality is mostly a matter of what people should receive—so-called distributive theories that apportion who gets what. In a very basic sense, a distributive theory of justice sees an enactment of equality take place when the organization or a state maintains or changes its distribution of rights, goods, or responsibilities to correct a social injustice of inequality. By definition, distributive theories of justice presuppose the passivity of the receiver in terms of being able to enact social justice in particular. Under passive-equality frameworks, the marginalized are objects of distribution rather than validated as able to enact equality through their own activities. As Todd May (2008) states,

Once people are thought to be objects of distribution rather than subjects of creation, then hierarchy is inevitable. The idea that those who distribute equality are simply performing an administrative task hides a deeper problem. It divides people into those who are politically active and those who are politically passive. And to be politically passive is not to be equal, in the creation of one's own life, to those who are active. (5)

May (2008) cautions that even when a liberal system might name all human participants as equals, the ability to practice social justice retains a division (though not an absolute binary) between active and passive. As a result, digital rhetoricians may frustratingly see themselves as limited in terms of enacting social justice. Under a passive-quality framework, researchers may view their work as political in the sense that the research is always embedded within power relations (Sullivan and Porter 1997) and as they critically call attention to and lobby for the inclusion of marginalized groups; however, a framework has yet to be put forth that enables researchers to view their own practices as actively producing social justice. In our anecdotal experience, students often voice frustration in relation to this need. It can be difficult to bring the idea of social justice into the digital rhetoric or technical communication classroom when the very modes of enacting social justice seem so far removed from the day-to-day writing practices and workplace environments of the students' future professions. Furthermore, even the use of mediums such as Twitter, which seem to place the public into more accessible forms, suffer criticisms of merely enabling outrage. Such is not to say these are not real or authentic dispositions. It is more to highlight that it is necessary to provide students not merely with kairotic medial needs but also with theories to aid their active practices of social justice if they choose such activity.

The Americans with Disabilities Act (ADA) is a perfect example of passive equality. Enacted as law by the US Congress in 1990 (with an amendment in 2008), the ADA "prohibits discrimination and ensures equal opportunity for persons with disabilities in employment, State and local government services, public accommodations, commercial facilities, and transportation" (ADA.gov 2014). The enactment of this law was a great success for those who lobbied for decades to recognize the equality of people with disabilities; however, as such acts are envisioned through a lens of liberalism, social justice was enacted only when it was sanctioned and enforced by government institutions. In contrast to passive-equality frameworks, we argue that digital rhetoricians can envision and productively enact social justice themselves without waiting for institutional sanction to change or better reflect a more ethical social arrangement. Many in technical communication scholarship, for example, have advocated active civic engagement as crucial to ethical technical communication (Bowdon 2004; Grabill and Simmons 1998; Rude 2004; Simmons and Grabill 2007). However, we argue that to fully realize such advocacy as enactments of social justice requires an alternative theory of social justice that shifts digital rhetoricians from passive objects of distribution to subjects of action, and we believe this theory is one that sees justice as a hexis.

RANCIÈRE'S HEXIS OF (SOCIAL) JUSTICE

In this section, we introduce a hexis of social justice for digital rhetoric that, like liberalism, is invested in equality. However, instead of seeing equality passively as something that is received or is only a long-term goal, this theory of social justice stems from active equality and sees justice as something in need of continual reenactment. The political philosophy of Rancière (1992; 1995; 1999) offers one useful framework for realizing this shift from passive to active. Instead of a framework in which the emphasis is on distributive methods or administration agendas, Rancière's theory politically enables those who need it the most, people whose equality is unrecognized by a system or the social order. An act of social justice, in Rancière's sense, is any act that makes visible the equality of even one person whose voice has been suppressed and whose equality has been erased or ignored. Rancière argues that political emancipation is not the freedom or liberation from restrictions, whether they be legal, political, or social. Rather, political emancipation is the moment one recognizes one's own equality, which enables "the verification of the equality of any speaking being with any other speaking being" (Rancière 1992, 58–60). After one is emancipated, others can be emancipated. All that is required for this emancipation to be verified is for one human being to "mobilize an *obligation* to hear" in another human being—for one being to incite another into seeing what they had not recognized before: a fellow human's equality (Rancière 1995, 86). It is important to note that this other human being can be oneself, for to verify the equality of another, one must recognize the presupposition at work in oneself: "Proving to the other that there is only one world and that one can prove the legitimacy of one's action within it, means first of all proving this to oneself" (50). Simply put, Rancière's thought helps digital rhetoricians actively engage in social justice practices without thinking they must wait for institutional permission or must work only through legitimized frameworks of redress.

Perhaps the best way to understand Rancière's political thought is to place it in context with those ideas, systems, and practices that are *not* "politics." As Rancière argues, politics occurs through dissensus and verifications of equality. However, these terms and processes are very different from the terms and processes researchers typically associate with politics, such as order, law, consensus, and the distribution of rights and resources. Usually, such a "set of procedures whereby the aggregation and consent of collectivities is achieved, the organization of powers, the distribution of places and roles, and the systems of legitimizing this distribution" is named "politics" (Rancière 1999, 33). These conventional forms of politics, with the liberal tradition as a case in point, maintain individuals as passive receivers. This point is important to stress. Processes as diverse as government elections, social safety nets, taxes, healthcare, and institutions that maintain law and order all work to organize, classify, and create social hierarchies among citizens. To be clear, one can undeniably find arguments and articulations of political equality within these organizational contexts, including examples like providing equal access to healthcare, administering voting rights, and enacting affirmative-action laws. However, these cases of equality are passive and require people in authority and institutional mechanisms to distribute this equality. Rancière's concern is that politics in the liberal tradition (and other political traditions) presuppose a structural order that ensures that someone controls another person, even if this control is born out of concern for that person's well-being.

By contrast, Rancière's philosophy is simply interested in reclassifying politics as an active form of the verification of equality any individual can practice. Thus, he has relabeled "politics" in the liberal sense of distribution and legitimization of passive equality through hierarchies as the "police order." Simply put, even societies with strong or weak democracies (see Barber 1984) have police orders. Not to be confused with individuals with badges who pull over speeding drivers, the police order is much more generalized, much more systemic. Rancière (1999) states,

> The police is thus first an order of bodies that defines the allocation of ways of doing, ways of being, and ways of saying, and sees that those bodies are assigned by name to a particular place and task; it is an order of the visible and the sayable that sees that a particular activity is visible and another is not, that this speech is understood as discourse and another as noise. (29)

Rancière's (1992, 1995, 1999) concern for making equality visible and sayable has to do with the ways in which police orders work to maintain what he calls "partitions of the sensible," the structuring, programming, and institutional dividing that decide which individuals count in a societal order or, in other words, the ways in which a system identifies their political equality and counts them as participating players.

Rancière's unique conceptual terminology is often easier to grasp through an example. Some obvious, explicit forms of the partition of the sensible include English-only education and "traditional" marriage laws. These laws legitimate certain people and groups (e.g., English speakers and couples who are identified as heterosexual), and these laws distribute powers across various social institutions and practices, influencing who qualifies for medical-insurance benefits and against whom a company can discriminate when hiring new employees. However, this partitioning of the sensible also occurs in what may, upon first glance, appear to be less oppressive and more implicit distributions of the sensible, such as in the designation of men's and women's public restrooms—distributions that make people who identify as transgender, for example, invisible in a social order. This distribution of the sensible is beyond exclusion in that the invisible are not even counted among what is excluded in a social order (e.g., women are excluded from a men's restroom and vice versa).

Thus, Rancière's notion of politics exists through what he calls dissensus to police orders that disturb (i.e., make visible) existing partitions of the sensible. Politics is not an overall strategy of governance but a habitual act of dissensus (resistance, disruption) born out of presupposition of equality: "Politics only occurs when these [police] mechanisms are stopped in their tracks by the effect of a presupposition that is totally foreign to them . . . the presupposition of the equality of anyone and everyone" (Rancière 1999, 17). As a result, politics occurs very rarely and is temporal, as Rancière has designated "the term *politics* for an extremely determined activity antagonistic to policing" (29). However, unlike liberal models of social justice, any individual or collective can take part in an active verification of equality as an act of social justice against partitions of the sensible in actual existence. Here, individuals do not wait for a state or institution to distribute human rights because this delay would legitimate police orders that leave digital rhetoricians as passive objects of distribution. Rather, Rancière's thought flips the script, enabling digital rhetoricians to become active practitioners of equality. It is a bottom-up form of social justice in contrast to a top-down distributive model of liberal or even libertarian justice. To be clear, Rancière does not mean any act of dissensus against an authority figure is an act of equality. One might imagine a digital rhetorician who destroys a photocopier at work in the spirit of the film *Office Space* (Judge 1999) in response to a mean-spirited performance evaluation. Such an act of dissensus is not political unless it is born out of a desire for equality.

To sum up, Rancière's political framework sees digital rhetoricians (or anyone) as able to enact equality actively rather than waiting passively for the distribution of equality from those in positions of power—it needs no policies to be put into action, and it requires neither a perfect system of distribution nor mechanisms from which to perpetuate order. Rather, enactments of social justice require the existence of beings who can communicate and thus presuppose and verify each other's equality. In the context of this book, it is Rancière's aim of making politics an individual and collective activity of constant reverification, rather than a permanently existing institutional achievement, that makes Rancière's work a tacit form of Aristotelian justice, that is, a hexis. In this regard, we view Rancière as offering one of the most significant updates and extensions of Aristotle's virtue ethics, particularly in political contexts. Rancière at once retains the sensibility to kairotic flexibility public rhetoric scholars desire, while at the same time advocating a specific ethics of justice (equality) that may be understated or latent within a great deal of digital activist scholarship. In this regard, Rancière's framework is ideal for digital rhetoricians because it acknowledges that many of us work in systems of inequality as employees or contractors or teachers or researchers, and this situatedness does not matter to Rancière in the least in relationship to our ability to practice social justice as a hexis. While he acknowledges that individuals may not always have the power to create institutional forms of the redistribution of justice, for Rancière, equality cannot be institutionalized, and thus social justice is never achieved in any permanent sense, even when laws or policies are improved. Rather, digital rhetoricians must be aware of human equality and work diligently to continually verify it through their work and research practices, no matter the institution in which they work.[5]

ENACTING EQUALITY THROUGH CLOSED CAPTIONING

In the following section, we suggest one medium and practice as crucial to developing a hexis of social justice in digital rhetoric: closed captioning in video production. As a growing number of researchers (notably Dolmage 2014; Meloncon 2013; Walters 2014; Zdenek 2015) have made clear, ableism is a critically underexamined form of marginalization within digital rhetoric and technical communication research on usability and the organizational contexts in which technical communicators practice. Liberal forms of redistributive justice have enjoyed success in this area. The Individuals with Disabilities Education Act (IDEA), the Rehabilitation Act of 1973, the Americans with Disabilities Act (ADA), and the Federal Communications Commission have required buildings to be planned with elevators, automatic doors, and ramps. While similar legislative efforts have enforced closed captioning in certain contexts, such as public education and television, there are multiple arenas in which people with disabilities are still not included as equals to able-bodied people. In Rancière's terms, such systematic exclusions are a product of partitions of the sensible, or the social structuring that determines who counts in certain contexts.

Closed captioning represents a particularly important site of mediation between deaf/hard-of-hearing communities and nondeaf communities. With respect to this emerging research area, Zdenek writes, "Despite the age of captioning technology, we still do not have a comprehensive approach to caption quality that goes beyond basic issues of typography, placement, and timing" (Zdenek 2011, para. 2). The 1996 Telecommunications Act requires closed captioning for all television broadcasts, but social media streaming is not yet held to the same standard. By extension, closed captioning is yet to be raised as a specific concern by digital rhetoric directly invested in social justice, though Zdenek is undoubtedly concerned with issues of inequality, particularly as they pertain to captioning.

While not in explicit dialogue with digital rhetoric scholarship in composition studies, it is worth noting that Zdenek's comments apply equally to the ways in which captioning issues remain somewhat on the margins of digital rhetoricians' emerging interests in video production. We do not want to diminish in any way these texts' important contributions to digital and visual rhetoric, but we must point out that major texts from Bump Halbritter (2012), David Blakesley (2007), and Sarah J. Arroyo (2013) do not reference captioning as part of the video creation or critique process. If mentioned at all, captioning remains bracketed as something external to video production rather than a fundamental part of the process of imagining how a viewer experiences a video. Some might argue that captioning is external or secondary to the video-production process; however, researchers such as Zdenek have countered that the failure to consider the deaf and hard-of-hearing communities as potential viewers during the production stages in effect figures deaf viewers as abnormal in comparison to able-bodied viewers (Zdenek 2015). To be clear, the above texts' subject matter would clearly lend them to supporting these practices. In other words, readers will not encounter direct claims that closed captioning is somehow external to the interests of video production. It is mostly in a tacit partition of the sensible that captioning remains bracketed as something external to video production rather than a fundamental part of the process of imagining how viewers can experience a video.

As an illustration of how partitions of the sensible operate in closed captioning, consider a digital rhetoric assignment in which a teacher asks their students to make a screencast of a set of technical procedures for making a recipe, such as a seafood gumbo. The students create the video and upload it to YouTube, and that is the end of the process. Their assignment is apparently complete. However, the students have omitted an important practice that is not required by YouTube and that, furthermore, has clear implications for social justice and ableism: composing closed captions. Hard-of-hearing YouTube lifestyle vlogger Rikki Poynter recently foregrounded this problem (Newcomb 2015). She told ABC News that even if users want to generate closed captioning through YouTube's automatic captioning algorithm, the result is "'a bunch of nonsensible mumbo jumbo'" (para. 2). In fact, comedians Rhett and Link (2011) have raised awareness of horrible YouTube translations in their "CAPTION FAIL" video series. They upload videos to YouTube and then revise their videos' audio scripts to correspond to the inaccurate YouTube autocaptioning transcription.

How then might a teacher help students use Rancière as a lens through which to think through social justice in this example? Or, more specifically, how might a teacher provide assignments that help students begin to cultivate a hexis of justice as equality? Well, the loose sort of institutional hierarchy Rancière criticizes is already in place. Echoing a liberal orientation, Rikki Poynter has lobbied YouTube and used her considerable clout to encourage her viewers to also petition, with few positive results (Newcomb 2015). The same ABC News article that features an interview with Poynter quotes YouTube product manager, Matthew Glotzbach, as stating that while the garbled translations were "'better than nothing . . . it is by no means good enough yet'" (Newcomb 2015, para. 6). In contrast to its inaction regarding the poor quality of its automated closed captioning, YouTube has made numerous improvements to increase video quality and prevent copyright infringement. With Glotzbach's response as a case in point, captioning technology or even giving video creators a strong motivation to caption accurately does not appear to be a top priority. Able-bodied users remain YouTube's implicit universal users—a clear partition of the sensible. To reiterate our point, Poynter's response to this injustice, while important, clearly relies upon a liberal passive-equality framework because Poynter is relying on institutional powers, in this case YouTube's, to redress the wrong of inequality in captioning.

In contrast (but in addition) to Poynter's approach, Rancière's philosophy offers ways for researchers, teachers, and digital practitioners who employ screencasting in their work (and YouTube video producers in general) to engage in social justice activism through the practice of creating rhetorically effective closed captions. Consider a web designer who is creating a site with five "how-to" videos for installing a piece of equipment. The videos are created either in house or by linking to existing videos created by another user. By default, YouTube's policies state that the user can specifically select an autocaption option as a conscious decision, or it "may" use its own algorithm to "add" closed captions if the user does not select this choice (YouTube 2016). While a typical uploader may consider that their role of participating in accessibility has ended because of the automated closed-caption feature, it is quite clear that leaving garbled captions still maintains a partition of the sensible. Thus, automated closed captioning still produces a form of social injustice as it privileges hearing users over deaf and hard-of-hearing users.

In this situation, the web designer can enact equality in multiple ways. Ideally, we claim that digital rhetoricians should consider producing closed captions as a vital practice of any form of video production—as a key component to video production from the start. Such considerations should begin in the storyboarding and planning phase. Thus, our web designer can use software such as Camtasia to create captions as an important part of the production of the video rather than solely cap them on as a second thought; alternatively, depending on their technological constraints, they can use the free online interface Amara.org to enter a video URL link and caption the company's videos accurately (as well as embed the videos with the Amara wrapper). However, in keeping with hexis as a dispositional practice rather than a temporary form of inspiration, this does not mean creating the captions should be the last step. For example, creating the text for captioning can and should be a part of the initial invention stages of video production. Rather than solely caption dialogue, the web designer also will follow Zdenek's call to caption all significant sounds and will do their best to caption each audio element that may be crucial to the making of meaning for deaf, hard-of-hearing, and global users (Zdenek 2011)

Recognizing that YouTube's automatic captioning feature works out of a presupposition of inequality regarding deaf users—a partition of the sensible that assumes viewers are hearing users—the web designer will intervene and verify their equality in her practice. Such actions do not eliminate the digital rhetorician's ethical obligation to also make an argument to the company. They might argue that effective captioning should not be an afterthought but a critical element the company should add to usability guidelines for design policies for web and social media production rather than placing the lobbying burden on Poynter and the deaf community. In other words, captioning should not just be a new policy but a hexis—a habitually formed disposition—for employees to critically cultivate. Contrary to passive paradigms, petitioning institutional mechanisms of distribution will not be the web designer's primary or only goal for enacting social justice.

Enacting a hexis of justice through a verification of equality can be as simple as an employee making it known that they are going to take the time to plan how to close caption any new videos in production (and perhaps delve into the archive where possible) as an active practice of verifying the equality of deaf and global viewers. Relying on a certain distribution of the sensible, an employer might view this decision as an act of dissensus. One might similarly imagine an employer saying, "We have no deaf users," questioning the use of resources for this purpose or implicitly believing the employee's time is better reserved for serving the majority of able-bodied consumers rather than a minority. To emphasize this distinction again, such appeals for equality no doubt appear similar to the practice of lobbying for social justice in liberalism. However, unlike liberalism, which requires sanctioned mechanisms and processes such as voting and law making to enact justice, Rancière's framework simply requires the ability to communicate. Certain manifestations of hexis-as-justice will appear as dissensus to an employer or client—they might make an employer go "Huh?" in the sense that an invisible form of marginalization has been actively made visible through a dissensual act. Simultaneously, the unheard user with a disability may say, "Someone's listening; I *am* equal to hearing users." The decision to compose rhetorically effective closed captions is a complex form of dissensus in an additional sense because the YouTube account owner must approve the uploaded captions for the captions to be viewed on their channel. In the case of the web designer linking to existing video content, the decision to produce accurate closed captions would again make visible a partition of the sensible to other content creators.

Indeed, even the decision to "add" closed captions may not ultimately overturn this partition of the sensible. *Adding* as a verb implies that closed captioning is an external or supplementary concern, akin to proofreading a research article before submitting it to a journal editor. For example, John-Patrick Udo and Deborah Fels offer a hypothetical example of an active theory of social justice in the context of the film industry (Udo and Fels 2010). Speaking specifically to digital rhetoricians' interests in video production, movie producers also support a de facto partition of the sensible by making closed captions an added postinventional or postproduction activity by relying upon independent contractors to produce captions. By contrast, Udo and Fels (2010) recommend that movie producers should be involved in the production of movie captions themselves. In our digital rhetoric practices, an active-equality framework would foreground or start with captioning alongside any analytical or productive use of videos, television programs, and related social media clips. Indeed, asking, say, digital rhetoric and technical communication students to storyboard their videos as a primary act of rhetorical invention should also include the production of rhetorically effective captions as a crucial part of the process. An active theory of social justice requires a dramatic shift in metaphors and practices of closed captioning. Such a shift envisions students viewing captioning in a video (or any multimodal audio/visual text) as a political site of complex and competing interpretations rather than a mere vehicle of transcription as a mechanical and formulaic practice.

It is important to affirm again that an active theory of social justice in no way replaces or eliminates the need to attend to liberal forms of political activism. To offer an example specific to the deaf community, as a result of decades of lobbying for accessibility reform, it is illegal under the Americans with Disabilities Act to even conceive of planning to build a structure without considering access for people with disabilities (e.g., wheelchair ramps). In other words, lawsuits are inevitable for any public or workplace building that does not factor in these concerns from the start. The ADA confirms that certain partitions of the sensible have been made and institutions have provided correctives, thereby eliminating the need to lobby for political equality in instances after the fact (e.g., after a building has been completed). However, such successes of liberal activism do not mean certain partitions of the sensible are erased.

Major research schools such as Harvard and MIT recently have faced lawsuits related to the lack of closed captioning in their online education and course-management software, such as Blackboard and Canvas (Lewin 2015). Beyond the context of YouTube, however, many other universities have begun to form policies in response to Section 504 of the Rehabilitation Act of 1973, 29 U.S.C. § 794, which obligates institutions "to be accessible to students and other individuals with disabilities . . . [and] provide necessary auxiliary aids and services for

individuals who are deaf or hard of hearing, including qualified inter-
preters, transcribers, notetakers, and provision of closed captioning or
other access for televised information" (National Association of the Deaf
n.d., para 3). While it is tempting to think a partition of the sensible has
been overturned because of this legislation, and that passive-equality
forms have been effective, the reality is that partitions of the sensible can
run far deeper than policy change.

In chapter 2, during our discussion of Viki, we offer the examples of
a university or company that has indeed changed its policies to require
closed captioning for all instructional videos, whether as a result of
political pressure or the desire to be seen as an advocate of accessibility.
Echoing our hypothetical manager above, a clear problem lies in convincing already overburdened professors and adjuncts that this partition
of the sensible is even important given the seemingly low numbers of
deaf students or accessibility needs in a given class, or other technological resource constraints. Thus, professors could understandably view
this requirement as an unnecessary step unless a deaf student is present.
Taking a step further, professors simply may not know how to caption
effectively (or have institutional resources to support these initiatives)
or how to change their pedagogies. Hence, any of these reactions—individual or institutional—would support a partition of the sensible even
when institutional permissions have been authorized.

These potential issues highlight the need to think of social justice
as an active and ongoing verification of political equality (as an ethical disposition, a hexis) within, alongside, and beyond institutional
redress. An individual professor interested in political equality does
not need to wait for the institution to ensure equality is distributed
(or supported) properly. Indeed, even Rancière is not an optimist.
He is clear in acknowledging that disturbing partitions of the sensible
undoubtedly will be accompanied by new variations of previous partitions of the sensible. Thus, active social justice is not a once-a-year act
of charity, such as an annual canned-food drive, but an ongoing and
evolving practice of verifying political equality across all parts of an
individual's workplace context. We do not mean to present a theory
of well-intentioned individuals who simply do the right thing in the
absence of institutional constraints and contexts. Nevertheless, the
existence of uneven implementation of accessibility, as well as the
possibility of individual or institutional resistance, confirms the importance of a terministic shift in emphasis for social justice as an active
practice for digital rhetoricians.

RACISM IN CLOSED CAPTIONING

In terms of captioning, deaf users are not the only community in need of verifications of equality. Highlighting again the need to think of ethics as the development of a virtuous disposition rather than as a deontological adherence to existing rules, multiple partitions of the sensible exist within the broader landscape of online streaming and closed captioning. Indeed, other users might find closed captions or written transcripts to be helpful. For example, one argument digital rhetoricians could use to petition employers or institutions to close caption could be couched in terms of search-engine optimization benefits. While casual users may never realize it, the World Wide Web Consortium (WC3) confirms that closed captions and other accessibility elements increase a website's search ranking for a given term, particularly for videos. The Discovery Digital Network also confirms that producing closed captions increases a YouTube video's ranking 13.48 percent (3 Play Media 2017, para 7). Alternatively, producing captions addresses the interest in intercultural and globalization practices. For instance, Viki, the online captioning collaborative, offers numerous Korean and Japanese television shows that have been captioned in English. They offer a potentially unlimited number of languages videos can be translated into, thereby enabling digital rhetoric practices to facilitate cross-cultural sharing. Online video hosts, like TED Talks, already do this to great effect. Simply put, Rancière does not require us to only acknowledge one partition of the sensible even if deaf or hard-of-hearing viewers are the primary partition of the sensible that might motivate our actions.

This point leads directly into a related point of significance for Rancière. Consider an additional digital rhetoric assignment. The teacher now asks their students to employ Rancière as a lens through which to read Poynter's criticism of ableist YouTube autocaptioning. The teacher combines Rancière with Zdenek to create an intervention assignment in which they instruct their students as content creators to create their own captions to any popular video in order to disturb YouTube's partition of the sensible. While this dissensual activity identifies one partition of the sensible, another related issue arises: if students or digital media professionals seek to employ specific captioning language to help the deaf and hard-of-hearing communities, how can they also be sure their transcription choices are still verifying political equality or enabling others to do so? In the podcast *Yo, Is This Racist?* on the racial equality network Earwolf, Andrew Ti (2013) discusses the possibility of whether certain instances of closed captioning in *The Wire* (Simon 2002) are racist. Ti speculates that a deaf individual might live in a racist bubble when closed captioning on a given episode, for example, translates the softer African American Vernacular (AAV) word *nigga* used informally by some African Americans into a "hard-R" *nigger*. In other words, merely adding nonautomated closed captions does not alleviate the need to constantly verify equality across all aspects of digital rhetoric practices. Enacting equality is not something one achieves and can dispense with in a given digital rhetoric project. Rather, it is an active and ongoing ethical practice.

Just as the decision to include closed-captioned dialogue and sound can function as a critical site of mediation among a range of bodies and abilities, transcribers must make decisions that have great significance for how individuals with disabilities and other caption readers encounter race and other aspects of culture. Indeed, Zdenek demonstrates that the same audio content within a given television episode may be captioned differently on television as closed captions than on a DVD with open digital subtitles (Zdenek 2011, para. 11). Simply put, these differences indicate important sites where race can be recoded through omission and selection—partitions of the sensible in Rancière's sense. This is not to say that by captioning we somehow make the experience equal for the deaf reader or the global audience (or other) viewer. In fact, measuring equality in this sense is not the goal of this article and is very far from Rancière's interest. By contrast, the goal is to convey that understanding the complex ways in which these possible differences maintain a partition of the sensible is key to attempting to verify another individual's equality through better closed captioning.

Working from Zdenek, Nicole Ashanti McFarlane and Nicole Elaine Snell and have coined the term "color-deafness": "the habits of production employed by screenwriters, subtitle producers, and closed caption transcriptionists as they routinely omit and insert racially significant sound information" (McFarlane and Snell 2014). As an example, McFarlane and Snell cite the popular television show *Breaking Bad*, which is about a former high-school chemistry teacher, Walter White (Bryan Cranston), who produces crystal methamphetamine. The show routinely offers encounters with stereotypical nonwhite drug traffickers and gang members. McFarlane and Snell focus on differences in captioning between the "wigger" characters, such as the Caucasian Jesse Pinkman (Aaron Paul), and African American characters. Wiggers represent white youth who superficially identify with elements of African American culture such as rap and hip-hop. Drawing on Geneva Smitherman (1994) and Jan H. Hill (1998) respectively, McFarlane and Snell reinforce that wiggers reproduce racism because they are not asked to interrogate their whiteness and that wiggers seem indistinguishable from what Hill calls "moth-eaten tokens of minstrelsy" (quoted in McFarlane and Snell 2014), a metaphor that characterizes whites' historic use of blackface to undermine the intelligence and political equality of African Americans (McFarlane and Snell 2014).

Intriguingly, more tensions between African American and wigger identities manifest for the deaf user because AAV is translated differently when used by Pinkman or African American characters. In one episode, Pinkman leaves as his voice recording, "Yo, yo yo, 148–3 to the 3 to the 6 to the 9, representin the ABQ, what up biatch? Leave it at the tone" (McFarlane and Snell 2014). McFarlane and Snell note that the use of "yo" as a standard greeting attempts to emulate AAV discourse (McFarlane and Snell 2014). Intriguingly, the closed captions in this episode and others translated accurately both Pinkman's use of AAV and moments when he employed Standard (white) English discourses. Yet, transcriptions for authentic AAV speakers and African American characters in episodes of *Breaking Bad* are far less accurate, particularly when African American characters employ Standard English. As a notable case in point, the character Huell Babineaux (Lavell Crawford) has many lexical items properly captioned, but significant mistakes occur. McFarlane and Snell comment,

> Certain morphological elements in the misrepresentation of verbs superimpose incorrect corrections of Huell's spoken language, such that "ain't" is captioned as "didn't" and "gone" is transcribed into "gonna." Oppositely, closed captioning of the [same] scene reveals the privileging of white speech as demonstrated by the perfectly rendered transcription of the scene's opposite character, Hank Schrader. (McFarlane and Snell 2014)

These seemingly small decisions with respect to the accuracy of translation for white and African American characters function to maintain a partition of the sensible with (implicit) forms of white privilege and racism for deaf viewers of *Breaking Bad*.

In this scenario, another clear opening exists for the practice of enacting equality, not in terms of offering access to the deaf community alone but in terms of the language and racism the deaf community encounters in reading closed captions. A digital rhetorician interested in practicing social justice through enactments of equality could respond to this situation as our web designer above approached the deaf community (e.g., actively captioning). Yet, it is not enough to manually correct YouTube's autotranslate feature. This effort must also include attention to how partitions of the sensible manifest with regard to specific language choices. To this point, it is important to acknowledge that it would be impossible to imagine how any individual digital rhetorician could account for all partitions of the sensible on behalf of all groups at all times with respect to closed captioning. Readers can easily imagine mistakes being made even when good intentions are motivating the enactments of equality. However, the key is being aware of such inequalities and realizing—in contrast to liberal social justice—that these injustices can be addressed immediately and by the individual on a moment-to-moment or work-assignment-to-work-assignment basis. Our point in referencing racism within the closed-captioning digital-communication situation lies in the need to affirm both calling attention to inequalities and correcting those inequalities by enacting and continually practicing verifications of equality. We contend that this practice should become habitual throughout all forms of digital rhetoric.

The issue of racialized partitions of the sensible in closed captioning is complex for an additional reason: the formalization of captioning protocols. The overwhelming tendency is to produce closed-captioned speech in Standard English, which Geneva Smitherman (1973) and other race-rhetoric scholars more accurately dub "standard white English" (SWE), given that the grammatical, lexical, and syntactic patterns map easily onto the language structures of the white middle and upper classes. Still, it is interesting that the *Breaking Bad* example should be against the letter of FCC law (which mandates the use of the four principles of accuracy, synchronicity, completeness, and placements), which notes, "If slang or grammatical errors are intentionally used in a program's dialogue, they shall be mirrored in the captions" (Federal Communications Commission 2014).

Nevertheless, both closed-captioning norms and practices can thereby reduce or eliminate the complexity of oral speech (pitch, gender, race, dialect, pronunciation, etc.) by even measuring AAV as "slang" against "proper" grammatically correct SWE. Where cultural differences such as AAV are acknowledged, they stand out like a gestalt in comparison to the near universal SWE. As with many partitions of the sensible (gender, sexuality), this state of affairs stems less from an intentional exclusionary act and more from normative practices or is even an inadvertent but unfortunate byproduct of a pragmatic need to create some form of standardized practices to avoid a closed-caption *lingua fracta*. Indeed, it is likely that SWE is deemed the most accessible for users to read in an era of hyperreading webtexts (Hayles 2010)and that closed-captioning departments may be underfunded and rendering speech phonetically takes time. Even the protocological constrictions of the caption field (line lengths, reading-speed guidelines) may play a role in creating partitions of the sensible. Rather than letting closed captioners off the hook, if anything, protocological partitions of the sensible confirm the need to consider the production of captions as a vital practice for all forms of video production, including screencasting.

VERIFYING EQUALITY AS A HEXIS OF JUSTICE

To sum up, any active verification of equality does not eliminate all partitions of the sensible. Just as one partition (e.g., YouTube's partitioning of the deaf community from its conception of the universal user) is disrupted by an act of equality, another partition may replace it in a moment, or the previous partition may be reinstated. Active equality as social justice, then, requires continual reverification to disturb these partitions. By extension, Rancière offers a particular form of hexis that can usefully support and extend digital rhetoricians' resurgent interests in social justice. Social justice in a Rancièreian sense is the hexis of continually verifying equality across various digital rhetoric situations, such as adding closed captions and making sure the language used to transcribe audio dialogue does not create additional partitions of the sensible. Rancièreian hexis is not universally applicable as a fixed set of analytical practices or heuristics of dissensus but rather functions akin to Aristotle's active "having": a hexis a digital rhetorician must constantly cultivate in order to practice active forms of social justice within workplace situations and research practices.

Rancièreian hexis as a form of active political agency is worthwhile to engage because it encourages a habit of enacting social justice whereas other theories of social justice urge digital rhetoricians to expend their energy on lobbying for passive redistribution. To revisit our earlier point, solely relying on long-term liberal notions of social justice can be incredibly frustrating to the digital rhetorician who might not see any long-term consequences of their day-to-day actions—actions in which they might very well be calling attention to and verifying other people's equality, acts which, from a certain point of view, are practices of social justice. Indeed, there is little motivation to develop this hexis of social justice when petitioning and lobbying may seldom translate directly into institutional change. By contrast, shifting from passive to active forms of equality—or perhaps, more accurately, employing these forms in conjunction—does indeed offer motivation to develop the sort of hexis that can engage in social justice without waiting for the method of distribution to realign itself. Beyond our discrete case study of captioning, we hope it is clear that Rancière's extension of Aristotle's justice can also apply to digital and procedural partitions of the sensible in a wide variety of interfaces. Indeed, we hope it is a clear that there is an exigency to begin cultivating this particular justice as a hexis.

4
CARE IN REMIX AND DIGITAL SAMPLING

In his book *Convergence Culture*, the media studies scholar Henry Jenkins (2008) opens with a memorable anecdote. He describes the wide online circulation of a Filipino high-school student's Photoshop collage of *Sesame Street*'s Bert engaging terrorist leader Osama Bin Laden. Images of the collage ended up (among other places) on an anti-American post-9/11 protest sign in another country and was broadcasted to US television audiences by CNN. Indeed, the neologism *photoshopping* functions as an almost clichéd umbrella term to describe how user-friendly multimedia production software is combined with networked connectivity as an everyday social media activity. A number of interfaces even seek to streamline these processes, such as Memegenerator, which offers templates that emulate the most popular memes. Users only need to add their own textual content to a gigantic stockpile of past and current meme images. Indiloop, an app and online sharing community, offers users the mantra of "everything is remixable," from Soundcloud audio, Vimeo films, and personal audio or video recordings taken with mobile phones (and computers). Highlighting Matthew S.S. Johnson's claims that video-game players are often skilled rhetors as well (Johnson 2008), Overclock Remix is an online community dedicated to users who wish to remix video game sounds and music. Countless community sites are also devoted to DJ cultures and other aspects of music or video sampling, often in ways that are not typical but that are no less important forms of sampling-like activity. Take Machinima, a site where players remix recorded video-game footage to create new forms of meaning. The popular video game livestreaming social media site, Twitch, for example, has a dedicated Machinima channel solely devoted to these types of sampling and remixing activities.

Such concerns are by no means new to digital rhetoricians, as the rhetoric of remix and cultural appropriation has become an integral part of the logic of the digital (Palmeri 2012). In the past, numerous scholars of digital rhetoric advocated for methods of "ripping" and

DOI: 10.7330/9781607328063.c004

remixing digital content into new compositions. Yet, the pervasive availability of software and media texts that enable sampling online media presents rhetorical and ethical challenges for rhetoricians as they struggle to select and use samples in their composition practices. Issues such as copyright, for example, come into tension. While reusing a single image to create new memes, for example, may seem fairly trivial, efforts to sample commercial films and videos have been more controversial. As a case in point, Professor Eric Faden of Bucknell University posted a video on the website of Stanford University's Center for Internet and Society called "A Fair(y) Use Tale." Mixing satire and education, "A Fair(y) Use Tale" recombined two-second clips from a wide variety of Disney films to highlight the complexities of contemporary copyright law versus artistic or political "fair use" (and, Disney, of course, is well known for its proprietary approach to such copyrighted material).

Beyond copyright issues, another important ethical issue for digital rhetoricians is the possibility of cultural appropriation. A prominent example lies in international music star Moby's sampling and remixing of African American musicians Bessie Jones and Vera Hall on Moby's award-winning album *Play*. It is not as if Jones or Hall or their descendants stand to earn any profit from Moby's album. Despite these challenges, versions of "limitless" invention practices have been promoted for use by those attuned to the inventive strengths of digital sampling and remixing practices demonstrated in hip-hop, DJ-ing, and other genres that incorporate the practices (Rice 2003; 2007; Sirc 2002; 2006). On the other hand, some have countered this idea by showing how these digital sampling and remixing practices are informed by a complex awareness of communal difference and cultural histories (Banks 2011; McFarlane 2013). The latter position has critiqued the former as potentially endorsing naïve cultural appropriation at best and, at worst, enabling the production of racist, sexist, and homophobic content.

Powerful benefits apply to both the free sampling argument and the cultural critique, however incompatible and polar opposite they may appear at first glance. In a scenario in which universal or axiomatic prescriptions ("cross-cultural sampling is always good"; "cross-cultural sampling is always bad") can hardly be said to apply, a hexis of care enables us to bring both digital-sampling positions into consideration to help digital rhetoricians produce and question inventive and more ethically aware multimodal compositions without prescribing a dogmatic morality (see Hawk 2012). In this chapter, we engage an understanding of care as a virtue through feminist care ethics in the context of digital sampling. Along with virtue ethics and capabilities approaches, a care ethics (which is considered an updated virtue ethics by some ethicists) is oriented toward the specific goods internal to our digital-sampling practices rather than relying solely on some external axioms or the external effects of an act (Vallor 2011). This latter position is informed by feminist philosopher Adriana Cavarero's later ontological work on vulnerability (Cavarero 2011). While her later work is not well known in the field of digital rhetoric, her earlier work has been taken up by a handful of rhetoricians in recent years (Anderson 2014; Burgess and Murray 2006; Colton 2016; Colton, Holmes, and Walwema 2017).

In this chapter, we suggest cultivating this particular hexis of care—not to defend the free-play invention strategies with the critiques its opponents have brought to bear but rather to look to care ethics as an ethical vocabulary for enabling discussion of these issues without rein-scribing rationality or prescribing an unyielding code of conduct. This hexis of care, while not falling neatly under deontological, rights-based, or consequentialist ethical frameworks, shares many of the characteristics and interests of virtue ethics. As Duffy (2014) might argue, a hexis of care is related to, if not completely consistent with, many of the normative positions other compositionists have worked from when engaging with problems of cultural appropriation, as there are no hard and fast rules to guide digital sampling; there are only ethical dispositions to work from. This hexis asks rhetoricians to place themselves in an empathetic relation with those they are responding to (i.e., sampling from); this hexis is motivated by an attempt to respect the difference of others and acknowledge a responsibility to those individuals and communities with which the rhetorician is in relation. Developing a hexis of care with respect to a digital rhetor's specific *disposition*, we suggest, offers a way to respond to these relations as they emerge in their local situatedness. In turn, the digital rhetorician can develop a theory and practice of "right action" with regard to appropriation, exercising virtues rather than abstract universal ethical categories. Two other concepts care ethics relies upon, reciprocity and empathy—also Aristotelian virtues—allow us to easily articulate Cavarero's care ethics as a dispositional practice for digital rhetoricians.

PERSPECTIVES AND DEFINITIONS OF SAMPLING AS A STRATEGY FOR RHETORICAL INVENTION

In *Rhythm Science*, Paul D. Miller (2004), also known as the writer, musician, and artist DJ Spooky that Subliminal Kid, defines sampling as a new way of doing something that has been with us for a long time: creating with found objects. "The rotation gets thick. The constraints get thin. The mix breaks free of the old associations. The script gets flipped. The languages evolve and learn to speak in new forms, new thoughts" (25). Claiming, "There is no such thing as an 'immaculate perception,'" Miller sees creativity in "how you recontextualize the previous expression of others" (33). He maintains that the DJ is an archetype of contemporary artists and writers who use multimedia, as the DJ's ability to create art is contingent upon a critical embrace of technologies that reproduce sounds and video from previous works: "DJ-ING IS WRITING/WRITING IS DJ-ING" (56). Along with the emphasis on artistic invention, other scholars have noted how the practice of sampling, under a broad umbrella of hip-hop culture, has been and can be used as a rhetorical means of political resistance to dominant societal norms of ownership, including those of language, identity, and property (Alim, Lee, and Carris 2011; Alim and Pennycook 2007; Pennycook 2007a, 2007b; Palmeri 2012).

Viewing writing as the sampling, remixing, and recontextualizing of others' works is not necessarily a new idea for readers familiar with the works of twentieth-century theorists such as Roland Barthes (1977, 1982) or Mikhail Bakhtin (1982; 1986), who each challenged modern notions of authenticity and authorial creativity in their critiques of writing. Barthes and Bakhtin each posit an always-present excess of historicity preceding and determining the meaning of any written or spoken utterance. More simply stated, who we are as composers (even when we are placing our own thoughts down on a blank sheet of paper) is partially shaped and conditioned by the particular cultures we dwell within. In this way, all forms of writing have a degree of remix about them. Shakespeare did not invent the sonnet form, for instance, and he drew upon established stories and historical circumstances to inform his famous plays. While these ideas by no means equate in totality to what a DJ does, they help explain why sampling as a means of multimodal rhetoric has found legitimacy in composition studies. Digital sampling as a rhetorical practice simply foregrounds this sampling more directly.

One of the most influential promoters of sampling as a means of rhetorical invention is Jeff Rice. In one important essay, "The 1963 Hip-Hop Machine: Hip-Hop Pedagogy as Composition," Rice promotes the importance of sampling and hip-hop as a method for developing alternative forms of meaning making through writing. Building upon Houston Baker's (1991) previous work in this area, Rice starts from a definition of sampling as "the hip-hop process of saving snippets of prerecorded music and sound into a computer memory. These sounds become cut from their original source and pasted into a new composition" (Rice 2003, 454). Rice then extends this definition beyond sound to include images and video, advocating a "take whatever you find and use it" method. This method enables digital rhetoricians to produce content at a moment's notice (especially through the use of computer, tablet, and other mobile technologies) even without necessarily having a specific thesis or end goal in mind; the term *whatever* works in youth culture as a word that evokes "a sense that something has eluded the meaning of the response or defiance, dismissal, and opposition" (455). As a method, then, *whatever* privileges "cutting a detail from its original source and recontextualizing it within a different setting," often critiquing, disguising, or hiding the original source in the process (456).

Rice (2003; 2007), who is highly influenced by Gregory Ulmer's electracy theory (Ulmer 1994), has not been alone in promoting the study and practice of sampling and remixing in rhetoric and composition studies. Sarah Arroyo (2013) and Alex Reid (2007) each similarly argue that "rip-mix-burn" (Reid 2007) is a primary method of understanding how invention works for digital rhetoric. Johndan Johnson-Eilola and Stuart Selber point out that studying the various genres using sampling, from hip-hop to film, enables digital rhetoricians to question the "often narrow perspectives on plagiarism" found in the history of composition (Johnson-Eilola and Selber 2007, 376; see also Hess 2006). Geoffrey Sirc (2006), similar to Rice, emphasizes invention via hip-hop sampling in numerous essays, pointing out that composers better identify with how the world works around them through an understanding of the content and practice of hip-hop sampling than they might through more formalist writing practices. Digital sampling also has been referenced as one of several ways digital rhetoricians can demonstrate popular-culture knowledge in multimodal composing (Williams 2014).

In tension with those above (particularly Rice and Sirc) is Adam Banks, who, calling on Carmen Kynard (2007), posits that "trying to scratch or sample the practices of the DJ, MC, or hype-wo/man in Hip Hop and drop them into our scholarship without thorough, searching attention to the discursive and rhetorical traditions from which they emerge" is "foolishness" (Banks 2011, 13). Banks is most critical of the "take whatever you find and use it" method Rice and others espouse. Banks argues that such "isolated sampling or ripping" risks uncritical cultural appropriation "if we somehow build our theorizing on individual practices without full recognition of the people, networks, and traditions that have made these practices their gift to the broader culture" (13). Nicole McFarlane goes further and maintains that when digital rhetoricians teach sampling without an awareness of the socio-political contexts from which the sampling and remixing borrow and appropriate, they risk uncritically "deliver[ing] assignments with sexist, homophobic, and/or racist content" (McFarlane 2013, para. 5).

Banks's and McFarlane's shared concerns that unchecked or uninformed digital-sampling rhetorics may result in uncritical cultural appropriation or worse are important and valid concerns. Sampling and remixing without regard for cultural differences can produce ethically problematic results. Poet Raymond McDaniel came under fire for sampling the personal histories of six African American survivors of Hurricane Katrina to compose the centerpiece poem of his *Saltwater Empire* (McDaniel 2008). Using narratives "stripped of names and context, and combined with one another," the nineteen-page, six-part poem presents the content as all from McDaniel's own imagination, observation, or experience with only a vague reference at the bottom of the copyright page to the website where the narratives were located (Young 2010, para. 4). David Hesmondhalgh also raises broader cultural concerns about unconstrained sampling practices. He applies legal and media studies research to question the problems of "cultural borrowing" inherent in digital sampling (Hesmondhalgh 2006). Like Rebecca Moore Howard (2000), Johnson-Eilola and Selber (2007), and Alastair Pennycook (2007a, 2007b), who have advocated for plagiarism-policy reform, Hesmondhalgh acknowledges that copyright laws that view digital sampling without permission from the original creator as unlawful often discourage the creative and political powers of African Americans and other marginalized groups. However, pointing to the example of Moby's use of Bessie Jones and Vera Hall on *Play*, Hesmondhalgh (2006) resituates the issue by demonstrating how fewer constraints on digital-sampling laws can actually perpetuate or increase the already-present dynamics of inequality that privilege dominant groups in a power relation.

For example, in his Grammy Award-nominated 1999 album *Play*, international artist Moby, who is white, samples and remixes a number of current and past African American musicians and then overlays their performances with his own musical compositions. The most praised and controversial samples are those taken from Alan Lomax's field recordings, the originals of which can be heard in a compilation called *Sounds of the South* (Lomax 2011). These field recordings are only used on a few of the songs on Moby's album *Play*, but it is those songs that received the most attention and praise from music critics. Controversially, however, the African American musicians sampled on those songs initially received little to no credit and very little compensation for their work, including Vera Hall. As one example of this sampling and remixing, Moby takes Vera Hall's vocals from "Trouble So Hard" and places those vocals over a dance-rhythm track. There are no effects added to her vocals (other than perhaps a light delay and reverb) that would make them distinguishable from the original, nor are there any added harmonies or complex edits made. In essence, Vera Hall becomes the lead singer for Moby's song "Natural Blues." In other words, if one listens to Vera Hall's performance of "Trouble So Hard" and then listens to Moby's remix in "Natural Blues," it is quite easy to see that the samplings of some African American musicians were by no means minor additions to Moby's creations.

Moby's use of sampling on the album *Play* conjures the kinds of questions we should be asking in our own digital rhetoric pedagogies and practices that draw on sampling—questions that interrogate how other cultures, traditions, and people are represented and acknowledged in our remixes and questions that ask why certain representations of certain communities or cultures are privileged in a remix. Because someone with Moby's access to power can more easily, in Rice's words, "take whatever he finds and use it" (Rice 2003) to produce, publish, and present art to an audience of millions, giving that person further license to digitally sample from anywhere and any person or group can work against the interests of marginalized groups' political and artistic interests.

These concerns distill down to a basic point: it is easy for digital writers or musicians with economic or racial privilege to borrow rhetorical practices spawned in or made popular by marginalized groups, and they can often do so without having to live through the economic or racial exclusions that provided the backdrop for the invention of these practices. Celebrity pop singer Miley Cyrus's 2013 appropriation of twerking in the music video *We Can't Stop* is a prominent example. While not an example of digital sampling per se, it is an effective illustration of how appropriation functions. As journalist Amy Lacount complained on *Bust*, "[Miley Cyrus] can twerk and pretend to be 'ratchet' but it only lasts for the three minutes and 34 seconds that you're on screen, and then you can take it all off and live life as the privileged white girl that you are. Other people of color can't do that" (Lacount 2017, para 12). Cognizant of this problem, Banks (2011) argues that, rather than employ the free-play sampling practices advocated by Rice and others, digital rhetoricians should follow and attempt to embody what Banks deems the virtues of a "digital griot." Banks describes griots as a combination of "storytellers, preachers, poets, standup comics, DJs, and even everyday people [who] all carry elements of the traditional griot's role in African American culture"—a multifaceted role Banks describes as equal parts historian, social critic, archivist, entertainer, and cultural interpreter (25). Adding "digital" to this identity, Banks shows how the griot's role persists and is critical in our multimedia age. Some of the values of the digital griot, for example, include the ability to demonstrate "knowledge of the traditions and cultures of his or her community" and "the ability to employ [technological] skills for the purposes of building community and/or serving communities with which he or she is aligned" (26).

One of Banks's aims in *Digital Griots* is to increase the awareness of ethics in rhetoric regarding how sampling and related practices are rooted deeply in historically black music and storytelling traditions. However, at other times, Banks's argument appears audience specific; that is, he articulates that he is "grounding a discussion of digital ethics for African Americans in a theoretical frame . . . that would encourage black people to make use of technological systems and tools" toward progressive political goals (Banks 2011, 123). We do not question the historical precedence or political exigency of either of these goals. Nonetheless, we think it is safe to say most digital rhetoric scholars would love to see the set of values Banks articulates emerge in most social media sampling compositions, that the characteristics of the digital griot should inform a dispositional ethics of any researcher or practitioner who produces digital-sampling works for personal enjoyment or professional practice.

How then might a digital rhetorician negotiate this balance between creative freedom and cultural sensitivity? We believe it is critical for digital rhetoricians to envision themselves as potential public sphere participants regardless of their background or experience. We believe a middle ground exists between creativity and sensitivity that does not hold digital-content creators accountable to the sometimes paralyzing standards of paying due "attention to the discursive and rhetorical traditions" from which they sample (Banks 2011, 13), let alone a standard of considering themselves "grounded deeply" enough in their own traditions that they feel authorized to "tell it," as Banks puts it (27). For the remainder of this chapter, then, we suggest that helping digital rhetors begin to develop a particular hexis of care is one way of enabling them to embody ethical stances in their digital-sampling practices. This hexis of care considers an awareness of empathy and reciprocity within communal relations as vital to ethics. A hexis of care also finds political and ethical value in acts of caring *and* wounding through an understanding of ontological "vulnerability," which, as we describe below, stems from the work of feminist philosopher Adriana Cavarero (2011).

A HEURISTIC OF VULNERABILITY

While there are a few prominent figures—such as Carol Gilligan, Nel Noddings, and Joan Tronto—who have each taken key roles in the development of an ethics of care framework, there is arguably no foundational text or key author. There are many facets to the ethics of care and many advocates of care. It has been articulated in different, even potentially contradicting, ways. Nevertheless, there are some common points of identification. For example, unlike deontologists and utilitarians, care ethicists have historically advocated specifically for accounting for special relationships such as family and community. Most care ethicists also share an interest in feminism and women's ways of knowing and being. Again, while there are a great number of differences in how care is conceptualized, there are some "tenets" of an ethics of care, which include some of the following: an appreciation of difference and marginalized voices, particularly with regard to valuing moral perception and decision making (Gilligan 1982); the privileging of *caring for*—a particular action directed toward attending to another person's needs—over *caring about*—an abstract positive feeling toward someone or something (Tronto 1987); a rejection (or at least a questioning) of ethical frameworks based upon abstract, impersonal principles (Noddings 1982); and an emphasis on understanding moral behavior as stemming from and directed toward receptivity, relatedness, and responsiveness in personal relationships (Noddings 1982).

Criticisms of care ethics include accusations of essentialism (with its focus on women's ways of knowing, for example) and an incompatibility with larger public issues of social justice, as much of care ethics is focused on "private" familial and communal relationships. Care ethicists have countered similar claims by noting that even though the ethics of care stems from feminism and women scholars, it does not need to be associated solely with women (Larrabee 1993). Others have argued similarly that stemming from a certain way of knowing (e.g., personal relationships) does not mean a certain ethic cannot be applied to broader issues, such as concerns of justice (Held 2006). As we argue, Cavarero's particular notion of care, stemming from a larger project of mapping ontological uniqueness (not individualism), resolves both the problem of considering care as only a practice within personal relationships and the problem of only extending care to larger societal issues of justice and morality.

Before we get to Cavarero, however, we want to add two qualifications. First, care has been taken up in rhetoric and composition studies in the past. Gesa Kirsch and Joy Ritchie write, "Unlike rule-bound ethics, 'caring' requires one to place herself in an empathetic relationship in order to understand the other's point of view" (Kirsch and Ritchie 1995, 21). Jacqueline Jones Royster's (1996) advocacy of respect for the difference of other singular beings and communities also is in line with the general tenets of care ethics). Similarly, Royster and Kirsch (2012) remind us that such ethical considerations remain important today and will be in the future, as this chapter hopes to reiterate. Second, while Aristotle did not name care as a specific virtue, contemporary care ethicists have been quick to make this connection (Ruddick 1989; Tronto 2006; Vallor 2011; 2016).[1] Indeed, as we make clear in following sections, Cavarero's vulnerability and ethics of care also link to Aristotle through hexeis of empathy and reciprocity.

We see the recognition of these ethical positions as first steps in developing a hexis of care, a disposition not inconsistent with a complex and mature ethos like that of Banks's digital griot. In many ways, we are arguing for a reconsideration, reapplication, and revision of a feminist ethics of care with regard to digital-sampling practices. In fact, the heuristic of vulnerability we describe below, which stems from Cavarero's notion of vulnerability, works toward developing such a disposition. We suggest that a heuristic of vulnerability can enable digital rhetoricians to work toward developing the kind of ethical disposition of care that can help bridge the seeming dissonance between free-play invention strategies and Banks's ethos of the digital griot. Most important, this heuristic also equips audiences with a vocabulary for identifying, anticipating, or responding to digital-sampling projects that have taken a turn for the worse, ethically speaking.

One inroad for understanding vulnerability in relation to care as a tacit virtue ethic of care lies in Cavarero's prominent aim to distinguish horror from terror. In *Horrorism: Naming Contemporary Violence*, Cavarero claims horror is not the same thing as terror, which "moves bodies, drives them into motion. . . . [Terror's] menace is directed, substantially, at life itself: it is a threat of violent death. He who is gripped by terror trembles and flees in order to survive, to save himself from a violence that is aiming to kill him" (Cavarero 2011, 5). In other words, terror isn't just that feeling one gets at a movie theater but is a primal fear of losing one's life. In contrast, horror is the fear of being maimed or having one's body parts removed. "Horror does not concern imminent death from which one flees, trembling, but rather the effects of a violence that labors at slicing, at the undoing of the wounded body and then the corpse, at opening it up and dismembering it" (12). Key to Cavarero's understanding of how horror is invoked and how horror as a metaphor affects issues of digital sampling and remix is her concept of vulnerability.

Influenced by the works of previous philosophers such as Hannah Arendt, Judith Butler, and even Thomas Hobbes, Cavarero posits that vulnerability is an ontological characteristic of being human. Cavarero's *Horrorism* follows up her work in *For More Than One Voice: Toward a Philosophy of Vocal Expression*, in which she maintains that voice is the primary characteristic that expresses a singular person's simultaneous uniqueness and necessary relation to others (Cavarero 2005). In *Horrorism*, Cavarero adds vulnerability as an additional characteristic of simultaneous uniqueness and relationality: "If . . . everyone is unique because, exposing herself to others and consigning her singularity to this exposure, she shows herself such, this unique being is vulnerable by definition" (Cavarero 2011, 20–21). This commitment to uniqueness does not equate to individualism; in fact, Cavarero rejects ontologies of individualism, which refuse "to admit dependency and relationship" (21). She argues, rather, that each human being is unique and singular, but each person's uniqueness and singularity are constituted in concert with the constant "relational exposure" to the difference of others. By "relational exposure," she simply means each person's identity and sense of self is formed by a lifetime of relations to the various people and institutions that make up who a person is and becomes: family, church, workplace and educational institutions, and the larger culture in general. Just as no human's voice is identical to another's, no two humans' lifetimes of vulnerable exposures to others are identical.

By designating vulnerability as an ontological category, Cavarero (2011) highlights that a significant part of being human is that throughout life "the singular body is irremediably open" to two responses: "wounding and caring" (20). Not only are no two persons' lifetimes of vulnerable exposures to others identical, but the degree to which people are vulnerable to others also changes depending upon life circumstances. In other words, though we are always vulnerable, context governs the degree to which we can be wounded and the degree to which we require care.

> Even though, as bodies, vulnerability accompanies us throughout our lives, only in the newborn, where the vulnerable and the defenseless are one and the same, does it express itself so brazenly. The relation to the other . . . in this case takes the form of a unilateral exposure. The vulnerable being is here the absolutely exposed and helpless one who is awaiting care and has not means to defend itself against wounding. (Cavarero 2011, 20–21)

As the above passage makes clear, "'vulnerable' and 'helpless' are not synonymous terms" (Cavarero 2011, 30). Vulnerability is not reducible to helplessness. One might say helplessness is the most extreme form of vulnerability. However, understanding vulnerability through a theme of infancy (and thus helplessness) enables Cavarero to theorize how, just as our degree of vulnerability changes depending on the context, the "drastic alternative between violence and care" can also shift in degree and change in character as an active response to another's vulnerability. For example, an attempt to "[refrain] from wounding" (Cavarero 2011, 24) can be an act of care or wounding, depending on the degree of vulnerability of the person to whom one is responding. In the context of an adult, the active response to wound or care may be the difference "between a hand that strikes and one that does not rise to do so" (24). But if the vulnerable person is an infant, or a group unable to defend itself, "the arresting of a violent hand is not enough" (24). As Cavarero points out, in such cases, "it is necessary that the alternative inscribed in [the helpless person's] primary vulnerability should also bring into account a hand that cares, nourishes, and attends" (24). This lifetime of vulnerability, characterized by the intertwining relationship among the degree of one's vulnerability, contingent circumstances, and responsive acts—always defined as caring and/or wounding, depending on those circumstances and the degree of vulnerability of the person acted upon—is best summed up in the following passage:

> As a body, the vulnerable one remains vulnerable as long as she lives, exposed at any instant to *vulnus* [wound]. Yet the same potential also delivers her to healing and the relational ontology that decides its meaning. Irremediably open to wounding and caring, the vulnerable one exists totally in the tension generated by this alternative. As though the null response—neither the wound nor the care—were excluded. Or as though the absence of wound and care were not even thinkable. And yet you might call that indifference, and even bless it, if it were just the absence of wounding, whereas, if it were the absence of caring, we would perhaps have to call it desolation. But exposure to the other that persists over the arc of an entire life renders this absence improbable. In fact, given that every human being who exists has been born and has been an infant, materially impossible. (Cavarero 2011, 30)

In any human-to-human relation, then, a response of wounding and/or caring is always taking place. While we as human beings are vulnerable throughout the entirety of our lives, and no human can escape vulnerability, the degree to which we are vulnerable is contingent upon the circumstances we find ourselves in; hence, we are "always vulnerable but only sometimes helpless, as contingency dictates and with a variable degree of intensity" (Cavarero 2011, 31). We cannot escape responding to another's vulnerability to which we are exposed. Even leaving someone alone is a response, and the degree to which our response is one of wounding or caring is contingent upon circumstances.

Here is where we want to put forward the consideration of vulnerability, based upon Cavarero's thought, as a heuristic for digital rhetoric, particularly digital-sampling rhetorics. To anticipate a likely objection, we are not equating sampling with the dismembering or disfiguring of vulnerable, physical human bodies—though there is always a physical connection between the labor of the producer and the materiality of the product. Both rhetoricians (Fountain 2014; Meloncon 2013; Pigg 2014) and media studies scholars (Farman 2012; Hayles 1999) have argued that any use of technology or medium always entails some relationship to embodiment. As Reid highlights in his introduction to *The Two Virtuals*, there are two virtuals in composition studies: the first locates virtual (immaterial, disembodied) forces solely on the space of the screen, and the second (Deleuzian) virtual views any instrumental rhetorical activities— "actualizations" in Deleuzian parlance (Deleuze 1966)—as reliant upon a prior space out of which all forms of meaning emerge (Reid 2007).

We do not claim that knowledge of this ontology guarantees or even provides us with the kind of ethics all digital rhetoricians should enact. Rather, the key here is to work toward making the practice of this heuristic of vulnerability a habit—in Aristotle's sense, a hexis, or dispositional orientation toward the world. As teachers and digital producers, we should strive to offer opportunities for the beings in the world around us to manifest these dispositions. However, in contrast to Cavarero's use of vulnerability to understand horror, when practicing a heuristic of vulnerability for digital sampling, rhetoricians may find certain instances in which an act of wounding—a determination that is, while very real, always a subjective construct—might function as an act of caring with another relation or in another context. For example, some might argue that what Lomax has done with his samplings of Vera Hall and Bessie Jones is an act of care. Some might argue that we would not even know about these singers if not for the sampling and remixing practices of Lomax and Moby. A lot of Lomax's recordings were of prison inmates, many of whom would never have otherwise had access to a recording studio. While it is easy for us to say the Lomaxes and subsequent samplers like Moby should have given more credit to those original performers, advocates of Lomax and Moby could argue that their use was an act of caring. (However, again, we stress that this viewpoint is by no means absolute. We mean this example purely in an illustrative sense.)

In addition, developing a hexis of care through the dichotomy of wounding is important. The visceral character of a term like *wounding* provides a more affective response for digital rhetoricians than do considerations of copyright law, for example, when justifying what and how to sample, even if no act is easily defined as one that solely wounds. Furthermore, just as differences between terror and horror exist for Cavarero, ignoring and erasing our relationship to others in our scholarship and pedagogies is different than sampling from others and disguising those relations for purposes of reappropriating meaning. While both practices are problematic and deserve attention, the concept of vulnerability can make a particularly productive impact on how we practice digital sampling and remixing—methods associated with genres such as hip-hop and DJ-ing—in which a lack of acknowledgment of the source material, or a masked acknowledgment, can be seen as an inventive strength and even an expected convention of the genre (Hess 2006, 282–86).

We suggest, then, that when digital rhetors apply a logic similar to Rice's *whatever* pedagogy ("take whatever you find and use it") as a method of invention to guide digital rhetoric practices (Rice 2003), we supplement this method with a hexis of care through the multifaceted idea of vulnerability. Such a practice views each composition from which we sample as in relation to a vulnerable human being and/or community and requires the sampler to develop the ethical habit of asking, In my sampling and remixing of this work, am I wounding or caring for the people who took part in the works I sample from? *and* In my remixing of these works into a new composition, am I wounding or caring for those people and others who might be exposed to my own remix? Such a disposition enables digital rhetoricians to work toward habituating a cultural consciousness, ideally toward ultimately developing an ethos like that of Banks's digital griot.

To reiterate one of Cavarero's (2011) important points, identifying an "original author" as vulnerable does not mean identifying that person as helpless—this is not a patronizing identification. Those from whom digital rhetoricians sample are not necessarily helpless (though they might be in certain contexts) and do not lose their agency when recognized as vulnerable. Rather, this presupposition is a recognition of all human beings' ontological condition, one that enables digital rhetoricians to consider their relation to those they sample from as a coconstitutive relationship. The sampled-from are not completely passive but agents who help constitute composers' own subject positions as multimodal writers and producers of new meaning. Such an ontological presupposition helps digital rhetoricians realize no creative work exists in a vacuum; rather, it is a coconstitutive relationship that simultaneously contributes to the recognition of each person's uniqueness and agential capacity to affect others.

Therefore, while in its essence, such a heuristic of vulnerability sounds simplistic, it is multilayered and a difficult hexis to develop. We cannot merely say we care for others but must continually work to ask ourselves, In this act, who am I caring for, and who am I wounding? and then reevaluate those actions. Of course, while such a lens or heuristic of vulnerability is motivated by a hexis of care, using the heuristic does not guarantee such a dispositional ethic will develop. Nevertheless, in applying this heuristic to their practices, digital rhetoricians are asked to recognize and interrogate the relationship between those from whom they take and the creation of their own inventions when they practice digital sampling—for to ask the question Am I wounding and/or am I caring? requires that digital rhetoricians ask a host of other questions regarding their sampling practices, enabling them to consider additional but related ethical concerns.

To understand whether they are caring or wounding in the activity of sampling and remixing, digital rhetoricians must identify or even address those people from whom they sample. Whether they sample from a speech by Martin Luther King Jr., footage of the Arab Spring, prison folk music, or a protest by the Westboro Baptist Church, answering this question requires individual research into various people or communities in relation to the images and sounds sampled. A digital rhetorician must ask Where did this come from? and Who took part in this work? The problems of ethnography and of "speaking" for others are real. Acknowledging for whom we are caring or whom we are wounding (even if just to ourselves) first requires some acknowledged and careful speculation and identification on our part—actions that expose our own subject positions and open us up to responses of wounding and caring from those exposed to a remix. Plus, a digital rhetorician must presuppose they are neglecting the recognition of someone, even if unintentionally.

An additional concern is that a digital rhetorician should be able to explain how their practices of sampling and remixing are acts of caring or wounding, or perhaps both. As Cavarero (2011) argues, an act of caring for one person may be an act of wounding for that same person in another context—or for someone else in a similar context—depending on the degree of vulnerability and the context in which the response takes place. Like the previously mentioned concern, to address this issue calls for additional research on the digital rhetor's part, beyond discovering the names of those who composed the media from which they are sampling. It also asks that a digital rhetorician researches (to the best of their ability and in the time given) the cultural values of those people and communities so the rhetorician might understand why the remix response could be construed as an act of caring and/or wounding. Now, no digital rhetorician will ever be able to fully discover the totality of the values of a community—as if there is such a thing—even if they identify as a member of that community. Consequently, attempting to discover these values and discern whether one's sampling and remixing are acts of caring or wounding necessitates great empathy (another hexis, we might argue) on one's part and an acknowledgment of the deficiency of one's subject position. "Empathy is not an unproblematic concept," as Kirsch and Ritchie (1995, 21) have noted, as we never understand another solely in the other's terms, hard as we may try. Kirsch and Ritchie's concern is with the ethics of the power relation of the researcher and research participant, which "can undermine, threaten or manipulate" that relationship, even if enacted through an expression of empathy (Kirsch and Ritchie 1995, 22). While the relations in the genres employing sampling are different than the kind of relations Kirsch and Ritchie are discussing—very likely the sampler will never meet the sampled-from—samplers can also find themselves in a similarly manipulative power relation.

It is true that Aristotle does not directly mention the hexis of care. Furthermore, while he ascribes great value to the notion of empathy, it is also true that the latter is not considered a strict virtue for some (see Vallor 2011). However, it is in Cavarero's (2011) insistence upon the centrality of her idiosyncratic notion of care and empathy through vulnerability that an Aristotelian precedent exists in his hexis of reciprocity. Aristotle's conception of ethical relations (both intimate and public/civic) are grounded in reciprocity (*antipeponthos*) (Aristotle 2002, 1155b34). While he takes certain elements for granted (friendship, desire for the good), he assumes human beings possess a natural inclination for valuing giving and receiving as ethical practices (1155a). Yet, in keeping with the second-nature requirement of hexeis, reciprocity is not just a natural impulse. Rather, individuals must cultivate it as a virtue, which enables a person to reciprocate the right goods in the right times and ways. Even acknowledging some of Aristotle's inegalitarian forms of friendship, his general framework nevertheless confirms that any good pair of friends must be capable of both giving and receiving benefits. It is only when reciprocity breaks down that Aristotle claims justice is necessary as a supplemental virtue.[2] In the context of sampling and care, reciprocity confirms that digital rhetors should strive to sample in a way that maintains the sample form's ability to reciprocate (e.g., engage, interpret, and read the work) without feeling as though its particular position has been negated or unproductively reappropriated.[3] In our reading, Aristotle's privileging of reciprocity is why we feel comfortable in identifying Cavarero as a tacit virtue ethicist even if she does not self-identify as one.

Recognizing that the sampler/sampled-from relationship can be one of manipulation, one's empathetic and reciprocal position, as a digital sampler, should also theorize how one determines an act of care actually may be an act of wounding. There is no perfect method for making this identification—this is a hexis, not a foundational rule. An ethical enactment will vary across different actors and rhetorical situations. Identifications of wounding and caring are not exempt from slippage of the signifier or multiple interpretations; however, both in production and teaching practices by digital rhetoric researchers, this slippage in meaning can be a strength. Such an acknowledgment of instability can help lead a class to discussions of cultural appropriation versus appreciation, property ownership, identity construction, and politics of (mis)representation, or as Stuart Hall describes it, "the way representational practices operate in concrete historical situations, in actual practice" (Hall 1997, 6). The key in these types of discussions is to move away from (or at least alongside) a sense of someone's owning a production, as we see in copyright law. Ellen Barton rightly reiterates that there is a great difference "between a context-based ethic of care and a principle-based ethics of rights" (Barton 2008, 598). In the context of digital sampling, this means a digital rhetorician ought to be cautious of worrying solely about who owns the rights to the product, or who "originally" created it in a legal sense, and rather be more concerned in their response with reciprocating with empathy.

Though the concern for legality should not be neglected, all too often some digital rhetorics confuse legal action with ethical action. Determining the rights of the "original creator," as well as what they "own," is extremely difficult and even controversial and should not be the sole identifier of ethicality. Examples abound in recent news media coverage of pop music, from the various Led Zeppelin lawsuits to the recent "Blurred Lines" controversy. The latter is a particularly effective example to discuss in class for differentiating between ethics and law. The "Blurred Lines" song is not only controversial in its potential endorsement of rape and the objectification of women, but the Marvin Gaye estate sued and was rewarded $7.4 million from the "Blurred Lines" writing team of Robin Thicke and Pharrell Williams for copying elements of Marvin Gaye's "Got to Give It Up." As pop-culture journalists Kal Raustiala and Christopher Jon Sprigman point out, in effect, the song "Blurred Lines" merely "sounds like" Gaye's earlier work. Williams and Thicke, who acknowledged Gaye's influence on that song and their work, neither sampled directly from Gaye's song nor copied the sheet music, leading Raustiala and Sprigman to conclude that the verdict sets a disastrous precedent: "The 'Blurred Lines' verdict may end up cutting off a vital wellspring of creativity in music—that of making great new songs that pay homage to older classics" (Raustiala and Sprigman 2015, para 3). Put simply, what is legal is not always ethical and vice versa.

Thus, instead of conflating ethics and law and pursuing an endless trail for authenticity, each of us can ask, as digital rhetoricians, how our sampling and remixing might affect certain persons, groups, or communities that have devoted their lives to the creation, reception, and meaning of a particular work. Admittedly, this practice can be exhausting, and developing hexeis of care and empathy is not only problematic but also difficult to embody. As Royster argues, empathetic recognition requires a subject position that admits that "what we think we see in places that we do not really know very well may not actually be what is there at all" (Royster 1996, 614). Such an admission might even speculate that the "original author" might not care what some teenager on social media does with their work, as long as the other remixing digital rhetorician does not financially profit from the sampling. This may be a legitimate claim, but to justify it, a digital rhetorician cannot help but negotiate with and reflect on the concepts of caring and wounding and on the sampled-from author's values. Such self-reflexivity is, again, not a guarantor of ethical action, but it is a first step toward embracing the complexity of ethical justification and working toward a more mature self-reflexivity that is the embodiment of a hexis of care.

Thus, in acknowledging that perhaps both caring and wounding are taking place through the idea of vulnerability, we should attempt to justify our actions ethically. Sometimes, a digital sampler may find wounding appropriate for a particular rhetorical situation, and negotiating such a claim is difficult. For example, were one to cut and sample footage of the Westboro Baptist Church community's funeral protests of what they insist on calling the "homosexual lifestyle" and then overlay it with loops of music and audio that imply a critique of the church's actions, one would acknowledge that such a sampling and remixing could easily be construed as an act of wounding the community associated with the church. Criticism and disruption are not inherently ethical acts. Such a criticism, disruption, or contestation of another's value system needs justification, even if contingent. This act would demand ethical and political reasons, in this case perhaps an acknowledgment of one's concerns for the inequality and the problems of hate speech perpetuated by the Westboro Baptist Church. Hopefully, a digital rhetorician would do this in a spirit of critical affirmation and try to understand the community's perspective, even as they may condemn it. From a certain point of view, one might argue that this act of wounding one group is (or at least we hope it is) an act of caring for that group and others, such as LGBTQ communities. This justification complicates the heuristic of vulnerability and ethic of care and ideally leads to questions about the problems of universal or foundational claims to identify certain practices as moral in and of themselves and the problems of identifying any practice as always virtuous, no matter the context.

It is important to reiterate that supplementing the "take whatever" forms of rhetorical invention with a hexis of care does not place a set of prescriptive norms upon the compositional choices of a digital rhetor. As we demonstrate in chapter 2, Aristotle's virtue ethics is in no way a deontological list of rigid ethical rules to follow. Rather, virtue ethics gives digital rhetoricians tools to think ethically about how their own ethical dispositions are already being shaped by unfolding and particular relations of vulnerability. The value we advocate is *care*, and this is a habitual practice that—like any rhetorical techne—can be used for good or for bad, as Richard Lanham's famous discussion of the "Q Question" reminds us (Lanham 1993). Care is not an attempt to impose on digital rhetors deontological norms, such as white folks should never sample from a person of color's texts, but rather to be mindful about the particular—not universal—relations of vulnerability such practices entail.

Equally important, a digital rhetorician should consider how they are exposing their own vulnerability (how might I be cared for or wounded?) in presenting a given remix. As we note above, any attempt to recognize and justify practices of sampling and remixing also exposes the sampler's own position of vulnerability in relation to composers and audiences. Thus, embodying a hexis of care in accounting for potentially wounding or caring for another's work increases the critical awareness of putting forth one's own work to be sampled from and remixed by others. This awareness should not discourage future digital rhetoricians from producing and sharing work but rather expose them to the realities of multimodal production and communication. This awareness should also lead to discussions in the digital rhetoric classroom of the ethics and politics of social media applications like Facebook, the technological dissolution of the border between public and private, systems of surveillance, and the practice of exposing our daily actions and identifying information on the Internet.

One benefit of teaching vulnerability in the digital rhetoric class-room is that it enables instructors to avoid didacticism and embrace the challenge of negotiating rhetorical invention with ethics. As Sheridan, Ridolfo, and Michel (2012) make clear with their notion of the "Kairotic Web" (68–69), so many elements contribute to the constitution of any multimodal composition that encapsulating the specific ethical responsi-bilities of the multimodal composer is never clear, leading to a very unsure ethic: "What is off limits one day is routine the next" (xvii). They argue,

> In multimodal compositions, the whole exceeds the sum of the parts, resulting in both challenges and new possibilities. Some of these challeng-es concern a set of ethical considerations that emerge from multimodal semiosis. Some of the potentials concern the reality that culture itself is multimodal, as are the cultural products of identity and consciousness. (xvii–xviii)

Sheridan, Ridolfo, and Michel (2012) are most concerned with multimodal rhetoric at large, but the ethical difficulties they explicate are exacerbated further by the conventional practices typically associ-ated with the genres that employ digital sampling—namely the practice of intentionally masking sources—which expose the opposite of one of the claims Sheridan, Ridolfo, and Michel make in the above passage. In conversation with their claim that "the whole exceeds the sum of the parts" (xvii), we argue that multimodal compositions very often fail to account for the sum of their parts, whose cultural implications and ontological relationality can far exceed the newly created "whole." This is why developing a hexis of care by applying a heuristic of vulnerability to digital-sampling practices works so well: in applying these insights, digital rhetors can find themselves changing their own minds about past identifications of acts of wounding or caring as well as how they justify those acts. Rationalizing those changes does not require that a digital rhetorician give an answer that best satisfies a given group's ideological viewpoint or fits a set of standards or rules. Instead, the digital rhetorician must regard the communal relations to their inventive practices—an engagement that will likely recognize that what one digital rhetorician sees as ethical, another may deem unethical, thus necessitating rhetori-cal engagement.

TOWARD A HEXIS OF CARE
Thinking through a lens or heuristic of vulnerability hopefully leads to embodying a hexis of care in practice so we can see results similar to Hesmondhalgh's suggestions for musicians who engage in digital

sampling—that is, giving due credit and compensation to the sampled-from musicians and communities, regardless of the current copyright laws (Hesmondhalgh 2006, 73). Our larger purpose in this chapter is to show how the ethical problems of digital sampling, a pervasive rhetorical activity in a networked age, can be addressed productively. Rice's "take whatever you find and use it" method for digital sampling (Rice 2003) need not lead to the kind of multimodal compositions with which Banks (2011) is concerned, or at least it need not lead to them in vain. We have suggested that one way to address ethically problematic digital compositions, as well as to help Rice's and Banks's seemingly irresolvable perspectives on digital sampling find some connection, is through a heuristic of vulnerability that asks digital rhetors to account for what might seem to be isolated free-association sampling decisions via a lens of caring and/or wounding. This heuristic, again, is motivated by the interest in developing a hexis of care.

Even if digital rhetoricians do not formally adopt care ethics or intentionally work toward developing such a hexis, if they engage with a heuristic of vulnerability, they will at least begin to develop a concern for how their own rhetorical choices can have ethically profound consequences and be perceived in terms of caring and wounding. Hopefully, this awareness also leads to questioning the ethical frameworks to which digital rhetoricians might already be committed. One of the main differences between a hexis of care and demonstrating rhetorical concern with caring is intent, which cannot be verified easily. However, by establishing conditions under which this hexis can be put into practice and habituated, digital rhetoricians will have, at minimum, considered their ethical relation to other communities and cultures they otherwise may have ignored or not even known existed. Such a reflection is a first step toward developing a hexis of care.

5

GENEROSITY IN SOCIAL
MEDIA TECHNOLOGY

One of the most commonly criticized yet resoundingly popular social media practices is slacktivism. Debated in the *New York Times*, the *Washington Post*, and numerous other journalistic and media outlets, slacktivism is generally defined as taking part in online actions that offer a political group or social cause superficial support, doing little to directly support the actual cause. In essence, an action is called *slacktivism* when it appears to affect the ego of the person taking part in the act more than the cause the person is tweeting about or commenting on. More specifically, slacktivism is "activism" on social media that is limited toward a simple activity of retweeting without necessarily requiring any "real" activist work (organizing movements, rallies, protests, etc.). Whether someone is posting a comment about #BlackLivesMatter or #OpKKK, #UmbrellaRevolution, or #icebucketchallenge, if their actions are seen as only token to the cause, then those actions are defined as slacktivism.

However, as we suggest in this chapter, many common criticisms of slacktivism turn to utilitarian values and question only the ends achieved as the overall metric for evaluating good and bad forms of activism. By contrast, virtue ethics, while it does not require us to conflate online and offline forms of activism, nevertheless helps us to see that a hexis such as generosity simply means something different in an online context and that this difference in comparison to offline activism is neither inherently good nor bad (or superior or inferior). Rather than looking only at the ends achieved through a given social media awareness campaign, virtue ethics instead directs us to examine how the structures of a practice such as slacktivism produce affective dispositions in users that cross the boundaries between online and offline activism.

In the first section of this chapter, we give a general summary of slacktivism with the well-known examples of KONY 2012 and the Ice Bucket Challenge. We demonstrate how criticisms and defenses of the ethical values in these two cases of slacktivism are couched in utilitarian

DOI: 10.7330/9781607328063.c005

terms. In the second section of this chapter, we place Aristotle's original discussion of generosity as a virtue in dialogue with the work of the contemporary philosopher and virtue ethicist Martha Nussbaum. She convincingly connects a hexis of generosity to contemporary issues of social justice, in particular, by dissociating generosity from what she calls "transactional forgiveness" (defined below).[1] Briefly summarized, Nussbaum (2015) challenges a commonsense notion of generosity as a transaction in which an act of generosity is only an ethical good if the giver can see an immediate change in the recipient (e.g., giving money to a homeless person causes them to get a job or change their behavior). By contrast, she counters that generosity as a disposition should exceed such conditional giving because generosity in and of itself is an internal good in the spirit of Aristotle's interest in what motivates the moral activity (as opposed to solely focusing on the end result).

In the third section of this chapter, we illustrate how an updated hexis of generosity functions in a case study of the blog *Humans of New York*. We have selected this blog because it represents one successful example of an online writing platform that repeatedly has many users contribute (via clicking!) to different causes. In other words, it appears as if the *Humans of New York* blog has succeeded in creating a set of conditions in which the disposition of generosity can be cultivated in what many of us would consider to be a stereotypical slacktivist space.

Overall, we demonstrate that, unlike utilitarianism (which emphasizes the end goal over the means to accomplish it), a virtue ethics framework is interested in the development of ethical dispositions, or hexeis, in the building of people's habits of giving to charities and doing so in a way that contributes to human flourishing, or eudaimonia. One of the goals of this chapter, then, is to describe such a hexis and place it in relation to slacktivism in social media. Through this specific hexis, we offer a larger argument that virtue ethics gives us a particularly helpful lens for understanding, evaluating, and hopefully enabling better rhetorical practices in social media and technology. Indeed, a recent study by communication researchers demonstrates how slacktivism, far from signaling the absence of a generous disposition, may increase the likelihood of individuals' engaging in offline forms of civic action. In other words, contrary to common criticism of slacktivism, it is entirely possible to argue that slacktivism is not a sign of the absence of a generous offline disposition but may serve as a reliable signal of the presence of the latter (or even help develop it).

BAD HABITS IN SOCIAL MEDIA: SLACKTIVISM

The term *slacktivism* is frequently used in criticisms of the so-called democratic social media revolution. As is confirmed by the title of media theorist Clay Shirkey's (2009) *Here Comes Everybody*, the emergence of decentralized peer-to-peer authoring and dissemination capacities of the Internet led to an assumption by many researchers in the humanities that a democratic public sphere could finally be realized apart from corporate or state-controlled media (Shirkey 2009). Individuals had the power to form their own political publics or counterpublics (Warner 2005) and to reach other audiences without needing to solicit access to expensive television broadcasting equipment. However, a number of critics swiftly began to question the political utopianism of these early democratic assumptions. As a case in point, decades after its invention, the Internet is dominated once more by large corporate content hosts and distribution forces (Google, Facebook, Instagram, YouTube, etc.) rather than decentralized individual actors.

Among many others, one lingering criticism is that while social media technologies enable digital rhetoricians to more easily simulate or produce a decentralized or bottom-up sense of political or social organizing, "real" engagement still only takes place if a user eventually occupies a visual or physical space of protest, goes door to door petitioning, or makes a donation at a charity fundraiser. In sum, the main points of this criticism are that slacktivism does not make a difference, is only self-serving, and is therefore a questionable pursuit and a case of working with technology that only simulates "real" action—clicking without engaging. When needing to call upon a well-known advocate of this antislacktivism position, critics often raise the name of media journalist Malcolm Gladwell. In his famous essay for the *New Yorker*, "Small Changes: The Revolution Will Not Be Tweeted," he draws a comparison to "actual activism" (his phrase), complaining that the social media revolution cannot be equated to sit-ins and street protests, partly because of the risk involved in the latter practices and the little to no risk in the former (Gladwell 2010). Similarly, popular podcaster Brian Dunning has said slacktivism is a waste of an individual's time at best, and in the worst-case scenarios, slacktivism has stolen "millions of dollars from armchair activists who are persuaded to donate actual money to what they're told is some useful cause" (Dunning 2016). In Dunning's view, many of the causes "slacktivists" donate to are filled with unreliable claims. He has been most critical of the KONY 2012 campaign. For those unfamiliar with KONY 2012, though anyone regularly participating in social media during that year could hardly miss it,[2] the campaign was centered around a documentary movie about a Ugandan militia leader and war criminal named Joseph Kony.

The KONY 2012 documentary (Invisible Children 2012a) went viral via Twitter and Facebook, accumulating over one hundred million views on YouTube as of this writing. The documentary exposes the acts of the Lord's Resistance Army (LRA), of which Kony is the leader, a group whose initial goals were to resist Ugandan government oppression. However, the group's acts have included rape and murder as well as the forced recruitment of children to become sex slaves or child soldiers. The end goal of the movie, beyond creating awareness, is to promote contributions to the Invisible Children organization's Stop Kony charity. However, as Dunning (2016) and others have pointed out, because donors are asked to send money to the filmmakers (Invisible Children) rather than a body of law enforcement, the gross receipts of over $30 million have not been directly used to stop Kony and the LRA. Instead, most of the money has gone toward programmatic costs, such as transportation for victims' speaking engagements, though some funding also went toward making another movie about Kony (Invisible Children 2012b)—a movie explaining (for some, ironically) Invisible Children's use of the charitable contributions.[3]

A similar criticism of slacktivism can be found in media theorist Evgeny Morozov's book *Net Delusion*. He cites an experiment by Anders Colding-Jørgensen, a Danish psychologist. Colding-Jørgensen created a fictitious Facebook group that protested the destruction of a historical monument, the Stork Fountain, although there were no plans to destroy it. From 125 members who joined the first day, his number of fans grew to 27,500. Citing this example, Morozov complains that if the barriers to communication are low (and, by extension, if commitments to prolonged or risky activity are low), slacktivism cannot be thought of as activism. At worst, then, some see slacktivism as an obstacle to forming a long-term habit of activism—an important concern we discuss below in more detail (Morozov 2012). Micah White argues that since there is so little connection between clicking and seeing political change, slacktivism can lead individuals to lose hope in the prospects of change rather than feel empowered (*Guardian*, August 12, 2010). These are some of the more prominent critiques of slacktivism, though there are many more from which to choose. A quick Internet search shows the critique has become almost as knee-jerk as slacktivism seemingly is.

On the other hand, some claim that to hold slacktivism to the standards of what Gladwell (2010) calls "actual activism"—sit-ins, protests, marches, fundraising events—is unfair. In one notable response, media researcher Leo Mirani argues that inasmuch as raising awareness is part of activism (and the slacktivism in the case of KONY 2012, for example, did raise awareness), slacktivism has an important role to play for political activism. Indeed, Mirani goes so far as to specifically criticize Gladwell's position by claiming "the revolution will indeed be Tweeted" (*Guardian*, October 2, 2010).

It is important to acknowledge that Mirani's position has some truth to it. We can indeed find evidence that some forms of slacktivism have made a difference, such as in the example of the Ice Bucket Challenge. The Ice Bucket Challenge, which began in the summer of 2014, is a movement designed to increase charitable contributions to help research toward earlier diagnosis and better treatment of amyotrophic lateral sclerosis (ALS), also known as Lou Gehrig's disease, a neurodegenerative disease that usually leads to death within three to five years. To participate in the challenge, an individual had to

1. accept the challenge (from a friend or colleague on social media);
2. record a video of dumping a bucket of ice over their own head;
3. upload the video to social media, tagging and challenging three or more friends; and
4. make a donation to support the ALS community. (ALS Association 2017)

The humor of this challenge, including the fun of watch a favorite celebrity, a friend, or a family member get soaking wet, led to mass sharing of the videos and the challenge itself going viral. However, these four steps have an exception. According to the ALS Association, social media users did not have to make a donation to participate in the cause. Rather, it was (seemingly) enough simply to raise awareness. This exception led to cries of enabling slacktivism. Critics from various global-journalism outfits denounced the challenge as "problematic in almost every way" (Davidson 2014), a waste of water and a cannibalization of better causes (Kosinski 2016), self-congratulatory (Gilmore 2014), and even what Willard Foxton (2014) calls "a middle-class wet t-shirt contest for armchair clicktivists" (quoted in Townsend 2014).

The problem with these criticisms—valid though each may be in a certain way—is that the Ice Bucket Challenge may have worked. A study in *Science* reports that the research funded by the Ice Bucket Challenge has advanced knowledge on ALS and even possibly enabled the achievement of a medical breakthrough (Ling et al. 2015). To offer a brief summary, the studies highlight the role played by a particular protein (TDP–43), which is linked to cell death in patients' brains or spinal cords. Designing a new protein and inserting it into these affected areas could help the cells return to normal. This discovery may possibly lead to new strategies in gene therapy, which the scientists hope will lead to a diagnostic test for ALS (though not yet treatment). Key to our interest in slacktivism in this chapter is that the scientists have been giving direct credit to the Ice Bucket Challenge for this recent breakthrough. The ALS Association reported over $220 million in donations within a year after the challenge began, and according to lead researcher Philip Wong, "Without [the Ice Bucket Challenge], we wouldn't have been able to come out with the studies as quickly as we did" (Gebelhoff, *Washington Post*, August 19, 2015). Simply put, the Ice Bucket Challenge offers concrete evidence that slacktivism—in certain cases—can produce meaningful forms of social activism.

Based upon the different examples of KONY 2012 and the Ice Bucket Challenge, how then should we ethically evaluate a practice such as slacktivism? Or, what in the practice of slacktivism should be valued? Is slacktivism productive and ethical? If so, how? In what ways? These questions have no obvious answers, or at least no answer that is right in all situations. However, one clear trend emerges when looking at the slacktivism cases above and others: whether it succeeds or fails, slacktivism is almost always evaluated upon the ends achieved. How much money did it raise? What did the money accomplish? In other words, the tacit framework being used to evaluate the ethics of slacktivism is utilitarianism. As we discuss in chapter 1, utilitarianism is an ethical system and framework that looks at achieving ends that are the greatest good for the greatest number of people, with an emphasis on the ends justifying the means. In other words, within a utilitarian framework, the emphasis is on the consequences rather than the means used to achieve them.

By no means do we argue that digital rhetoricians should eliminate such utilitarian perspectives in discussions of charity or other forms of activism. The end goals of a charity are obviously of great importance. But in situations such as KONY 2012 and the Ice Bucket Challenge, one cannot easily predict the ends to be achieved before or even in the midst of the practice, nor is utilitarianism invested in the habits formed by the people involved in the practice of charity. In other words, utilitarianism is more concerned with the final product than with the practices themselves. At least in the discussion of KONY 2012 and the Ice Bucket Challenge, utilitarianism fails to help us understand the ethics of slacktivism as a charitable rhetorical practice and behavior. In the case of KONY 2012, a utilitarian framework would evaluate the charity as a failure and even unethical, a diagnosis many have given. In the case of the Ice Bucket Challenge, those using a utilitarian framework have only evaluated the charity as an ethical practice in light of the recent success of the researchers who relied on the funding from the challenge. Obviously, we will not and even cannot always see perfect means-ends connections; we will not always find the perfect charity to donate to (i.e., a charity that most efficiently uses our money). Of course, this qualification does not mean researching charities is an unworthy goal, and as we mention below, such discernment is necessary for a virtue of generosity, the focus of this chapter.

Now, as the reader of our previous chapters may already infer, in looking at the cases of KONY 2012 and the Ice Bucket Challenge, we are presented once more with a situation in which virtue ethics is able to play an explanatory, and perhaps even a normative, role. Put differently, virtue ethics may help us better understand the motivational thrust of slacktivism—why and when people want to be charitable—and it may give us a better framework for engaging with and enabling online charity work—for creating the conditions to develop a hexis of generosity in individuals. This framework makes sense considering that the sole ethical motive to judge the success or failure of slacktivism seems to turn around utility. At minimum, we suggest additionally taking a look at slacktivism through a lens of virtue ethics. In contrast to our instinct to evaluate phenomena such as slacktivism by their utility, KONY 2012 and the Ice Bucket Challenge obviously show the problems with relying solely on such a framework. These movements were similar in method but opposite in result. Should every person interested in donating to an online charity take these and other similar reasons into consideration, people would rarely participate in online charities through social media. People cannot evaluate the ethical merits of a charity only by a guaranteed end, an end often at best unpredictable. Otherwise, they would become paralyzed with indecision regarding when to donate to which charities.

Once again, it is the plurality of motives across contingent rhetorical situations that enables virtue ethics to offer such a powerful language for discussing social media ethics in the context of slacktivism. Virtue ethics' point of reference is not a concrete or fixed rule, obligation, or end goal but rather facts about our shared existence we might agree on—dispositions such as caring for others, being just, and so forth—in the goal of working toward eudaimonia, or human flourishing. Even as different individuals from different cultural backgrounds may disagree on what a friendly person might look like (i.e., friendliness is not an essential trait with a universal set of qualities), in most instances, those same people will agree that hexeis such as patience, fairness, and generosity are dispositions important for friendship and that cultivating such hexeis is beneficial to communities as much as it is beneficial to any specific individual.

As we note in chapter 2's discussion of her three exigencies, Vallor (2010, 2016) has made a particularly strong case for the use of virtue ethics in social media technologies. In making her argument, she notes that if people are to benefit from a virtue ethics of technology, such an ethics needs "to be able to successfully identify dispositions generally recognized as important to the ability of human beings to flourish in relevantly similar technological situations" (Vallor 2010, 161). Thus, with regard to the multifaceted situation of slacktivism, or charity in online environments in general, we identify one of Aristotle's original hexeis, generosity (often translated as liberality), as a key disposition for rhetoricians to develop and cultivate in our age of social media.

ARISTOTLE, NUSSBAUM, AND THE VIRTUE OF GENEROSITY

For Aristotle (2002), generosity (or liberality, *eleutheriotes*) means to be free from material and monetary attachments (1119b30). Individuals demonstrate a hexis of generosity when they show excellence in dealing with money, especially in giving it to others (although Aristotle considers the temperament in how one receives money as well). Consistent with the internal/external goals of virtue ethics broadly (see chapter 2), he argues that individuals find pleasure in giving to others. Giving is an internal end of nobility or beauty in generosity itself. However, this practice also has positive external ends, such as helping others in their lives. Together, the internal and external ends contribute to eudaimonia. (As an aside, it is important to note that while Aristotle does not discuss care as a specific virtue, as we do in chapter 4, we differentiate care and generosity by the latter's specific orientation toward money and wealth. We might assume a person who has developed a hexis of care is also invested in developing a hexis of generosity, but they are not the same disposition.)

The vices in relation to the mean of being a generous person are that of prodigality or wastefulness (*asotia*)—a vice of excess—and miserliness or stinginess (*aneleutheriotetos*)—a vice of deficiency. In other words, generosity is the virtuous mean between wastefulness and stinginess. This virtue manifests itself in giving appropriate amounts of one's wealth to the appropriate people at the appropriate time (Aristotle 2002, 1120a26, 1106b20–23). Notably, the vices are not equally unethical. If one had to choose between the vices, Aristotle notes it is better to be wasteful in what we give than to be stingy (1121a20). Those who are seen as embodying a disposition of generosity, although they may be wasteful at times, are still appreciated by others (1120a16), as their giving is helpful to others (1120a22).

A key point for Aristotle when discussing certain virtues, including that of generosity, is the motive of *kalon*, the beautiful or noble. This is a point he reiterates throughout the *Nicomachean Ethics*. Aristotle argues that to inhabit the disposition of generosity is *kalos*. Individuals' generosity is viewed as beautiful and noble by themselves and by others. An individual who has not developed a hexis of generosity likely feels pain when giving to others rather than a sense of beauty or nobility (Aristotle 2002, 1120a24).

A person with a generous disposition prefers giving to receiving (Aristotle 2002, 1120b8), but this disposition does not mean they do not ask for benefits when necessary. Similar to acts of giving, they only ask for an appropriate amount of help from the appropriate people, at the appropriate time (1120b1). This type of discrimination—choosing the right amount, right people, and right time—is a key part of a hexis of generosity. Other than imparting advice to avoid giving to and receiving from criminals (1121b33), Aristotle is (likely deliberately) vague about telling his readers what exactly those right amounts, people, and times are. While vagueness could be a source of frustration for some readers, it is also helpful to remember virtue ethics is not fixed but is to be determined in each contingent situation by those involved (1104a3–7).

While some readers may admire Aristotle's goal of developing a hexis of generosity in order to be free of monetary attachments, our contemporary understanding of political economy and the more recent turn to materialism and objects in digital rhetoric research, for example, confirms that no one is ever "free" of material constraints, as Aristotle seems to want. With respect to some of the limitations of Aristotle's conception, it is understandable that subsequent virtue ethicists have offered some important updates. For example, the Scottish philosopher David Hume's book *An Enquiry Concerning the Principles of Morals* offers the claim that the cultivation of a disposition such as generosity—he often uses the term "benevolence"—should not be cultivated as a way to free oneself of material constraints; rather, he suggests virtues such as generosity should proceed from concern and sympathy for others (Hume 1983, II.1–5).

A fuller account of Hume's extension to Aristotle's original approach to generosity can be found in the philosopher Martha Nussbaum's recent book *Anger and Forgiveness: Resentment, Generosity, Justice*. In the spirit of Hume, who sees generosity as important to and developing from social concerns, as well as personal concerns, Nussbaum contends that communities' abilities to develop dispositions of generosity and unconditional forgiveness have bearing on their ability to produce a just society (Nussbaum 2015, 9). While Nussbaum's larger argument is that justice and forgiveness cannot be built upon anger and resentment—a controversial argument, to say the least, considering the important work of critical theorists such as Audre Lorde, bell hooks, and others who have shown the value of anger—Nussbaum does add a crucial element to understanding what it means to embody a generous disposition, which we believe is important to take up here.

One of the key points of Nussbaum's argument regarding generosity is that she distinguishes it from dispositions and behaviors that are often mistaken for generosity but that actually deter one away from developing a generous disposition. According to Nussbaum, generosity should not be mistaken for forgiveness or, in particular, what she calls "transactional forgiveness." In her definition, transactional forgiveness "exacts a performance of contrition and abasement, which can itself function as a type of payback. (Often, too, the payback mentality is combined with a focus on status, in the form of abasement and lowness" (Nussbaum 2015, 33). To inform this concept, Nussbaum looks to ancient Greco-Roman and Judeo-Christian texts to historicize how forgiveness is so often viewed as transactional. However, she also finds pockets throughout those texts in which generosity and unconditional forgiveness are shown to be different from transactional forgiveness. For a starting definition, she turns to the work of philosopher Charles Griswold (2007), who argues that forgiveness "is a two-person process involving a moderation of anger and a cessation of projects of revenge, in response to the fulfillment of six conditions. The person who seeks [transactional] forgiveness" should

1. Acknowledge that she was the responsible agent
2. Repudiate her deeds (by acknowledging their wrongness) and herself as their author
3. Express regret to the injured for having caused this particular injury
4. Commit to becoming the sort of person who does not inflict injury and show this commitment through deeds as well as words
5. Show that she understands, from the injured person's perspective, the damage done by the injury
6. Offer a narrative accounting for how she came to do wrong, how that wrongdoing does not express the totality of her person, and how she is becoming worthy of approbation (Nussbaum 2015, 57).

While Nussbaum elaborates on this basic framework of forgiveness throughout her book, her general point is that if we think of forgiveness or generosity as transactional, our emphasis is on keeping score of another's acts and omission of acts in response to our "giving." If we see forgiveness and generosity as transactional, we are overemphasizing the effect of our actions over any value in the actions themselves. Similarly, virtue ethics sees the development of hexeis as working toward both internal and external goals. If the development of a disposition of generosity is motivated only by the normative effect it has on others—Are they changing their behaviors? Are they promising to work harder or be better next time?—then such a disposition is solely built upon external aims. As a case in point, Nussbaum argues that such a transactional view of forgiveness and generosity is consistent with those who demand "confession, weeping and wailing, and a sense of [another's] lowness and essential worthlessness. The penitent is tormented simply by penitence. The person who administers the process is controlling and relentless toward the penitent, an inquisitor of acts and desires" (Nussbaum 2015, 73).

Nussbaum, of course, finds this view of transactional forgiveness as having religious roots. Nevertheless, this religious context has also taken hold of contemporary culture's view of how forgiveness and generosity are economic practices (and, indeed, herein lies the clear link to understanding the significance of evaluating slacktivism in terms of the ends achieved alone). To really highlight how distinctive this approach to dispositional ethics is, consider how Nussbaum would encourage us to read a cultural practice like mass incarceration. In the United States, we currently have over two million individuals imprisoned, which is roughly 22 percent of the global prison population (US Bureau). According to Nussbaum (2015), anger, as Aristotle defines it, has three parts, which, in turn, help explain why acts of imprisonment stem from anger:

1. You think you've been wronged.

2. The damage was wrongfully inflicted.

3. It was serious damage to something you care about. (quoted in Green 2016, para 4)

For Nussbaum (2015), anger comes with a desire for payback. Someone commits a crime—say, robbing a bank—and we justify imprisonment as a way to remedy this wrong (as well as to rehabilitate). Nussbaum counters that this type of mentality is already focused on the wrong point of ethical relevance for generosity. How we view and justify mass incarceration does not come from a disposition of generosity or fairness. To be clear, our goal in raising this example is not to wade into the thickets of research on this topic. Rather, it is more important to note some researchers have convincingly argued that focusing on the punishment instead of on improving the structural economic, nutritional, educational, and cultural factors that give rise to garden-variety crimes fails to solve the crime problem. In other words, payback as motive in responding to crime may not adequately solve the problem, which is evidenced by the number of repeat offenders and, especially, the systemic incarceration of poor and nonwhite populations (e.g., see Alexander 2012). While this topic is very important, as we move forward in this chapter, our point in looking to Nussbaum to extend the hexis of generosity is simply to see that a disposition of generosity is not invested in payback or demonstrations of betterment from those to whom we give.

To recap the claims we make in this section, it is clear each thinker's notion of generosity is characterizing the same kind of disposition. Aristotle and Nussbaum would probably both recognize generous dispositions in the same kinds of people. However, Nussbaum differs from Aristotle in that she is not committed to the notion of generosity as part and parcel of a larger goal of metaphysical separation from materiality. Rather, Nussbaum sees human communicative connectedness and the sympathy that arises from that connectedness as the motive to produce a generous hexis. While Aristotle's general description of a hexis of generosity rings true (giving the right amount of one's wealth to the right people at the right time), his larger goal of metaphysical separation from one's worldly attachments is not consistent with our contemporary situation, in which we know even our material surroundings, including wealth, constitute who we are. Thus, an understanding of generosity as stemming from epideictic rhetoric with others and the sympathy that results in such communication—in other words, Nussbaum's understanding of the development of a hexis of generosity—is more appropriate to the concerns about and criticisms of slacktivism so prevalent in social media today.

DEVELOPING HEXEIS OF GENEROSITY THROUGH SOCIAL MEDIA

To return to our chapter's subject matter of slacktivism, our goals in turning to Aristotle, Nussbaum, and a hexis of generosity are quite modest. As our examples above demonstrate, and our more thorough example below confirms as well, slacktivism as an ethico-political practice is almost universally discussed in terms of utilitarian ethics—either explicitly or tacitly. However, we contend virtue ethics uniquely locates the emergence of ethical behaviors within slacktivism in a way that exceeds this either/or binary. This complexity is demonstrated in the social media presence of *Humans of New York* (*HONY*), a blog by the *New York Times* photojournalist Brandon Stanton. In Stanton's own words in a 2016 post on the blog,

> Humans of New York began as a photography project in 2010. The initial goal was to photograph 10,000 New Yorkers on the street, and create an exhaustive catalogue of the city's inhabitants. Somewhere along the way, I began to interview my subjects in addition to photographing them. And alongside their portraits, I'd include quotes and short stories from their lives.

Upon first glance at *HONY*, it seems to be nothing more than that which is described above: a blog cataloguing and narrativizing the lives and experiences of various people in New York and around the world. However, describing *HONY* as just a blog seems reductive. *HONY* is a network in which readers access the blog from social media sites such as Instagram and Facebook. While Stanton began the project as a blog on New Yorkers, "he might have simply called it Humans" (Kingma 2015), for as his project gained in popularity, he began photographing people in many different countries, including those he visited on an eleven-country tour (including Iraq, Kenya, Ukraine) with the United Nations in 2015 (Kweifio-Okai, *Guardian*, September 5, 2014). At the time of this writing, the blog has over seventeen million followers on Facebook, over five million on Instagram, and over four hundred thousand on Twitter. Most interesting to our concerns in this chapter is that while *HONY* began as a photography project, it has turned into a go-to site for philanthropic interests and charity in general.

HONY highlights the stories of individuals and their families within various series, titled "Refugee Stories," "Syrian Americans," "Pediatric Cancer," "Inmate Stories," and more. Each story is told through multiple images and quotes from the photographed subjects. As Stanton learned about the people in his photographs, many of whom are in dire circumstances, he began launching charities that would directly help the individuals he was photographing and writing about. Readers who follow *HONY* on social media receive updates for new stories and opportunities to donate to the charities that will help the specific person, family, or community they read about on *HONY*. At times, *HONY* continues to follow the subjects of each story as the charity begins to affect their lives. Thus, the readers of *HONY* (many of whom donate to a particular cause) can sometimes see their and others' donations take effect, including the reaction of those who are benefitting from their charitable donations, and then see change take place.

For example, Vidal Chastanet, (at the time) a thirteen-year-old from Brownsville, New York, was photographed and interviewed by Stanton in January 2015. When Stanton asked Vidal who his greatest influence was, the following conversation ensued:

VIDAL: "My principal, Ms. Lopez."

STANTON: "How has she influenced you?"

VIDAL: "When we get in trouble, she doesn't suspend us. She calls us to her office and explains to us how society was built down around us. And she tells us that each time somebody fails out of school, a new jail cell gets built. And one time she made every student stand up, one at a time, and she told each one of us that we matter." (Ellis 2015)

Stanton was inspired to meet with Principal Nadia Lopez, and with the school's director of programs, they created an Indiegogo fundraiser (most of the *HONY* charities go through Indiegogo) with the goal of raising $100,000. The money would be used to take the sixth-grade classes at Mott Hall Bridges Academy on field trips to visit Harvard University over a period of three years as a way to inspire the students toward a future of learning beyond secondary education. Vidal's story and the fundraiser were shared on the *HONY* blog and in various social media outlets, and within one month, the fundraiser accumulated over $1 million from over fifty thousand contributors, far exceeding its original goal (Ellis 2015). The money has funded and will continue to fund trips to Harvard and other schools of higher education and is also being used to fund scholarship opportunities.

Now, we neither share this story to advocate for readers to donate to a specific *HONY* charity nor to qualify *HONY*'s charitable actions as more ethical than others. A utilitarian perspective may urge us to draw these sorts of conclusions, as almost every one of the charities associated with a story on the *HONY* blog exceeded its charitable-donations goals (and to reiterate this point once more, a utilitarian approach can be productive in this context at times). We also do not share this example to uphold Stanton as someone who has developed a hexis of generosity. He may very well have. He definitely appears to have made generosity a habit, whether one likes his version or not. Rather, we wish to suggest that those behind the *HONY* project have begun to tap into the kind of rhetorical practices that produce the conditions for developing generous dispositions in social media through slacktivism. Furthermore, it is our claim they are doing this in a manner that supports Nussbaum's nontransactional generosity and parallels the kinds of environments Aristotle and Hume each describe for producing such a hexis.

First and foremost, *HONY* is effective in offering a mechanism through which to cultivate a hexis of generosity in its readers, by enabling people to give the right amounts to a charity, to the right people, and at the right time, as Aristotle argues. By the right amounts, we simply mean that by going through a service such as Indiegogo, one can donate a minimum of $1 to a cause. When considering donations, donors also see their donations in the context of others, which may motivate the donors to dig a little deeper. Because donors can donate anonymously, they can do so without any fear such a donation will be seen by others as too little.

Timing (kairos, if you will) is also crucial for *HONY* in developing hexeis of generosity in its readers. This includes the fundraiser deadline, which should parallel the needs of the people affected by the charity, the people in the narrative whom the donor has likely been discussing on social media with other potential donors. Timing is also important in making such charitable considerations a habit for readers. Flooding Facebook, Twitter, and Instagram too often with images, links, or appeals to donate to a specific cause can make even the most interested party want to hide such news items from their social media feeds. However, providing enough repetition and identification—for example, showing readers how a story they've read about is progressing—can engender a sense of expectation in the reader/donor and even make them look forward to giving to a similar charity in the future.

Perhaps most important is providing the means for donors to feel as if they are donating to the right people. The main means for *HONY* to produce this sense of giving to the right people is through storytelling. Rather than ask the reader to donate to an abstract cause, *HONY* provides a narrative about individuals, their families, and their communities accompanied by images that appeal to the emotions of the reader and are in line with the topic at hand. While other organizations that provide means for charitable or political contributions also use storytelling as a device to ask for donations, many of them, such as change.org, stitch together a quote or two from the people or parties in need and dedicate a paragraph at most to their story. In contrast, by dedicating four or more significant posts to the same person and story—composed by the people in need themselves—each story develops a larger narrative arch for who is involved and what they need to solve their problems. In this way, *HONY* gives the reader a greater sense of commitment to the particular people the story is about and to their cause.

With this example as a case in point, it is clear social media also plays an important part in creating a sense of donating to the right people. While for Aristotle freeing oneself from the constraints of wealth may be a motivation for developing a hexis of generosity (perhaps especially in those most likely to be associated with material interests), as Hume (1983) points out, social motivation is key. Social media provides not only the opportunity for people to discuss a particularly interesting story on *HONY*—for example, the victims of Hurricane Sandy, a boy who wants to own a horse, or the fight against bonded labor in Pakistan—but also for them to post that they gave to a particular charity. While the cynics among us might be critical of this seemingly boastful aspect of social media, Hume is quite clear that the desire to be admired by others (and to have one's actions praised) is powerful in motivating one to be generous and then to repeat that generosity to the point of it's becoming a habit, a disposition, a hexis. Admittedly, boasting can have a negative effect on some, but unlike a PBS fundraising drive for which the donor receives a DVD set of *Downton Abbey*, when one donates to a cause via social media, generosity becomes part of one's dispositional identity for others to praise (or criticize). Liking someone's act of generosity that had real consequences for what appears to be very real people with real lives, in other words, a life story, also means the acts of that person are more likely to pop up in one's Facebook or Instagram feed and potentially induce a habit of more sustained reading of a *HONY* cause by others.

Critics of *HONY* have pointed out that the blog relies too much on emotional appeals and that this somehow invalidates *HONY*'s causes (Boyle 2016; Smyth 2015). No doubt *HONY* should consider any critique leveled at it, and there is truth in these critiques. However, such critiques would do well not only to consider how rhetoric functions beyond mere appeals to logic but also to consider how ethical dispositions are formed. We can reason about ethical behavior all we want, but in order to develop hexeis of justice, care, and generosity (to name a few), critical reasoning is not enough. Habits and nonconscious affect play a huge role. If pathos-heavy narratives enable people to continually look to be generous and charitable in their lives, we must be careful about how quickly we dismiss such causes—even if we don't see them working toward our preferred systemic change.[4] In fact, such pathos-heavy narratives that encourage charitable donations may very well be working toward systemic change via the development of people's hexeis.

To help illustrate this claim, we close this section by featuring the findings of a recent study on slacktivism. In 2013, communication researchers Yu-Hao Lee and Gary Hsieh presented research findings on whether a slacktivist act (a one-click donation to a charitable or political cause) affected a person's subsequent choice to continue to donate. Lee and Hsieh (2013) wished to discover three things: (1) whether under certain conditions, moral balancing would occur—in other words, whether people felt they had done their good deed and no longer needed to consider participating in civic action (this research question addresses the biggest critique of slacktivism: that it only makes people feel good about themselves, so they can go about their day afterward); (2) whether an effect of consistency and commitment occurred—whether a donor's act to participate in a charity online, a charity they might not have otherwise contributed to, actually encouraged further action on the same issue; and (3) whether participating in slacktivism in general increased people's interest in participating in other more traditional civic action. The results they discovered are intriguing for thinking about dispositions of generosity.

> Fortunately, contrary to critics' concern, we found no evidence that performing one form of slacktivism (i.e., signing online petitions) will undermine a subsequent civic activity (i.e., donating to a charity). In fact, we found scenarios where "slacktivism" can actually *increase* likelihood of participation in a subsequent collective action. . . . In addition, what has been often overlooked in the discussion of slacktivism's efficacy is its effects on the people who decline to participate. In this study we found that when people are invited to sign a petition and decline to do so, they actually subsequently donated more to an incongruent charity. (Lee and Hsieh 2013, 8)

It is true that Lee and Hsieh are not virtue ethicists (or, more accurately, they are not advocating such a framework in this article). However, their interest in questioning critics of the knee-jerk response to slacktivism as either ethical/unethical or not real activism is definitely in line with the interests of virtue ethics. Simply put, their findings direct us to consider the broader role of slacktivism in producing or eroding dispositions of generosity rather than merely assuming the existence (or absence) of a disposition based upon the observation of a slacktivist action.[5]

These findings raise an additional point we need to clarify: a virtue ethics orientation is still very invested in systemic change. However, rather than focusing only on large structural changes, virtue ethics asks us to look in a different direction, toward individual and communal dispositions that are being developed—dispositions that might better enable such structural change. What this focus means for slacktivism is that it is possible to view it for what it is: a means of creating a particular type of sociopolitical relation, enabled by certain mechanisms, that takes part in the development of people's habits—whether of virtue or vice. Whether particular instances of slacktivism succeed or fail has remarkably little to do with the actual act itself; rather, the success of slacktivism depends on whether these activities encourage more generous hexeis in those involved and those exposed to their involvement. The larger question for virtue ethics is whether slacktivism stems from this sort of disposition rather than from a capricious action, as critics of slacktivism would have it. For example, are individuals who engage in slacktivism more or less likely to engage in other forms of political-awareness raising? Lee and Hsieh's work indicates yes, but more should be done. Rather than simply dismiss slacktivism as not real activism, we hope more people will seek to understand how the structures in place that produce slacktivism lead or do not lead to more ethical dispositions of generosity.

A generalized approach to cultivating a hexis of generosity through online petitions and related forms of slacktivism can shift the typical question behind slacktivism: that if we only participate politically or in social causes online, that participation has no impact on our offline identities. *It is this type of thinking virtue ethics wants to push back against.* We want to carefully avoid accepting any link between online and offline behaviors with an a priori negative behavior (antisocial behavior, addiction, etc.). Rather, we should be interested in seeing how various networks enable the cultivation of a hexis of generosity—online and offline. Developing such a hexis of generosity will not come about solely from critical reasoning, and that is a key point for virtue ethics.

This hexis of generosity applies in particular to, well, us: students and researchers of digital rhetoric. We are interested in things like slacktivism because we are trying to determine what is happening to the people participating in slacktivism. How does it affect their habits, their dispositions, their hexeis? Might the development of such hexeis lead to more ethical systemic change rather than enforcing our ideologies through other means of systemic change? Whether for virtue or vice, we believe it is the actual dispositions social media encourages us to form that will play an important role in the types of political and social change we may wish to support or challenge.

6
A VIRTUE OF PATIENCE IN ENVIRONMENTAL NETWORKS

While we reference the nonhuman turn and the human-technology relationship at multiple times in this book, admittedly our case studies drawing upon Aristotle and other theorists (Rancière, Cavarero, Hume) tend toward anthropomorphic ethical concerns (i.e., those focused primarily on human-centered values and concerns). Yet, as a growing number of digital rhetoric and rhetoric and composition scholars have shown (Weisser and Dobrin 2002), anthropomorphism can be a problem if digital rhetoricians intend to contend with the environmental impact of digital technologies. We may use our mobile phones and laptop computers to perform important rhetorical activities in networked spaces or, as we show in the previous chapter, to even raise awareness or money on behalf of various deserving social causes. However, the production and disposal of these same devices implicate us—whether we choose to acknowledge this fact or not—within actual material, environmental, and ecological contexts that, as we demonstrate in this chapter, do indeed carry ethical duties and responsibilities with significance for virtue ethics. Here, anthropocentrism functions as something of an instrumental blind spot for ethics. As a number of scholars both in digital rhetoric and in the broader humanities have argued, if we only focus on our individual means-ends use of a technology to achieve some rhetorical goal, such as posting a photo of our pets or food on Instagram, we avoid contending with the full political and ethical range of consequences that support, condition, and enable our digital rhetoric practices.

How then, might we start to take account of how our digital rhetoric practices are interconnected with the ethical concerns of the world around us? In this chapter, we explore the cultivation of a hexis of patience (*proares*), or slowness to anger, to help us think through the environmental situatedness of digital rhetoric. To highlight the stakes of this hexis, we explore one social media rhetorical practice that can benefit from a hexis of patience in particular: shaming and outrage in response to environmental conflicts. In the first section, we explore the

DOI: 10.7330/9781607328063.c006

use of Twitter and other social media platforms in the wake of the 2013 California drought to express outrage at wealthy celebrities or home-owners who refused to reduce their water usage to appropriate levels. In the second section, we suggest that the way to start thinking about out-rage (e.g., a lack of patience) productively is not to avoid it but to better ground it within the emotional and embodied networks that structure us as digital rhetors.[1] In brief, we revisit debates by rhetoric and com-position scholars on the role of emotion in rhetoric, particularly those who have challenged paradigms of rhetoric that turn upon a separation of rationality and emotions. By contrast, alternative conceptions, such as Jenny Rice's (2014) articulation of the "figure of public exception," offer clear and compelling reasons to view digital rhetors as inherently emotional beings structured through our particular encounters with dynamic environments and ecologies. Indeed, Rice's concept shares a specific connection to Aristotle's treatment of emotions (thumos) as an unavoidable part of rhetoric to be negotiated, even its extreme manifes-tations of anger (*orge*).

In asking researchers to "develop some new habits" of thinking about our entanglement with the environmental world, to use Rice's phrase, we suggest in the third section that these efforts can be understood as a tacit call for a hexis of patience. Toward this end, we compare the online shaming of Los Angeles to the political philosopher Jane Bennett's (2010) discussion of outrage in the context of another environmental situation: the great Northeast electrical blackout of 2003. While our first instincts in these sorts of accidents might be to find a human scapegoat (i.e., an object for an expression of outrage), Bennett instead preaches patience against moral outrage (what she states comes from Plato's thumos, which is a point we examine in detail below). Drawing on her new materialist philosophy, Bennett argues that outrage far too often causes us to miss examining the full range of agencies—human and nonhuman—that are affected by and that affect environmental disas-ters. She offers us a particularly important method of cultivating a hexis of patience to help channel outrage on social media to more productive and nonanthropomorphic ends.

SHAMING AND OUTRAGE

Outrage is a clear dispositional ethics problem in social media and the Internet as a whole and is not unrelated in the least to forms of slacktivism. "Don't read the comments" is a commonly repeated refrain among social media users—advice that even applies to what one would conventionally think of as the more enlightened discourses of the online-comments sections of *Inside Higher Ed* or the *Chronicle of Higher Education*. While outrage can take many individual forms, including trolling, hate speech, or political rants, we are interested in one particular form that often takes on collective momentum: shaming. In large part due to the ability of nearly anyone with an Internet connection to transmit and post public-facing messages (and with potential anonymity), shaming has emerged as a popular response to, well, virtually any perception of socially irresponsible behavior that catches the attention of a critical mass of users. Even people who do not use social media are likely familiar with the 2015 public shaming of Martin Shkreli, the CEO of Turing Pharmaceuticals. Shkreli infamously purchased an AIDS- and cancer-patient drug and hiked the price per pill from $13.50 to $750. He was resoundingly vilified on social media, even earning at one point the "most hated man in America" title, according to many newspaper reports (Thomas and Swift 2015).

Shkreli's case has a clear analogy in environmental outrage at the rich Los Angeles water wasters. Beginning around 2011, Los Angeles and a large part of California had begun to experience one of the worst droughts on record. In response, city officials began to urge citizens to limit water consumption and set water-usage targets. Yet, famous celebrities in Hollywood and other citizens in wealthy suburbs were initially unresponsive. In the years following 2011, various public-relations campaigns and other pathos-laden appeals to community sensibility failed overwhelmingly in Beverly Hills. As a case in point, the state passed a mandatory 25 percent reduction in water usage in June 2015. Yet, in March 2016, Matt Stevens of the *LA Times* reported that Beverly Hills had yet to meet the required savings target as late as January 2015. Finally, frustrated state regulators levied a fine on the city, and, in turn, the city eventually registered a 26 percent water cut after local city officials levied extreme fines on individual water wasters.

While legislative fines eventually curbed the behavior, a driving force in prompting state and local legislators to hold the rich and famous accountable were a number of social media shaming campaigns that gained national news. While the city had already allowed (and even endorsed) vigilante-style reporting of individual offenders, in which details and photos could be submitted to www.savewater.ca.gov, #DroughtShaming became a trending Twitter hashtag during the summer of 2015. On May 11, 2015, Veronica Rocha of the *LA Times* reported that celebrities had been targeted by this campaign over the previous weekend . The *New York Post* also ran a spread on the lush green lawns of

LA celebrities during a time when average citizens were being subjected to extreme water-use quotas.

Clearly, shaming has some sort of rhetorical and ethical function that was effective in this case. But what type? Let us start with an obvious question: is outrage always an effective rhetorical form as a remedy for a perceived act of social injustice? Related to this question, is effectiveness even the best ethical measure to employ in assessing the rhetorical value of social media shaming? To revisit an earlier example, Shkreli had to perform public damage control, including affirming that he was not a bad individual (even though certain actions he performed may have been perceived as negative), affirming the benefits of free-market capitalism, and making other epideictic gestures that often accompany a shamed individual's attempt to restore their ethos. Despite Shrkeli's public acknowledgments, however, he did ultimately lower the price of his company's product in response to public outrage. (In fact, market competition may prove to be a better rhetorical motive, as Imprimis Pharmaceuticals has started selling Daraprim for $1 a pill.) Scholarly discussions of the effectiveness of outrage offer mixed results on this topic as well. Marketing professor Americus Reed argues, "Social media amplifies the illusion of outrage, making it seem more dangerous and risky than it is" (quoted in Wharton 2015). In confirmation of Reed's claim, the amplification of outrage over Shkreli's actions perhaps made various interested US publics believe their online activities (and subsequent gatekeeper reporting and interviewing) were more effective in stimulating some sort of redress than they actually were. In this scenario, it is clear social media enables millions to express their politics by stating their feelings, while very few rhetorical actors (politicians, other pharmaceutical companies, etc.) may have the ability to do anything in response that creates traction.

In rhetorical studies, it is important to note that outrage has been viewed as a part of rhetoric or language more generally from Plato's discussion of thumos (spiritedness) through Kenneth Burke's discussion of scapegoating. Along these lines, a recent study by marketing professor Pinar Yildirim demonstrates that public shaming on social media is not substantively different from previous nonnetworked and nondigital shaming practices, with the sole exception of speed (from Wharton 2015). Indeed, she goes on to discuss how shaming is a fairly common rhetorical practice that helps communities reduce antisocial behavior or even increase the likelihood of prosocial action. Yildirim affirms, "'This is true for a wide range of domains, from enforcing charitable donations to preventing petty crime, keeping traditions and even improving financial outcomes for groups'" (quoted in Wharton 2015). Digital rhetoric scholar Jodie A. Nicotra makes a similar claim, stating, "Virtual public shamings can be conceived as epideictic, the architecture of Twitter helping to performatively enact not just norms and values, but a community, one 140-character message at a time" (Nicotra 2016). Indeed, there is also a potentially democratic element to rhetorical shaming. Certain acts of shaming can be—but are not exclusively—designed as a way for individuals who do not have the ability individually or even collectively to resist a given negative action (e.g., by passing legislation or accessing lawmakers directly) to have some sort of impact. Social media shaming at times can create enough views to signal what Karine Nahon and Jeff Hemsley in their book *Going Viral* call social media "gatekeepers" (traditional television media, larger social media content contributors like Slate.com or BuzzFeed, etc.) to take up the issue in order to impact offenders such as Shkreli (Nahon and Hemsley 2013).

Yet, clearly, shaming is not an unequivocally ethical practice, even when it is effective in curbing a given antisocial behavior. Among many possible ethical objections to shaming, a clear problem with shaming and outrage lies in the potential of reducing complex social issues to a few cathartic scapegoats. For example, while it could be argued that #DroughtShaming worked to influence perceptions—and maybe even actions—of well-known Hollywood stars, the initial social media campaign excluded the role played by global food and beverage company Nestle, who did not seem—until very late in the shaming process—to gain much negative attention in comparison to individual citizen offenders. In the midst of the drought, Nestle took to eighty million gallons of water each year from Sacramento aquifers (O'Connell 2014). Simply put, the ability to vilify a few famous citizen names on social media may not paint an entirely accurate picture of all of the relevant actors involved in the drought political issue. We can also raise the fairly obvious point that shaming targets are not always correctly identified, or conversely, that the effects of public shaming may be greatly disproportionate to the offending action. Jon Ronson (2016), the author of *So You've Been Publicly Shamed*, highlights this danger by chronicling the very real damage to individuals' lives and careers that can be caused by social media outrage—even if the behavior shamed is clearly unethical or wrong. Furthermore, shaming, not unlike other negative social media practices such as trolling or hacktivism, is often easiest to support as an ethical practice when we personally agree with the cause it is used for. Suffice to say, it is difficult to offer a totalizing ethical condemnation or acceptance of social media shaming.

RECASTING OUTRAGE THROUGH EMOTIONS
IN COMPOSITION STUDIES

As the running theme across the various hexeis we have covered in this book, our claim once more is that virtue ethics offers us an important normative basis for thinking through ethical judgments in ambiguous situations such as social media shaming, especially in the context of environmental and sustainability issues around examples such as #DroughtShaming. In general, Aristotle's ancient views on emotions still have a great degree of relevance for helping us think through the ethics of shaming. In response to outrage, anger, and shaming, it is likely some readers may be tempted to call for a more "objective," "dispassionate," fact-based, rational, or logical sort of approach. That is, if outrage causes us to scapegoat individual celebrities or actors while ignoring the broader forces of capitalism, waste management, corporate lobbying, corrupt politicians, global warming, or, indeed, even our own complicity in producing environmental problems, it stands to reason that perhaps we must take emotions out of the equation in order to produce a better or more accurate understanding of the situation.

By contrast, it is critical to note Aristotle in no way allows digital rhetoricians to separate logic or reason from emotion and embodiment. As an aside, splits between emotion and embodiment are quite common to how many researchers understand rhetoric and writing. For example, Gretchen Flesher Moon (2003) finds that many writing textbooks used in high-school or college classrooms around the country—if they even teach the subject of emotion—follow Aristotle's treatment of emotion as an irrational *pisteis* (proof) in contrast to more rational proofs of logos and ethos (Aristotle 2006, 1156a22). For example, one textbook encourages a writer to replace the description "'fat cats'" with the more neutral and objective description "'those who control most of the nation's resources'" because the former is "'crudely emotional'" (Moon 2003, 35). In contrast to the ways hexeis form, such an emphasis also privileges rationality by directing digital rhetors to view writing as a transparent expression of thought (e.g., clear, logical, objective).[2]

Inasmuch as we note in chapter 2 that Aristotle's ethos is most often read as a proof, a parallel exists for how many contemporary researchers have picked up Aristotle's view of emotions. Classical-rhetoric scholar Jeffrey Walker (2000) observes that the etymological root for "'enthymeme,'" the mode of argumentative reasoning (in contrast to the Platonic dialectic) used by the sophists, is the term *thumos*, which is "'often linked to both the production and reception of passionate thought and eloquence, persuasive discourse'" (quoted in Moon 2003,

33). Thumos (heart, spiritedness) is the faculty of the soul that enables love and friendship along with aggression, ambition, and anger. Here, there is no split between thought (reason, rationality) and emotions. Aristotle argues that his students, the wealthy young men of Athens, "need intelligence and a spirit of *thumos* if they should be led toward laws by a legislator" (Aristotle 2000, VII.7.1327b26).Walker maintains that, far from subordinating emotions to rationality, Aristotle sees "all practical reasoning is pathetic reasoning" (Walker 2000, 91). Because of the central role of thumos in shaping the self, Eugene Garver (2006), another classicist, even offers "personal identity" as a more accurate translation of thumos (see also Baecker 2007). Simply put, if we cannot find a space of enlightened discourse or reason through which to disinterestedly examine #DroughtShaming, that is, if we cannot ever divorce our thinking from its constitution by thumos, then rhetoric and, as we point out momentarily, ethics must acknowledge and negotiate emotions, from extreme *orge* (anger) to passive disinterest, rather than try to eliminate the role of emotions in digital rhetoric.[3]

A major problem with explicitly or tacitly bracketing the emotions from rhetoric is that a rhetor's or an audience's ideological beliefs are inseparable from their habituated embodied and spatial contexts, regardless of the type of rhetorical forms instructors seek to place them in contact with (e.g., effective argumentation, cognitive modeling, logic, symbolic action). Highlighting the unavoidable role of emotion, a number of philosophers and media theorists, such as Marshall Alcorn, Peter Sloterdijk, and Gregory Ulmer, have noted that rational arguments do not always move us, even when we recognize sound logic or facts that contradict our opinions. Alcorn (2002) argues that we do not just receive a deposit of an ideological idea that can be removed when we encounter another idea that causes us to revise our world-views, in the way one withdraws money from a bank. Such ideologies are unevenly entangled with our embodied, emotional, and psychological practices, many of which have become habitual or, simply, part of our ethical dispositions. Again, from Aristotle's point of view, both virtue and vice result from dispositional formations.

Rice's (2014) *Distant Publics* offers a more recent elaboration of Alcorn's thinking through her discussion of the public figure of exception. Drawing upon contemporary affect theorists, such as Sara Ahmed, Rice argues, "Insofar as affect is structured at multiple points of institutional, cultural, social, and educational sites, the libidinal attachments to discourse may run much deeper than we even know" (97).[4] While affect theories differ from one another, a general illustrative division is between emotion, or a consciously felt discrete emotion like sadness or anger, and affect, a more generalized prepersonal realm of relationality that conditions our various emotions as well as cognitive states. Since our emotional states and ideological beliefs evolve through repetition over time and space, Rice contends that "changing people's minds requires more than exposing ideological structures behind discourse. . . . In order to change people's minds, you have an effect at an affective level, which is much more challenging" (97). One extremely valuable contribution of Rice's work lies in calling writing and rhetoric teachers' attention to the ways in which our framing of various political topics succeeds or fails in asking students to see themselves as affectively constructed beings. In the context of urban-development rhetoric, Rice argues that the use of "victim" narratives, such as evil corporations who wage war on a helpless Mother Nature, may cause students to produce an emotional response (apathy, outrage) at a distant environmental target for catharsis, thereby failing to connect environmental issues to their own daily lives. This framing leads to the production of what she calls the figure of "public exception," when audiences feel as though they have participated politically by feeling an emotional response rather than acknowledging how development and environmental issues always already structure their daily lives.

REVITALIZING ECOLOGY THROUGH A HEXIS OF PATIENCE

Simply put, we cannot bracket outrage in our attempt to understand how we might think through the ethics of rhetorical responses to environmental problems. Because hexeis produce behaviors in localized and particular environments, we suggest a clear connection exists between the desire to challenge the rationality/emotion binary and the goals of better theorizing environmental ethics as an ethical disposition rather than a cognitive possession. Here, hexis adds to thumos an additional dimension. Specifically, hexis explains how our emotions are given semipermanent yet changeable forms by our localized and repeated behaviors in a given ecology both within the classroom and outside it. If we want to avoid the potential problems of appeals to rationality or unproductive outrage scapegoating while nevertheless retaining the ability to make normative ethical judgments about the environment, we believe one particularly valuable approach lies in cultivating a hexis of patience.

Aristotle's hexis of patience can be updated for contemporary issues of sustainability through Jane Bennett's (2010) new materialist philosophy, which has been engaged by other rhetoricians, including Laurie

Gries (2015), Nathaniel A. Rivers (2014), and Thomas Rickert (2013). However, these conversations have yet to connect Bennett's work to virtue ethics. Bennett offers what we view as a fairly straightforward extension of some of Jenny Rice's ideas (as well as the works of other rhetoricians who have engaged material rhetorics in recent years), though Bennett's work is directed primarily at a political science and critical theory audience. We see this point of overlap in her suggestion that the discursive frames we use to examine the environment should locate us as embodied and material beings. However, Bennett adds a more specific focus on the ontology of nature. Borrowing actor-network theorist Bruno Latour's term *actant*, Bennett argues that matter (*physis*) possesses its own agency, or more accurately, she disagrees with existing political models that have characterized the human-world relationship as one in which the human acts and the environment is a passive object that is only acted upon (instrumentally). Understanding the agency of matter enables us to better understand how our hexeis form from environmental sources. She declares, "To begin to *experience* the relationship between persons and other materialities more horizontally, is to take a step toward a more ecological sensibility" (Bennett 2010, 10). Similarly seeking to avoid a public figure of exception, Bennett invokes the French thinkers Gilles Deleuze and Felix Guattari's concept of assemblage (Deleuze and Guattari 1987) to demonstrate that environments are not fixed or static but actively composed by various human and nonhuman actors, each of whom are coming and going and continually becoming: "Assemblages are ad hoc groupings of diverse elements, of vibrant matter of all sorts. Assemblages are living, throbbing confederations that are able to function despite the persistent presence of energies that confound them from within" (22–23). Many who have responded to her work cite her memorable description of an assemblage in the great 2003 Northeast electrical grid blackout (25–28). Here, it was not merely human errors or caprices of nature (a lightning strike to the grid) that led to the blackout but the ways in which these activities intersected with various other nonhuman elements, including the active and reactive power of electricity. Bennett locates electricity's aleatory agency, for example, which at one point acted in ways that surprised technicians and avoided carefully devised circuit-protection plans, as an ethical actant as well.

The strength of Bennett's (2010) analysis lies in extending the idea of ethical dispositions to contend that the ways in which writers form ethical habits also must include how nonhuman actors shape these and other habits as well. In the 2003 blackout, naturally politicians and popular audiences wanted a scapegoat, such as the notorious company FirstEnergy, which had been siphoning energy from the grid to maximize profits (26). Yet, Bennett cautions that we must accurately trace the full assemblage and, furthermore, that human-centered outrage may distract us from this goal (38). While she does not mention the virtues, multiple lines in her book lead us to believe her argument to be consistent with virtue ethics thinking. For example,

> In a world of distributed agency, a hesitant attitude toward assigning singular blame becomes a presumptive virtue. Of course, sometimes moral outrage, akin to what Plato called *thumos*, is indispensable to a democratic and just politics . . . . A politics devoted too exclusively to moral condemnation and not enough to a cultivated discernment of the web of agentic capacities can do little good. (38)

Bennett offers no detailed explanation or footnote about her use of the term *thumos*. As Plato discusses in both the *Phaedrus* and *The Republic*, he sees the soul as being composed of three parts: intellect (*nous*), appetite (*epithumia*), and thumos. Bennett, we infer, is thinking about various Greek writings in which thumos refers to a specialized form of spiritedness, which is more like when anger seethes, boils, or rages, such as when our sense of personal honor is violated. Yet, we suggest that what Bennett is thinking about, in terms of emotional states to avoid, is probably closer to the irrational *orge* in Baecker's (2007) article we discuss above. Thumos, by contrast, more so in Aristotle (although, Jeffrey Barnouw [(2004)] adds, it can mean something more like "visceral reasoning" even in Plato), signals not only that emotions cannot be avoided but also that they are composed differently—through the hexis.

Here, we believe this link to thumos provides a natural corollary for using Aristotle's discussion of patience to highlight the virtuous practice of patience Bennett is after. In the *Nicomachean Ethics* (Aristotle 2002), Aristotle discusses anger as the sphere of feeling or action that requires patience as the golden mean. Patience lies between an excess of irascibility and a lack of spirit. Patience characterizes this disposition of not responding with extreme anger—outrage—while nevertheless not bracketing emotion's role from the rhetorical cultivation of the self. In a loose analogy, if Plato acknowledges thumos is what inspires us to take up arms against those who violate our honor, the hexis of patience for Aristotle is what enables us to take up such actions ethically.

> With regard to anger also there is an excess, a deficiency, and a mean. Although they can scarcely be said to have names, yet since we call the intermediate person good-tempered let us call the mean good temper; of the persons at the extremes let the one who exceeds be called irascible,

and his vice irascibility, and the man who falls short an irascible sort of person, and the deficiency irascibility. (Aristotle 2002, II.7.1108a.4–9)

Later on, Aristotle (2002) clarifies that the gentle person will in fact get angry (Aristotle 2002, IV.5). The person who does not get angry does not feel pain—or, rather, feel anything at all. As a result, similar to how thumos demonstrates that we cannot teach students to separate emotions from who they are as writers, a hexis of patience confirms that we also cannot separate emotions such as anger from the human.

This fact, once more, serves to demonstrate the differences between virtue ethics and post-Enlightenment forms of rationality. It is ingrained in our Enlightenment-influenced discourses to use our rational and dispassionate (objective) judgments in order to arrive at the proper ethical determination. Obviously, this claim has a ring of truth. If, say, a vigilante were to become angered at a coal-mining company in West Virginia for polluting the water without facing consequences due to its heavy political contributions (an event that happened in 2015) and were to let this anger drive them into an unfortunate act of violence, the claim for Aristotle that anger plays a role in ethical judgment is not the same as claiming we are ruled entirely by our impulsive reactions and extreme feelings. Again, Aristotle's virtue ethics requires that a *disposition* should govern our actions rather than spontaneous anger. Patience is this disposition.

Thus, what Bennett profoundly adds is a method for developing hexeis of patience. She updates Aristotle by acknowledging patience can emerge out of our attempts to account for the multiple social and environmental relations that cultivate our various dispositions. Once we trace the ways in which our ethical obligations take shape as digital rhetors, we can begin to gain a glimpse into how our habits of environmental dwelling shape us to a far greater extent than any rational model of writing can explain. Shifting agency from a rational possession to something distributed through networks of affects, she maintains, "does not thereby abandon the project of identifying (what the philosopher Hannah Arendt called) the sources of harmful effects. To the contrary, such a notion broadens the range of places to look for sources" (Bennett 2010, 37). Like Rice, Bennett is concerned not with letting FirstEnergy escape responsibility for its part in the great Northeast blackout but with advocating as a virtue the realization that we are produced by these nonhuman systems before we seek to form (or to *teach*) political or ideological judgments.

Furthermore, along the lines of Rice's (2014) goal of avoiding the figure of public exception, Bennett declares, "The ethical responsibility of an individual human now resides in one's response to the assemblages in which one finds oneself participating: Do I attempt to extricate myself from assemblages whose trajectory is likely to do harm?" (2010, 37). Indeed, Aristotle lists the golden mean of patience between the action of anger, which when excessive is irascibility, and a lack of spirit, but the golden mean is this slowness to anger. Slowness to anger does not mean rebracketing emotions from rationality or that there is no place for outrage; rather, it is a cautious anger that acknowledges the fundamentally dispositional nature of rhetors' beliefs and habits of engaging one another as writers and readers in fundamentally environmental networks. To teach sustainability as writing is first and foremost to cultivate a specific disposition of patience when writing in and about environments.

While Aristotle's ethics has been read as anthropocentric and subjective, Bennett (2010) echoes other environmental virtue ethicists who have observed that eudaimonia, which we discuss in chapter 2, does not mean a subjective feeling of well-being but fundamental recognition of flourishing as exceeding our personal subjectivity. We not only need social structures to offer us the ability to cultivate virtuous habits; we need physical environments conducive to thriving as well. For example, in her book *Gut Feminism*, the philosopher Elizabeth A. Wilson (2015) points out that recent empirical studies have demonstrated a close link between physiology and habit (disposition, hexis). Wilson observes that our digestive systems shape our dispositions for acting in the world, just as the former are shaped by our habits of dwelling in the world. She points to a 1990 study in which 44 percent of patients with gastrointestinal problems (abdominal pain, constipation) reported a history of sexual abuse. Not to belabor our point, it is not a stretch to declare that gut functionality expresses and conditions our predispositions to transact with the world in particular ways that contribute to a person's style, manner, and even character of being (i.e., hexis) (Wilson 2015, 264). The way abused bodies form within various environmental assemblages can influence these actors' abilities to flourish and signal. Environmental networks are no different, and a hexis of patience is the ethical disposition to cultivate to make sure we see the full range of human and nonhuman agencies at play. Here, patience refers to the ability to see how various harms and cares impact the ability of various bodies to flourish within specific environments as a normative basis for thinking through how environments produce the ways in which we think, write, and dwell.

RETHINKING SOCIAL MEDIA SHAMING
FROM THE PERSPECTIVE OF HEXIS

Once more, our argument, following Aristotle's virtue ethics, is not that social media shaming is not useful for galvanizing support for environmental causes—far from it. For example, some evidence points to the ways in which social media has helped make environmentalism a worldwide movement. Environmental author and founder of 350. org., Bill McKibben, used social media to organize and stage over five thousand environmental protests in 181 countries in less than two years (Whitford 2013). We also acknowledge that shaming has certainly worked in some instances. As another example, consider British Petroleum's (BP's) efforts to rebrand their image for a US audience following the 2010 oil-rig leak off the Gulf Coast of Mexico. In 2000, BP launched a $200-million effort to rebrand its image as "beyond petroleum," a claim with which the Gulf oil spill simply ran at odds. To challenge this rebranding, a number of social media campaigns, including Greenpeace's Rebrand the BP Logo contest in 2010, have served to consistently remind the public of the gap between BP's self-image and its actions. One corporate marketing blog accurately assessed the impact of social media on this type of campaign:

> That injury to the future BP corporate image will endure *because of the way Greenpeace collected the contest entries*. Greenpeace asked the contest entrants to submit their entries to a photo group on Flickr, the social photo and image sharing site. When the contest ended on June 28, 2010, there were approximately 2,500 entries in the two Flickr.com photo groups, "Behind the Logo 1 & 2," that Greenpeace had set up for their purpose. . . . These Flickr groups will live on long after the contest ends, drawing page views and damaging BPs image for years to come. (Telofski 2010; our emphasis)

At the time, these images earned about six hundred thousand views in the first three weeks, and to this day, the images live on the larger social media ecosystem (i.e., copied and used on other websites).

Clearly, social media shaming can lead to behavioral change in some cases, and furthermore, Greenpeace is not an isolated example of such effectiveness. Other examples include YouTubers UCB Comedy, who did a popular parody video, "BP Spills Coffee," with twelve million views on a coffee spill (UCB Comedy 2010); an anonymous Twitter account (á la the activists The Yes Men) called BP Public Relations (@BPGlobalPR), who picked up one hundred eighty-five thousand followers at one point (BP Public Relations 2010); Facebook's Flash Protest of BP Oil Hemorrhage; the Black Oil Firefox plugin; and countless others. In part, these examples confirm that shaming through various media apparatuses on behalf of environmental causes can effect change. By extension, our goal is not to dismiss the potential of outrage to motivate ethical actions or to secure what seem like effective or positive ends. Indeed, emotional appeals of any kind, more so than statistics or facts, may instill in certain audiences a desire to act. One only needs to take a look at the enormous amount of money raised for the American Society for the Prevention of Cruelty to Animals in response to Sarah McLaughlin's ad campaign against animal cruelty (Strom, *New York Times*, December 26, 2008).

Rather, our contention, following Bennett's work, is that outrage in response to shaming water wasters—[here, feel free to insert any corporate offender of your choice]—should go beyond the utilitarian ethical problem of effectiveness or ineffectiveness in order to avoid abstracting social media outragers from their own implication within environmental networks. Thus, cultivating this hexis of patience does not mean we do not get angry when we see acts that should be added to the #DroughtShaming hashtag. The implication, however, of a hexis of patience is that we need methods to learn how to channel this disposition at effective, appropriate, and multiple levels toward various forms of expression that may lead to change in the plural, starting with our own personal change, that of our own daily habits.

Rather than getting angry on social media as a sole motive for rhetorical activity, a hexis of patience highlights the need to trace networks carefully and determine which networks we ourselves want to affect, write about, and participate in so we do not just limit our emotional reactions to the excessive behaviors of others. Patience is required on multiple levels of rhetorical affectivity with regard to how our writing agencies are entangled with human and nonhuman actors. Being quick to shame may also be being quick to diffuse (and drift into passivity or Rice's figure of public exception). Conversely, someone with a hexis of patience might be justified in being angry but also be hesitant in their response (not blaming the first person in view, etc.), realizing the process for real change will take some time. In other words, the hexis of patience works in developing the habit of not being too quick to anger but also in developing the habit of being able to commit long term to a cause.

7
FUTURE APPLICATIONS OF THE
HEXEIS IN NETWORKED SOCIETIES

Throughout *Rhetoric, Technology, and the Virtues* we have made our arguments for the enduring relevance of virtue ethics for digital rhetoric as well as the existing need to expand this framework by drawing on contemporary theorists whose work engages this set of concerns in all but name. In concluding this book, we affirm once more that we are featuring virtue ethics as *one* important and neglected framework among many other possible ethical approaches digital rhetoricians must contemplate. In chapter 4, for example, we observe that cultivating a hexis of care in the context of digital sampling *can* help individuals negotiate the ethical problems of cultural appropriation. We acknowledge in our analysis that discussing other ethical aspects of digital copyright may also require the use of ethical and political frameworks grounded in the language of personal rights found in deontology. In other circumstances, we may need the language of utilitarianism. Furthermore, we are in no way claiming or even implying that the virtues are an absolute substitute for the use of alternative ethical frameworks, such as postmodern thought. However, in as far as specific behavior-based ethics emerge through practices of repetition that then influence phronesis and judgment in these systems, regardless of the ethical or political framework in place designed to regulate them, we contend virtue ethics has an important and neglected role to play in present research conversations in these areas.

Above any other contribution our book offers, we believe virtue ethics is useful to help us attend to the local and the particular, especially when it comes to avoiding the tendency to impose offline ethical systems onto online situations. As Kristie S. Fleckenstein puts it expertly in her discussion of cyberethos in the context of Julian Dibbell's "A Rape in Cyberspace," "Members of a discourse situation cannot 'read' each other, cannot regard each other as prudent, virtuous, and of good will, unless they exist at that moment as part of the same *ethos*" (Fleckenstein 2005, 333). As we interpret her thinking, this claim does not mean we cannot form ethical decisions about behavior in virtual gaming worlds

DOI: 10.7330/9781607328063.c007

if we are not gamers. For example, we do not need to be gamers to condemn the violent antifeminist behavior of the #GamerGate movement, which is devoted to attacking any woman in the game industry or surrounding rhetorical world (notably, video-game blogger Anita Sarkeesian) who offers even a hint of a critical voice about patriarchal values in classical and contemporary video games. In other words, our ethical reasoning does not have to emerge from directly participating in these systems. Rather, when we judge ethical behaviors as moral or immoral, good or bad, we must take into account how the various players and conditions within particular assemblages (communities, networks, and other relations) produce ethical behaviors within the context of those particular assemblages.

If the virtues—or even the expression of the same virtue—differ from technology to technology, it is entirely reasonable to conclude that future researchers who are interested in digital ethics will need to constantly be on alert for how to adjust the virtues to contemporary technological shifts. For example, with the development of Ryan Omizo and Bill Hart-Davidson's "Hedge-O-Matic" as a case in point, machines are now able to detect written arguments (Omizo and Hart-Davidson 2016). Available as an app on the journal *enculturation*, users can input text from any journal article and the Hedge-O-Matic can locate the use of qualifiers and hedges within around an 80 percent degree of accuracy. Computers can also compose stock templates for AP news articles and, in time, may make ethical decisions about how to shape certain news stories for human audiences. Algorithms may also (by some accounts) function rhetorically by creating "filter bubbles" through algorithmic selections that correspond to our browsing behaviors (Google Page Rank, etc.) and, in turn, influence the type of political content we are exposed to within social media. Our own online behaviors will increasingly change in complex adaptive feedback loops within these types of rhetorics. Finally, Google is making self-driving cars programmed like utilitarian ethicists. In response to an impending accident, which these cars detect faster than human perception can, a self-driving car might make a decision that harms its owner if doing so spares the lives of five pedestrians (Sample, *Guardian*, June 23, 2016). For this reason, some contemporary virtue ethicists, such as James J. Hughes (2011), have even begun exploring what they call "transhuman virtue ethics" to start theorizing what it means when machines can make real-time ethical decisions faster than the expression of human dispositions can be realized.

In closing this book, we offer our thoughts about a few of these emerging ethical threads in relationship to contexts we believe are important to the interests of rhetoric and composition scholars. We also wish to tie together a few loose ends to help those who plan to extend virtue ethics to different digital rhetoric contexts. In the first section, we discuss more directly how the virtues work together—a point that might not be apparent now, given the ways in which our chapters address one specific virtue at a time. We examine how Bennett's new materialism, which we discuss in the previous chapter, combines with Rancière's politics as an implicit example of what these overlapping virtues might look like in practice. In the second section, we use this example as a bridge to argue against using our framework as a rigid ethical heuristic. Indeed, we believe one of the important pedagogical values of the virtues lies in having students articulate their own conceptual frameworks for the virtues within the contexts of their own lives (which extend beyond the classroom). We specifically feature and extend Vallor's efforts to trace some new virtues of communication within social media dispositions and argue we should follow this process of helping our students learn how to engage in similar processes.

In the third section, we look at how the virtues change our understanding of algorithmic forms of producing behaviors in networked spaces (i.e., the ways machines are writing traces of our digital behaviors without our conscious attention), as well as at the rise of what digital publishing guru Tim O'Reilly (2013) calls "algorithmic regulation" in the context of the sharing economy. Here, we also examine the growing ethical quandaries surrounding big data, which are often discussed in utilitarian terms or liberal-democratic terms of individual rights. Through the lens of virtue ethics, we contemplate whether behavior tracking can be used for virtue as opposed to just vice, the latter of which is a perspective more or less adopted by many critics of the networked age. We see trust may be a virtue that emerges in the sharing economy by giving users access to more data about prospective peer customers. However, more data also allow racial (and gendered) bias to creep into the question—the emergence of a vice. In part, we use this discussion to highlight the ongoing need to be wary of how the presence of new digital habits (the sharing economy) may allow for novel reinscriptions of older unethical habits (racism).

Finally, we close this chapter by offering a specific engagement with one of the most recent texts on the ethics of digital rhetoric—Brown's *Ethical Programs* (Brown 2015). As we have acknowledged in chapter 2, Brown offers—in tacit form—a similar viewpoint to the one we are advocating but focused specifically on software and not necessarily on users' dispositions. In part, we suggest a final hexis to extend Brown's thinking in the language of dispositional ethics: a hexis of fairness. Found in the work of Bruno Latour (2004b), this hexis of fairness works alongside Bennett's (2010) hexis of patience (see chapter 6). A hexis of fairness draws our attention to the networks and actors that produce ethical action in a given situation rather than give too much agency to the human or nonhuman. While we do wish to avoid privileging one virtue over another (unlike Aristotle), we believe fairness is a particularly critical hexis to cultivate now so we may respect the hospitable relations of what Brown calls our "ethical programs."

NOT ONE (VIRTUE), BUT MANY

While we have examined certain virtues in this book in isolation (i.e., one distinct virtue in each chapter), we acknowledge in this section that the virtues will and should overlap. It does us little good to develop a hexis of patience with Bennett's new materialist philosophy as we discuss in chapter 6 if we do not also cultivate a hexis of justice in Rancière's sense that we explore in chapter 3. Indeed, in her final chapter in *Vibrant Matter*, Bennett (2010) offers such an effort to combine Rancière and new materialism. If we use the language of hexis here, a literal reading of Rancière's human-centered politics of equality is not interested in the electrical-grid assemblage's ability to surprise us with the aleatory activities of electricity. He would not care that electricity is an autonomous agent that defies human instrumental aims. Rather, Rancière would be much more interested in any resulting poverty and in how the government might "save" the electrical company at the expense of perpetuating inequalities among other humans. In Rancière's terms, saving the electric company at the expense of others would be an act of policing and maintaining the partitions of the sensible (see chapter 3). The grid going offline might serve as a trigger or catalyst in Rancière's thinking, but it would have no specific political significance for justice other than as the means to maintain a certain distribution of the sensible.

While Bennett argues that the surprising agency of nonhumans can call our attention to new political publics, it is clear that for Rancière, these surprises do not necessarily challenge political inequality. From a political perspective, a police order between human and nonhuman is simply not as important or necessary for enactments of political solidarity as a police order between humans because Rancière's world-view presupposes value in equality. We might envision—hypothetically—an enactment of politics in which poor Latinx people in California, the last to get power restored and last to be recognized, decide to act politically out of a presupposition of equality. The challenge could happen in many ways. While we might imagine large acts or protests, a verification of political equality could be made visible to two people. One person turns to another on a city bus and says, "It's not right that they took care of the folks in NoCal before us." Such a claim would be a recognition of their own measure of equality with other humans, an expression of their hexeis of justice that enables them to condemn this action.

Nevertheless, this human-centered aspect of what we are calling Rancière's *hexis of justice* is what Bennett takes issue with. Bennett complains that for Rancière, nonhumans cannot count as part of the *demos* because any dissensual political act must be accompanied by, in Rancière's words, a "'desire to engage in reasoned discourse'" (quoted in Bennett 2010, 104). Bennett endorses Rancière's notion of politics as a disruption of the ordinary, "but his description of the [political] act increasingly takes on a linguistic cast . . . . It is an 'objection to a wrong,' where a wrong is defined as the unequal treatment of beings who are equally endowed with a capacity for *human* speech" (Bennett 2010, 106). She advocates a Latourian alternative of political "publics as human-nonhuman collective[s] that are provoked into existence by a shared experience of harm. [She] imagine[s] this public to be one of the disruptions that Rancière names as the quintessentially political act" (xix). However, because she focuses intently on the element of Rancière's politics interested in the dissensual *effect* generated, she maintains that humans are not the only ones who have the ability to enact "surprises" (Latour's word) in politics that expose human/nonhuman partitions of the sensible. Bennett argues,

> A political act not only disrupts, it disrupts in such a way as to change radically what people can "see": it repartitions the sensible; it overthrows the regime of the perceptible. Here again the political gate is opened enough for nonhumans (dead rats, bottle caps, gadgets, tires, electricity, berries, metal) to slip through, for they also have the power to startle and provoke a gestalt shift in perception. (106–7)

These provocations can lead toward cultivating a more complex set of dispositions. Imagine the man on the bus notices a newspaper article discussing the plight of deer and says, "We shouldn't build large systems that we can't control because they hurt wildlife we need to keep our ecosystem going." A hexis of justice here serves as a supplementary ethical awareness to this sort of partition of the sensible. Our own concern for the environment engages our interest to preserve equality with each other. In our interest to preserve the environment, a presupposition of equality with one another is required to act in solidarity to effect positive

change to the environment. Yet, at the same time, it is unlikely a distur-
bance of a partition of the sensible produced by nonhuman actors will
be noticed if this individual reading the newspaper does not already
have a hexis of patience for the aleatory actions of nonhuman actors.
Both hexeis of justice and patience—not one or the other or one over
the other—are necessary to form a disposition that acts with respect to
the harms and cares of humans and nonhumans within an environmental assemblage.

Following from this example, we want to acknowledge it is not necessary to create a hierarchy of new virtues in which one virtue is always
privileged over another. This desire to privilege some virtues over others
is one of Aristotle's failings because it leads to an unmistakable sense of
foundationalism. Some groups and individuals may choose for political
and ethical reasons to privilege some virtues at various times and not
others. Inevitably, though, the virtues will overlap. Some may even come
into conflict with one another at times. Charity and care can sometimes
contradict justice. Furthermore, even groups devoted to cultivating
some eudaimonic practices may still subscribe to ethical habits of vice.
We do not intend in any way to reject or endorse the politics of the radical egalitarian Occupy Wall Street movement in Zuccotti Park, but it is
telling that the movement eventually had to initiate a series of meetings
in which only women were allowed to speak and men had to stay silent
to listen (McVeigh, *Guardian*, November 30, 2011). This occurrence
reflected the fact that a political movement that advocates for the economic equality of marginalized groups (including women and persons
of color) still can be largely dominated by white male activists in terms
of public speaking, leadership, and media interactions. The hexis of
justice as equality, therefore, does not just exist in our ideological positions but in the behaviors enacted multiple times and in multiple spaces
and practices.

ARGUING FOR NEW HEXEIS OF SOCIAL MEDIA COMMUNICATION

Just as Aristotle argued that politicians must make sure individuals have
opportunities in a society to cultivate virtue, we similarly believe first and
foremost that discussions of virtue ethics in digital rhetoric should be
collaborative and egalitarian in nature—perhaps in line with Rancière's
sense of political equality and the hexis of justice. Indeed, Shannon
Vallor (2010), in her article "Social Networking Technology and the
Virtues," which, along with John Duffy's writing studies work on ethical
dispositions, served as inspiration for our own book, actually takes the

step of inventing some new virtues of communication for social media. Following her lead, as well as our own efforts in this book, we recommend envisioning this pedagogical process as an active collaboration rather than arguing for or teaching students to analyze or cultivate a particular list of static virtues. As we note in chapter 2, contemporary theorists are often dissatisfied with Aristotle's original taxonomy of the virtues. Charity, for example, was later added by Thomas Aquinas, David Hume recast generosity, and feminists Carol Gilligan and Nel Noddings each introduced care. Similarly, Vallor argues for a new definition of what she calls the "communicative virtues" as "patience, honesty, empathy, fidelity, reciprocity, and tolerance," some of which stem from Aristotle while others do not (Vallor 2010, 164). She notes that certain original hexeis, such as courage, may not be as emphasized in online spaces as in Aristotle's original context, in which he was thinking about war practices (164). While we do not want to draw a line between material and immaterial forms of communication or affectivity, or between hexeis formed in offline habits with those formed in online habits, it is absolutely true that the courage of a first-person-shooter video-game player to take on a horde of enemy game combatants is of a different order from the courage of actual soldiers in the field of battle. In fact, hexeis can and will emerge that are specific to either forms of routine in ways neither a priori better or worse than one another (or, conversely, more linked toward eudaimonia). Nevertheless, there may be overlap depending on the type of video game and the game mechanics involved. Indeed, the military has long been interested in video-game simulators as a form of training. In any case, to return to Vallor's new hexeis, she notes there are nonmoral skills individuals cultivate in social media, such as self-understanding, but in as far as interpersonal communication has been ignored, she wants to refashion the virtues.

Following from these sorts of discussions, and to bring our discussion back to pedagogy concerns, it is a great exercise to have students look at which virtues are useful to cultivate in the digital rhetoric classroom and public sphere and then try to determine testing scenarios regarding the conditions for cultivating these virtues. Understanding ethics through virtuous hexeis as active having (from *echein*) is as crucial to explore as it is hard to grasp. Take honesty, for example. Reckless candor can be found in employers who relentlessly comb the Internet and social media, looking for ways to screen out candidates whose online posts or pictures demonstrate less than virtuous characteristics. Simply put, such employers are looking for individuals whose data presences seem to confirm a prudent existence—likely preferring people who post photos

of a glass of wine in moderation with friends rather than a raging frater-
nity party kegger with obvious binge-drinking connotations. In as far as
digital rhetoricians, such as Gregory Ulmer (1994), enjoin us to update
practical wisdom (phronesis) for the literacy apparatus of the digital
(electracy), it is fair to say part of this challenge will involve the need to
continually redraw what is meant by the virtues in digital arenas.

BEHAVIOR TRACKING AND THE VIRTUES OF TRUST

Echoing Vallor's creative extensions of the hexeis, we believe the ways
in which machines are beginning to trace (or produce) behaviors
requires a need to think through how the virtues change with activities of machine reading and writing. While writing is often thought to
be an activity human rhetors or writers do through a computer, it is
equally as true that these machines are *writing us* (so to speak), taking
part in producing hexeis in us. The GPS coordinates in our phones
write traces of our locations to various app providers or cellular towers.
Each time first-year composition students search SAGE Publishing or
Google, their activities are tracked, compiled, and employed to refine
search-engine results, which, in effect, change those students' search
habits. Algorithmic real-time monitoring is even used to shape collective behaviors in ethical and political ways. Take, for example, electronic
publishing industry guru Tim O'Reilly's (2013) notion of "algorithmic
regulation," in which real-time behavior monitoring is supposed to offer
more efficient ways to solve social problems like parking space availability in busy metropolitan areas. He offers the example of taxi regulation:

> Ostensibly, taxis are regulated to protect the quality and safety of the con-
> sumer experience, as well as to ensure that there are an optimal number
> of vehicles providing service at the time they are needed. In practice, most
> of us know that these regulations do a poor job of ensuring quality or
> availability. New services like Uber and Hailo work with existing licensed
> drivers, but increase their availability even in less-frequented locations,
> by using geolocation on smartphones to bring passengers and drivers
> together. But equally important in a regulatory context is the way these
> services ask every passenger to rate their driver (and drivers to rate their
> passenger). Drivers who provide poor service are eliminated. As users
> of these services can attest, reputation does a better job of ensuring a
> superb customer experience than any amount of government regulation.
> (O'Reilly 2013, 195)

Thus, algorithmic regulations, which consequently relate to the rise of
the sharing or "gig" economy, are directly changing some of the conventional ways in which we think about dispositions such as trust.

In his new book, *The Sharing Economy,* NYU business professor Arun Sundararajan (2016) describes how trust is established in the sharing economy, using examples such as the ride-sharing platforms Uber, Lyft, and many others. One of his specific case studies is BlaBlaCar, a city-to-city ridesharing platform that works in twenty-two countries. Citing a survey of 18,289 users across nine European countries, he points out that a complete digital profile (e.g., user ratings from previous riders, social media validation, a brief bio, a picture, and, especially, a verified mobile number) positively impacted how trustworthy users deemed their anonymous peers. Even if users did not know their peer driver, they indicated they trusted a digital profile "significantly more" than they trusted their offline relationships with known individuals, such as colleagues and neighbors, even ranking this trust as high as trust in families and close friends.

However, with a new virtue (or the evolution of an old one) emerges a new opportunity for vice. An additional problem, as cultural studies and critical media studies scholars are quick to observe, is that algorithms may indeed monitor behaviors, but they are nevertheless coded by race, gender, and other hierarchies of exclusion. The sharing economy is supposed to result in the freedom of individuals to pursue their own jobs on their own time in accordance with strict supply and demand monitored by algorithms (Uber, Lyft, Airbnb, etc.). Industry journalist Susie Cagle complains that "'the sharing economy doesn't build trust—it trades on cultural homogeneity and established social networks both online and in real life. Where it builds new connections, it often replicates old patterns of privileged access for some, and denial for others'" (quoted in Becker 2014). It seems that in this case, no virtue of "openness" is possible here.

One Harvard Business School study by Benjamin G. Edelman and Michael Luca similarly confirmed that "non-black hosts earn roughly 12% more for a similar apartment and similar ratings and photos relative to black hosts" (Edelman and Luca 2014). They also found that Airbnb guests with distinctly African American names are 16 percent less likely to be accepted than identical guests with distinctively white names. Similarly, a search of the #AirbnbWhileBlack hashtag on social media platforms reveals a common phenomenon when nonwhite users book flats only to have their reservations canceled by white users once they discover the former's racial identity. Save for the use of explicit racial terms, this de jure racism is permissible within Airbnb's operating guidelines because owners have wide license to cancel rentals for a variety of undisclosed reasons. In response, entrepreneur Rohan Gilkes went so far as to start Noirebnb, which specifically operates under the guidelines of racial inclusivity (Guynn, *USA Today*, June 6, 2016).

In these circumstances, we remain convinced that one of the best features of the virtues is that the medium (digital, nondigital; algorithmic, nonalgorithmic) is not as important as the hexis that motivates the ethical behavior. Indeed, consider a different approach to the problem of racism in the sharing economy. Other researchers have argued that the sharing economy can reduce the impact of preexisting dispositions such as racial bias. In the introduction to their edited collection, *Blinding as a Solution to Bias*, behavioral science professors Christopher T. Robertson and Aaron S. Kesselheim offer the example of a fingerprint examiner in a courtroom setting (Robertson and Kesselheim 2016). If the examiner hears an eyewitness confirmation of the perpetrator's identity, they are more likely to make a faulty determination (i.e., to find a match if the evidence is less than certain). Why? Studies have indicated that eyewitness testimony may offer an unconscious influence. Working from this analogy, the authors claim that if information with no useful purpose can nevertheless lead us to engage in discrimination, we should simply leave the former out.

On the surface, this claim sounds counterintuitive. Most of us are used to thinking about informed decision making in terms of gaining more information, like the former First Lady Michelle Obama's push to make nutrition information more transparent or visible. However, Robertson and Kesselheim (2016) (in tacit confirmation of Jenny Rice, Alcorn, Sloterdijk, and other affect theorists) suggest it is not always the case that more information makes us change our minds. Simply put, changing the entire design of the online marketplace of Airbnb may be a way to fulfill this aim. They suggest, for example, that a guest does not need to see a host's picture in advance of booking or even to know the host's name (which might allow for an inference of race or ethnicity). The company could reduce racial discrimination by expanding its Instant Book option, in which host sites, like a hotel, accept guests without screening them first. Airbnb can also conceal guest names, along with other information, such as e-mail addresses and phone numbers. Or, more basically, Airbnb could follow eBay's lead and simply use pseudonyms. Echoing Rancière's hexis of justice grounded in equality from chapter 3, while there may be larger capitalist forces at work under algorithmic regulation that we should continue to critique, there are more ethical ways to design these interfaces to help alleviate the problems of racial recoding and influence the development of more ethical hexeis.

In any case, virtue ethics avoids abstracting the question of whether Uber—or the sharing economy as a whole—is a good or positive social force in totality. Leftist critics among academics, for example, frequently complain that Uber erodes collective bargaining and offers workers no health benefits or permanent job security (witness, for example, the current legal debates over whether Uber drivers count as independent contractors or employees). There is an undeniably libertarian sensibility beneath O'Reilly's (2013) (quoted above) enthusiasm for algorithmic regulation as well (see Holmes 2014b). Algorithmic regulation offers companies and state institutions the ability to map collective behaviors and then intervene in existing collective habits without necessarily relying upon legislative changes because they seek to work at the level of nonconscious behavioral prompting—what Richard H. Thaler and Cass R. Sunstein call a "nudge" (Thaler and Sunstein 2008). By contrast, consider the rhetoric of "computationalism," as critical media theorist David Golumbia (2013) puts it, or the unquestioned belief that computers are better ways to solve social problems than other means, including democratic deliberation, conversation, or the distribution of wealth and other resources. To sum up, new challenges to the hexeis serve as a reminder that we still need to have discussions about how eudaimonia functions in this capacity both for users and drivers.

FAIRNESS AND HOSPITALITY TOWARD THE MACHINE

It is easy to overreact to algorithmic behavioral monitoring, as well as racial recoding, within these networks with fear, outrage, or, unfortunately, even ambivalence, which is why the final hexis we advocate in *Rhetoric, Technology, and the Virtues* comes from Latour—*fairness*—and from Brown's more recent notion of "hospitality" through digital networks. Networked computing, Brown suggests, takes up an ancient problem, hospitality: "the problem of others arriving whether we invited them or not—over and over again" (Brown 2015, 2). For the philosopher Levinas, whom Brown draws upon, our proximity to one another brings up a presymbolic relation when we try to identify or know the other: "a relationship with singularity, without the mediation of any principle or ideality. In the concrete, it describes my relationship with the neighbor, a relationship whose signifyingness is prior to the celebrated 'sense of bestowing'" (2). Thus, Brown concludes that "the guest has already arrived" and forced this relationship, even if we did not intend it. We are hostages to one another. Answering the phone when someone else calls us is to already say yes. It is what the theorist Avital Ronell

(1991) calls the problem of "answerability"—the duties, obligations, and taxes that are imposed upon us and obligate us to respond (even if we just hang up!). The importance of Brown's work is to confirm that computational networks place similar demands upon our hospitality. To enter into networked life is to worry about placing spam filters, blocking trolls, or unfriending or unfollowing individuals who keep posting articles from political sites we disagree with.

Out of this discussion, Brown (2015) coins the term "ethical programs" to think through the computational procedures of software and our own procedures to develop programs of action to deal ethically with them: "An ethical program, computational or otherwise, is a set of steps taken to address an ethical predicament" (5). Humans and nonhumans can both enact ethical programs. In addition to Levinas, he turns to Derrida's "law of hospitality." On the one hand, we must welcome everything that is Other. Brown writes, "Networked technology would not exist without the Law of hospitality, since connectivity is necessary for such technology to function" (5). Yet, on the other hand, everything we receive is filtered, shifted, and sorted by algorithms, such as those that try to catch spam e-mails in our university e-mail accounts. Thus, the law of hospitality is undermined constantly. These laws, he suggests, are fundamentally rhetorical in nature. If we lose the password to our university e-mail account, "the university server . . . examines the situation and determines the best course of action is to lock [us] out" (9).

What then makes for an ethical program? It is impossible to answer in universal categories and axioms, but we agree with Brown that we can certainly start to develop a provisional vocabulary to deal with these situations in which nonhuman actors are increasingly writing us as we write through them. In support of his framework, we add one more virtue along these lines: Latour's (2004b) "fairness." In some ways, Latour draws more freely upon the language of virtue ethics than do any of the other thinkers we have discussed in our book to this point. We make this claim not because Latour has stated he is a virtue ethicist—he has never said such a thing, at least not to our knowledge—nor to be opportunistic, as the nonhuman is currently a strong point of interest in the field of rhetoric and composition. We make this claim because like Rancière, Cavarero, and Bennett, each of whom we have argued tacitly makes a case for a particular virtuous hexis in their work (justice, care, and patience, respectively), Latour also advocates such a hexis, that of fairness toward things, toward objects, toward the nonhuman in critique, in the analysis of an event. Yet, unlike those other thinkers, Latour offers vices of excess and deficiency in relation to the virtue of fairness. In other words, his virtue of fairness toward objects is situated as a mean between two vices. At least on this point, his ethical conceptualization is more consistent with Aristotle's thought than are the conceptualizations of any of the previous thinkers we have discussed.

An articulation of this hexis is perhaps clearest in Latour's (2004b) most popular essay "Why Has Critique Run out of Steam?," in which Latour argues for a reevaluation of the purpose of academic critique and pushes for a new way forward that sees critique as a more affirmative undertaking (i.e., not solely to debunk but also to build structures). In making this argument, he advocates for a specific kind of disposition when engaging in critique: to be fair toward the nonhuman. Before he articulates this virtuous hexis, however, he gives us a set of hexeis that are vices, in which our critical consideration of the nonhuman is either excessive or deficient, to use Aristotle's terms. Latour's impetus for discussing these unethical habits is that theoretical critique has not given objects their due attention. He states,

> When we try to reconnect scientific objects with their aura, their crown, their web of associations, when we accompany them back to their gathering, we always appear to weaken them, not to strengthen their claim to reality. I know, I know, we are acting with the best intentions in the world, we want to add reality to scientific objects, but, inevitably, through a sort of tragic bias, we seem always to be subtracting some bit from it. Like a clumsy waiter setting plates on a slanted table, every nice dish slides down and crashes on the ground. (237)

Latour goes on to say that one of the causes for this inability to discuss objects in terms of their reality is that researchers seem to habitually place objects in one of two positions: "90 percent of the contemporary critical scene fixates the object at only two positions," which he describes as "the fact position and the fairy position" (237). The fairy position is a deficient disposition for giving the object serious consideration of its agency in the networks of a specific event. When a theorist discussing objects is placing objects in the fairy position, they are discussing the meaning of an object merely as a projection of human desires, as a fetish, or merely as a passive instrument. For the theorist with a fairy position, the object is indifferent. The fairy position sees any meaning or agency in an object as only due to its relation to the human ability to attribute meaning and agency to it. In sum, a researcher fully inhabiting the fairy position sees the human subject as "so powerful that he or she can create everything out of his or her own labor" and sees the object as "nothing but a screen on which to project human free will" (241). In terms of virtue ethics, this fairy position would be seen as a vice of deficiency, as not enough attention is paid to the objects, the social phenomena, or the environment for understanding a specific rhetorical situation. This unethical disposition seeks out an understanding of blame, attribution, and agency only through the human subject.

Of course, the habit of not taking the meaning and agency of objects seriously enough and attributing sole agency of a rhetorical act to humans is all too common in the field of rhetoric and composition. Study of this neglect of the rhetorical impact objects can make has been one of the major contributions of work on the nonhuman in our field, including Brown's call to define ethical programs. Additional calls to include the nonhuman in rhetorical analyses and composition pedagogies are now abundant (see Brown and Rivers 2014; Gries 2015; Holmes 2014a; Lynch and Rivers 2015; Rickert 2013; Rivers 2014). However, Latour does not stop there. In terms of treating the nonhuman fairly in critique, yes, a disposition that does not give objects enough attention or argues that their meaning is merely a projection of human desires is a vice; it is unethical. However, Latour also identifies as unethical a disposition he calls the fact position:

> But, wait, a second salvo is in the offing, and this time it comes from the fact pole. This time it is the poor bloke, again taken aback, whose behavior is now "explained" by the powerful effects of indisputable matters of fact: "You, ordinary fetishists, believe you are free but, in reality, you are acted on by forces you are not conscious of. Look at them, look, you blind idiot" (and here you insert whichever pet facts the social scientists fancy to work with, taking them from economic infrastructure, fields of discourse, social domination, race, class, and gender, maybe throwing in some neurobiology, evolutionary psychology, whatever, provided they act as indisputable facts whose origin, fabrication, mode of development are left unexamined). (Latour 2004b, 238)

This fact position, in contrast to the fairy position, is one in which facts—biological facts, geological facts, psychological facts, social facts—take on so much agency humans become merely pawns who act unwillingly in the face of the force of the power of objects, whether one is discussing social construction or natural phenomena such as genes and the environment. When researchers embody the fact position, they consider the human subject to be "nothing but a mere receptacle for the forces of determinations known by natural and social sciences" and the object to be "so powerful that it causally determines what humans think and do" (241).

In "Why Has Critique Run out of Steam?" (Latour 2004b), "Morality and Technology" (Latour 2002), and *We Have Never Been Modern* (Latour 1993), the ethics of the situation (seen in moral language such as "cruel treatment," "immoral," etc.) in relation to objects is a major exigency for Latour. It is not that he is anthropomorphizing objects, at least not in the sense of human feelings and desires for democracy; rather, he simply is calling for us to take them seriously, not just as objects of desire (i.e., fetishes) that block someone from knowing their true self nor as things so powerful as to determine all human action. Rather, a virtuous disposition is fair to the nonhuman in how the various nonhuman elements have agency and have impact on all situations, whether political, educational, or everyday life. It means to take objects seriously in the construction of gatherings and collectives, to recognize our communities are comprised of more than the human element. Vices can come in the form of deficiency and excess in terms of how we deal with objects. In the first, we privilege the human too much; in the second, we do not necessarily privilege the object too much, but we must be careful not to name objects in excess to the point of losing any specificity in a network.

Latour concludes that it is for these reasons—either the human is given so much power that the agency and meaning of objects is reduced to mere human projections, or the objects are given so much power that humans are unwilling pawns—that theoretical criticism has lost its force in our world. No one wants "to see our own most cherished objects treated in this way" (Latour 2004b, 240), so critique is taken less seriously. However, there is some hope. For Latour, between the vices of the deficient fairy position and the excessive fact position is a third way, what Aristotle would call a "golden mean." Latour simply advocates this mean for better considering objects in one's research a *fair* position. To embody this more ethical disposition toward nonhumans and to make this more ethical disposition a habit, Latour argues that it is not enough just to critique the fairy and fact positions. Rather, we must be willing to "seal the leaks" (243).

Conversely, we tend to see an implicit topoi figuration of the fairy position when attributions of agency are made to technologies. While we are hesitant to designate any scholar in rhetoric and composition as fully committed to such a (dis)position, the influence of social construction has often led to understandings of agency in objects as only existing when humans attribute such agency to them. For example, in Carolyn Miller's essay "What Can Automation Tell Us about Agency?," Miller (2007) is committed to a notion of agency as a kind of kinetic energy that emerges through relationality and attribution. She argues agency is "the kinetic energy of rhetorical performance" (Miller 2007, 147). For Miller, this means agency is a "property of a relationship between rhetor and audience" (150) that emerges as a property of the event in the performance of the rhetor and audience. Noting that our notion of agency comes from the Greek word *ethopoeia*, which basically means the production of one's character through discourse, Miller suggests that for agency to exist, there must be mutual attribution—in other words, in a rhetorical situation, for agency to exist, there must exist beings who can verbalize or communicate a recognition of agency. Miller bases her argument upon a survey of answers various university speech instructors gave when questioned about an automated speech-assessment machine, which was actually fictional. The largely incredulous responses instructors made were predicated upon this belief that agency is a property of human rhetors or writers and the human audiences the former communicate with. Thus, if a computer takes over the evaluation of speeches, this human bias causes no small degree of anxiety. In a very descriptive statement, Miller declares "that our resistance to automation is rooted in a commitment to agency, or more specifically that we find it difficult (and perhaps perverse) to conceive of rhetorical action under the conditions that seem to remove agency not from the rhetor so much as from the audience" (141).

To be clear, Miller's discussion is more diagnostic than prescriptive. She productively identifies a trend, but, to be accurate, she also does not take up directly—as Latour does—the question of whether a nonhuman actor does have rhetorical (and ethical) agency. As a point of clarification, the fairy position can be seen throughout many different areas in the field. In examining Latour's usefulness for visual rhetoric, for example, Laurie Gries helpfully observes that many widely taught composition textbooks tend to treat rhetorical agency as a form of human recognition and instrumentality (Gries 2015, 8). As a case in point, she points to Christine Alfano and Alyssa O'Brien's *Envision: Writing and Research Arguments* (Alfano and O'Brien 2013) (which both of us taught in first-year composition as graduate teaching assistants at Clemson University) (Gries 2015, 296–97). While it is not incorrect to isolate visual objects in order to interpret or analyze them, there remains the implication that pictures lack agency unless agency is projected upon the pictures.[1]

To sum up then, the cultivation of dispositions such as fairness and the realization that our participation within social media helps shape those dispositions—for better and for worse—allows us to grapple with the complex ethical demands and dispositions of digital rhetoric in the present moment. As we extend ethical considerations to machine rhetorics and production to understand how our bodies and selves are written by computers, we believe hexeis such as fairness and seeing ethics through a virtue ethics lens will continue to offer ways to think through normative values without reinscribing fixed rules or without relying on the myth of the autonomous rational subject. Thus, while we want to avoid creating a hierarchy of the hexeis, if we had to choose one to focus on first, it might be Latour's virtue of fairness. The way to form realistic ethical commitments with respect to political publics surrounding social media and networks lies in looking at how networks and actors support behaviors as opposed to relying upon previously settled topoi alone. There is no better indication for us of the enduring relevance of the virtues, and there is no better exigence to intervene in the various forms of ethical programs, than that of digital writing in the present moment.

NOTES

CHAPTER 1

1. Gamification is the use of game mechanics in nontraditional game contexts. Viki offers participants badges and levels for their contributions. Each user interface for any viewable video on Viki also prominently displays the total percentage of captioned content to encourage viewers to caption while they watch.
2. See Ian Bogost (2010), Douglas Eyman (2015), Laura J. Gurak (1997), Richard Lanham (1993), Elizabeth M. Losh (2009), Gregor Ulmer (1994), Kathleen Welch (1999), and James P. Zappen (2005) for further reading.
3. In the January 2017 issue of *College English* (after the initial drafts of this book were written), John Duffy published a similar essay that is getting deserved attention: "The Good Writer: Virtue Ethics and the Teaching of Writing."
4. For example, Donald Morton and Mas'ud Zavarzadeh argue that "critique (not to be confused with criticism) is an investigation of the enabling conditions of discursive practices" (Morton and Zavarzadeh 1991).
5. See James Berlin's (1992) "Poststructuralism, Cultural Studies and Composition Classroom."
6. This history of avoiding normative ethics in the field of rhetoric was previously recognized by Michael Bernard-Donals and Matthew Capdevielle (2008) (though not in a negative sense). Digital rhetoricians have yet to fully engage claims by some, such as literary theorist Michael Roth (2014), who believes that "if we humanities professors saw ourselves more often as explorers of the normative than as critics of normativity, we would have a better chance to reconnect our intellectual work to broader currents in public life" (quoted in Felski 2015, 16).
7. Mike Markel (2000) and Paul Dombrowski (1999) each have written about virtue ethics in their technical communication textbooks, but neither actively endorses virtue ethics or emphasizes the importance of habit formation in ethics.

CHAPTER 2

1. For example, we have not mentioned Jeffrey Pruchnic's (2014) *Rhetoric and Ethics in the Cybernetic Age*. Pruchnic draws (accurately and convincingly) on a wide number of thinkers and theorists both in and alongside the rhetorical tradition and continental theory. Pruchnic's ethics is more Foucauldian and historical. He tends to map the ways in which rhetoric and technology have always had a relationship to how ethical forms of subjectivity are produced in a given moment. In this sense, he stops short of theorizing a full-fledged ethical framework (such as we might see in utilitarianism, deontology, virtue ethics, etc.), and he seems more in step with the postmodern frameworks we suggest virtue ethics will extend. We view our book as a supplement to this type of scholarship, not unlike Brown's book (2015). Pruchnic argues that rather than resist dominant forms of technology and new media, we should "replicate and appropriate" these forms through a better-informed orientation to them. Our book provides more specificity toward such an orientation, via the virtues.
2. While we do not have the time or space to expound upon Davis's work here, most political systems stem directly from ethical frameworks (e.g., liberalism from

deontology, libertarianism from utilitarianism). At their most basic, politics might be considered the systematic expression or advocacy of a community's ethical values. This is not the case for Davis's work. As we note, she writes that "one cannot derive a political system such as liberalism or libertarianism from the notion of ethics as 'response-ability'" (Davis 2010, 120). This claim does not make her work on this presymbolic ethico-rhetorical relation unrelated to political thinking necessarily, though it raises questions of applicability. For Davis, the knowledge of this relation means any rhetorical agent is "infinitely responsible for responding to the call of the other" (115), and thus any judgment in which one must choose one person's interests over another's—and such judgments must take place in politics and elsewhere—is "always a betrayal of the other" and "never not terrible, never not tragic" (119, 142–43), even if such a judgment takes place within a particular political system in which we might recognize that judgment as just.

3.   Aristotle's hexis is now finding a number of contemporary enthusiasts among various theorists who are interested in habit as a creative and generative ecological force. For example, in describing the eighteenth-century philosopher Felix Ravaisson, who inspired many ontological views of habit for twentieth-century theorists (such as in the work of Merleau-Ponty, Bergson, Deleuze, etc.), Elizabeth Grosz argues, "Habit is a concept that has been difficult to address for much of what passes as postmodernism, for it grounds us firmly in a pre-representational real, a real made up of forces that stimulate and transform living beings through their ability to accommodate routines, activities, projects that the emergence of life amidst the real requires" (Grosz 2013, 218). Habit is an actual force in the world and not a purely discursive or cognitive phenomenon.

4.   Of course, others have made critiques similar to Berlin's. This conflation of virtue ethics with other ethical systems that depend upon reason and universal values separate from contingent rhetorical situations has led to a misguided and premature dismissal of virtue ethics in rhetorical theory and beyond. As Eugene Garver notes, contemporary approaches to Aristotle's virtue ethics tend to locate ethical realization in depoliticized individual agents "without the ties to happiness, the soul and external goods" (Garver 2006, 199). Such a reading even comes from one of Aristotle's most famous twentieth-century champions, Hannah Arendt, who recommended that politicians leave happiness to the private lives of individuals—an argument that also appeals to libertarian and utilitarian political theorists (see chapter 1; see also Depew 2008, 185). Others, in line with Berlin and Vitanza, respectively read Aristotle's list of virtues as forming precisely the supposedly dreaded deontological normative frameworks stemming from Kantian maxim making or Habermasian consensus much criticized in postmodern rhetorical theory (see, for example, Davis 2000).

5.   This adoption of a postmodern rhetorical ethics that avoids the term *ethics* also has a great deal to do with a general skepticism of reason. Michael Bernard-Donals and Matthew Capdevielle (2008) observe that after the atrocities of World War II, scholars in literary and rhetoric studies made an "ethical turn" but that this turn was comprised of a deliberate avoidance of Kantian imperatives, utilitarian logics, or overarching foundational moral principles brought about by reason, as this same reason was arguably put to the service of Nazi agendas. Bernard-Donals and Capdevielle claim that as a result of this skepticism of reason, the ethical turn privileged "an investigation of individual human encounters, an ethics of situation, in which language is seen as the medium of the encounter as such. Ethics, in other words, moved from the normative to the descriptive, and ethical investigations focused attention on the epistemology of the moment of human engagement itself, with all of its contingencies, possibilities, and the myriad ways that intended

consequences are diverted by the smallest details of the quotidian realm" (2). In other words, rather than explicitly advocate particular values or ethical standards (even if the postmodern ethical turn arguably has certain moral standards, such as the affirmation of difference, inclusion, etc.), rhetoricians turned to deep descriptions of the underlying ethics in a particular situation or descriptions of conditions that made possible the privileging of certain values over others and certain peoples over others. The goal, of course, was usually to critique those values as not natural, inherent, or universal.

6. While one might easily contest the identification of Ricoeur as a virtue ethicist (for he never identified as such), his continual reference to "the good life" and "*phronesis*," as well as his own advocacy of friendship and justice as key virtues for the development of well-being in his discussion of "little ethics," definitely puts him in conversation with virtue ethicists.

7. For example, Heidegger writes, "Hexis determines the authentic being [Eigentlichkeit] of Dasein in its structure aspect of being composed in readiness for something; the various hexeis as various ways of our being able to adopt a composure. Hexis is, in as an altogether fundamental sense, a determination of the Being of our authentic Being. . . . Our being composed is not arbitrary or indeterminate; within our hexis lies a primary orientation toward the kairos: 'I am there, come what may!' This being-there [DaSein], being vigilant in one's situation with regard to one's issue of concern—this characterizes our hexis" (176).

8. See Thornton Lockwood (2013) or Steve Holmes (2016) for more on the relationship between ethos and hexis.

CHAPTER 3

1. Following Bruno Latour's call to rethink criticism as assembling (see chapter 1), we argue that while digital rhetoricians concerned with politics and social justice have done a persuasive job exposing the problems with other political paradigms, they have only started to articulate alternative "arenas in which to gather" (see Latour 2004b, 246) for the purposes of producing, or what Latour might call "composing," political justice (see "An Attempt"). This call for more application of rhetorics for "practical use" is of course not new. Classical theorist Vincent Farenga (1979) argues that the origins of rhetorics emerged "out of the desire for democracy" (1035). Indeed, Latour (2204a), as well as digital rhetoricians who have engaged his work (notably Sheridan, Ridolfo, and Michel 2012; and Rivers 2014) is also interested in democracies (of things—*dingpolitik*), as we engage in greater detail in chapter 6, and as his unique reading of the Gorgias dialogue in *Pandora's Hope* (Latour 1999) makes clear.

2. While we do not have the space to address this issue in full, it is worth noting a few qualifications. To call justice a hexis, as Aristotle does in Book V, can clash with our modern-day understandings. For example, when we are discussing virtues, we are usually talking about the dispositions of individuals. However, even liberal theorist John Rawls sees justice as "the first virtue of social institutions" (1971, 3), so "justice as a virtue" can function in both individual and social contexts.

3. More recently, we can find a similar approach within social justice that has enjoyed an increasing number of references among technical communication and rhetoric scholars, with a particular focus on producing or enacting social justice.

4. Drawing on Michel de Certeau (1984), Miles A Kimball (2006) theorizes "tactics" through technical communication as an active form of resistance against corporate strategies of oppression and control. In support of Kimball's work, Rancière helps determine a particular ethic behind a tactic. In other words, it is not always clear in

de Certeau's thinking whether a tactic is motivated out of selfish interest, anticapitalism, Marxism, liberalism, anarchy, or some other ethico-political motivation.

5. It is worth noting that Rancière's vision has a degree of overlap with the body of work of another contemporary rhetorician, Patricia Roberts-Miller (2010). Briefly summarized, Roberts-Miller is concerned with privileging consensus as democratic. In *Fanatical Schemes*, she highlights ways in which proslavery (and antiabolitionist) movements were brought about through a rhetoric of consensus through appeals such as "manhood" or "honor." Roberts-Miller similarly highlights the need for rhetorical scholars to more closely examine spaces in which an abundance of consensus was found within proslavery rhetorics and, in turn, to help privilege spaces of what Rancière would call dissensus.

CHAPTER 4

1. To be clear, however, this connection is not without challenge. Specifically, Maureen Sander-Staudt (2006) has noted that feminists have resisted this connection to avoid diluting care ethics as a specific ethical subfield (see also Held 2006).
2. Other subsequent thinkers have picked up Aristotle's framework, such as the philosopher Lawrence Becker (1990). The latter claims that the centrality of reciprocity to human sociality carries an ethical obligation to promote and maintain social structures that support it.
3. See also Shannon Vallor's recent inclusion of care as a virtue (Vallor 2016).

CHAPTER 5

1. Thomas Aquinas (2005) is another thinker to have noted that either Aristotle's notion of generosity needed updating or there needed to be a new virtue, that of charity.
2. Anyone who follows Oprah Winfrey, George Clooney, or a handful of other stars would have had multiple posts about KONY 2012 on their social media feeds.
3. Others criticized the original KONY 2012 movie for false depictions of the Ugandan political climate.
4. See, for example, the arguably knee-jerk criticisms of Melissa Smyth (2015) or Robert John Boyle (2016), who each argue for unfollowing *HONY* because it does not address the particular systemic change Smith and Boyle desire.
5. See also rhetorician Stephanie Vie's (2014) defense of slacktivism in the case of memes affecting LGBTQ marriage-equality activism.

CHAPTER 6

1. In part, we offer a more specific reading of an ethics that builds on other scholarship that has recently focused on rhetoric and outrage, including Jeff Rice's Indiana Digital Rhetoric Symposium talk on social media, outrage, and Roland Barthes's mythology (Rice 2015).
2. This privileging is also seen in Sharon Crowley's (1990) well-known criticism of current-traditional rhetoric.
3. Readers who are professional researchers in rhetoric and composition will likely be more interested in another application nonacademic readers will likely not be. We can see how difficult a process it is to teach emotions as something that constitutes who writers are if emotions remain downplayed to rational assessment. This can be seen clearly in in our field's early engagement with ecocriticism. As Weisser and Dobrin (2002) describe, ecocriticism typically involves teaching texts of canonical "nature writing" fiction (e.g., Millhauser, Wordsworth, Thoreau, Muir, Leopold) alongside nonfiction writing that examines local and global environmental issues

to create critical awareness alongside regional or local environmental texts. While these pedagogical practices reflect ecocriticism's early roots in the discipline of literature (see Weisser and Dobrin 2002), similar expressions can be found in work by compositionists, including Randall Roorda (1997) and Derek Owens (2001). A quick glance at the American Society for Literature and Ecology website's sample syllabi on writing reveals the presence of many of the aforementioned practices.

While Weisser and Dobrin (2002) (and the authors of this book as well) in no way question the value of ecocriticism, they caution writing teachers, warning that ecocriticism historically tends to subordinate the actual teaching of writing to literary or critical analysis. As an example, they analyze Betsey Hilbert's description of teaching environmental literature in a community college writing classroom (Hilbert 1995, 121). Hilbert organizes her course thematically around various environmental texts and nature writers, while privileging student outcomes such as "'Student must prove that he or she is able to appraise critically and evaluate pieces of nonfiction prose with attention to content, organization, and style'" (quoted in Wiesser and Dobrin 123). In a sense, Hilbert's emphasis on reasoned analysis over composition also reflects Moon's (2003) diagnosis of the rationality/emotion division above.

4.   To differentiate emotion and affect, we echo Rice (2014) in distinguishing (á la Brian Massumi and other affect theorists) between emotion as a consciously felt and temporary emotion and affect as a largely nonconscious form of relationality.

CHAPTER 7

1.   Further support for our position can actually be found within one of the earliest treatments of rhetoric's material character in terms of nonhuman agency: Richard Marback's (1998) essay "Unclenching the Fist." In considering how we discuss rhetorical agency in the 2004 defacement of the monument to Joe Lewis (*The Fist*) in Detroit, Marback muses about the interconnected and entangled relations among the vandals (who were white), the objects (*The Fist* was covered with white paint), and the motives for action (the vandals placed a photograph of two slain Detroit police officers at the base). Marback's musing was prompted by an AP reporter who contacted him for a quote in answer to a question about whether *The First* symbolized Black Power. Marback's answer was "Not exactly." The reporter was seeking confirmation of an implicit fairy position: if the actions of the two men were motivated by still de jure racial segregation (whites in suburbs; nonwhites in the city), the two vandals' actions were motivated by racism. This first hypothetical newspaper headline would read, Marback muses, "They did it because they live here" (47). Conversely, it could be about the simple moral failings of two individuals ("They did it because of who they are") (48). In both examples, the report—in a perfect rehearsal of the fairy position—desires to see meaning not within the monument itself but "somewhere in the ethereal realms of interpretation, representation, and signification," or else no agency can be attributed at all (50). Even the monument's creator, Robert Graham, sided with semiotics, commenting that he wanted viewers to project their own ideas upon the image rather than offering a definitive meaning or symbol for it ("'Intentions and understandings are brought to it, it is made to mirror meanings'") (50). Yet, pushing back against this similar logic that undergirds the fairy position, Marback argues that objects "are more than just featureless repositories of consequential response" (51). The main key is not that the statue has no relationship to Black Power. It is more that *The First* does not exist in some unchanging definitive interpretation. Rather, *The Fist* participates in shaping the perceptions and agencies of those it interacts with as it is enacted and articulated in the perpetual present. To reach this later view is something closer to the middle

ground Latour wants to negotiate between the fact and fairy positions—precisely the middle ground of ethics we believe virtue ethics can support and extend for students, teachers, and researchers in rhetoric and composition studies.

REFERENCES

ADA.gov. 2014. "Introduction to the ADA." https://www.ada.gov/ada_intro.htm.

Agboka, Godwin Y. 2013. "Participatory Localization: A Social Justice Approach to Navigating Unenfranchised/Disenfranchised Cultural Sites." *Technical Communication Quarterly* 22 (1): 28–49. https://doi.org/10.1080/10572252.2013.730966.

Agboka, Godwin Y. 2014. "Decolonial Methodologies: Social Justice Perspectives in Intercultural Technical Communication Research." *Journal of Technical Writing and Communication* 44 (3): 297–327. https://doi.org/10.2190/TW.44.3.e.

Alcorn, Marshall Jr. 2002. *Changing the Subject in English Class: Discourse and the Construction of Desires.* Carbondale: Southern Illinois University Press.

Alexander, Michelle. 2012. *The New Jim Crow: Mass Incarceration in the Age of Colorblindness.* New York: The New Press.

Alfano, Christine, and Alyssa O'Brien. 2013. *Envision: Writing and Research Arguments.* 3rd ed. Boston: Pearson.

Alim, H. Samy, Jooyoung Lee, and Lauren Mason Carris. 2011. "Moving the Crowd, 'Crowding' the Emcee: The Coproduction and Contestation of Black Normativity in Freestyle Rap Battles." *Discourse & Society* 22 (4): 422–39. https://doi.org/10.1177/0957926510395828.

Alim, H. Samy, and Alastair Pennycook. 2007. "Global Linguistic Flows: Hip-hop Culture(s), Identities, and the Politics of Language Education." *Journal of Language, Identity, and Education* 6 (2): 89–100. https://doi.org/10.1080/15348450701341238.

ALS Association. 2017. "ALS Ice Bucket Challenge—FAQ." http://www.alsa.org/about-us/ice-bucket-challenge-faq.html??referrer=https://www.google.com/.

Anderson, Erin. 2014. "Toward a Resonant Material Vocality for Digital Composition." *enculturation: A Journal of Rhetoric, Writing, and Culture.* http://enculturation.net/materialvocality.

Anscombe, G. E. M. 1958. "Modern Moral Philosophy." *Philosophy* 33 (124): 1–19. https://doi.org/10.1017/S0031819100037943.

Aquinas, Thomas. 2005. *Disputed Questions on the Virtues.* Translated by E. M. Atkins. Cambridge: Cambridge University Press.

Aristotle. 2000. *Politics.* Translated by Benjamin Jowett. New York: Dover.

Aristotle. 2002. *Nicomachean Ethics.* Translated by Joe Sachs. New York: Focus Philosophical Library.

Aristotle. 2006. *On Rhetoric: Toward a Theory of Civic Discourse.* Translated by George A. Kennedy. Oxford: Oxford University Press.

Arroyo, Sarah J. 2013. *Participatory Composition: Video Culture, Writing, and Electracy.* Carbondale: Southern Illinois University Press.

Baecker, Diann. 2007. "'Can You Hear Me Now, Ms. Monster?' Anger, *Thumos*, and First-Year Composition." *Composition Forum* 17 (Fall). http://compositionforum.com/issue/17/can-you-hear-me-now.php.

Baker, Houston. 1991. "Hybridity, the Rap Race, and Pedagogy for the 1990s." *Black Music Research Journal* 11 (2): 217–28. https://doi.org/10.2307/779267.

Bakhtin, Mikhail. 1982. *The Dialogic Imagination: Four Essays.* Edited by Michael Holmquist. Translated by Caryl Emerson and Michael Holmquist. Austin: University of Texas Press.

DOI: 10.7330/9781607328063.c008

Bakhtin, Mikhail. 1986. *Speech Genres and Other Late Essays*. Edited by Caryl Emerson and Michael Holmquist. Translated by Vern W. McGee. Austin: University of Texas Press.

Ballif, Michelle. 1998. "Writing the Third-Sophistic Cyborg: Periphrasis on an [In]Tense Rhetoric." *Rhetoric Society Quarterly* 28 (4): 51–72. https://doi.org/10.1080/027739 49809391130.

Banks, Adam J. 2011. *Digital Griots: African American Rhetoric in a Multimedia Age*. Carbondale: Southern Illinois University Press.

Barber, Benjamin R. 1984. *Strong Democracy: Participatory Politics for a New Age*. Berkeley: University of California Press.

Barnett, Scot. 2010. "Toward an Object-Oriented Rhetoric: A Review of *Tool-Being: Heidegger and the Metaphysic of Objects and Guerilla Metaphysics: Phenomenology and the Carpentry of Things* by Graham Harman." *enculturation: A Journal of Rhetoric, Writing, and Culture* 7. http://enculturation.net/toward-an-object-oriented-rhetoric.

Barthes, Roland. 1977. *Image-Music-Text*. Translated by Stephen Health. New York: Hill and Wang.

Barthes, Roland. 1982. *Camera Lucida*. Translated by Richard Howard. New York: Hill and Wang.

Barton, Ellen. 2008. "Further Contributions from the Ethical Turn in Composition/ Rhetoric: Analyzing Ethics in Interaction." *College Composition and Communication* 59 (4): 596–632.

Barnouw, Jeffrey. 2004. *Odysseus, Hero of Practical Intelligence: Deliberation and Signs in Homer's Odyssey*. New York: University Press of America.

Becker, Lawrence. 1990. *Reciprocity*. Chicago: University of Chicago Press.

Becker, Olivia. 2014. "Not Everyone Is a Fan of the Sharing Economy." *VICE News*. https://news .vice.com/article/not-everyone-is-a-fan-of-the-sharing-economy.

Bennett, Jane. 2010. *Vibrant Matter: A Political Ecology of Things*. Durham, NC: Duke University Press.

Bentham, Jeremy. 2007. *An Introduction to the Principles of Morals and Legislation*. New York: Dover.

Berlin, James A. 1988. "Rhetoric and Ideology in the Writing Class." *College English* 50 (5): 477–94. https://doi.org/10.2307/377477.

Berlin, James A. 1990. "Postmodernism, Politics, and Histories of Rhetoric." *Pre/Text* 11 (3–4): 170–87.

Berlin, James A. 1992. "Poststructuralism, Cultural Studies, and the Composition Classroom." *Rhetoric Review* 11 (1): 16–33. https://doi.org/10.1080/07350199209388984.

Bernard-Donals, Michael, and Matthew Capdevielle. 2008. "Bakhtin Ethics Rhetoric." *Russian Journal of Communication* 1 (3): 307–22. https://doi.org/10.1080/19409419.2 008.10756719.

Bernard-Donals, Michael, and John Drake. 2008. "Ethics, Redemption, and Writing after Auschwitz: The Case of Emmanuel Levinas." In *Judaic Perspectives in Rhetoric and Composition*, edited by Andrea Greenbaum and Deborah Holdstein, 129–50. Cresskill, NJ: Hampton.

Bina, Olivia, and Sofia Guedes Vaz. 2011. "Humans, Environment, and Economies: From Vicious Relationships to Virtuous Responsibility." *Ecological Economics* 72(C):170–78. https://doi.org/10.1016/j.ecolecon.2011.09.029.

Bizzell, Patricia. 1992. "The Politics of Teaching Virtue." *ADE Bulletin* 103:4–7. https://doi .org/10.1632/ade.103.4.

Blakesley, David, ed. 2007. *The Terministic Screen: Rhetorical Perspectives on Film*. Carbondale: Southern Illinois University Press.

Bolsin, Stephen, Thomas Faunce, and Justin Oakley. 2005. "Practical Virtue Ethics: Healthcare Whistleblowing and Portable Digital Technology." *Journal of Medical Ethics* 31 (10): 612–18. https://doi.org/10.1136/jme.2004.010603.

Bowdon, Melody. 2004. "Technical Communication and the Role of the Public Intellectual: A Community HIV-Prevention Case Study." *Technical Communication Quarterly* 13 (3): 325–40. https://doi.org/10.1207/s15427625tcq1303_6.

Boyle, Robert John. 2016. "Unfollow Humans of New York: The Site Engages Sentimentality with Real Political Matters—Empathy Is Much Harder." Salon. https://www.salon.com/2016/01/24/unfollow_humans_of_new_york_the_site_engages_sentimentally_with_real_political_matters_empathy_is_much_harder/.

Bernstein, Adam. *Breaking Bad.* 2008. Titles of episodes, season 1, episodes 1 and 2, aired January 27. AMC.

Bogost, Ian. 2010. *Persuasive Games: The Expressive Power of Videogames.* Cambridge, MA: MIT Press.

BP Public Relations. 2010. @BPPublicRelations. Twitter. Accessed August 15, 2017. https://twitter.com/bpglobalpr?lang=en.

Brooke, Collin Gifford. 2009. *Lingua Fracta: Towards a Rhetoric of New Media.* New Dimensions in Computers and Composition. Cresskill, NJ: Hampton.

Brouwer, Daniel C., and Robert Asen. 2010. "Introduction: Public Modalities, or the Metaphors We Theorize By." In *Public Modalities,* edited by Daniel C. Brouwer and Robert Asen, 1–32. Tuscaloosa: University of Alabama Press.

Brown, James J. Jr. 2015. *Ethical Programs: Hospitality and the Rhetorics of Software.* Ann Arbor: University of Michigan Press. https://doi.org/10.3998/dh.13474172.0001.001.

Brown, James J. Jr., and Nathaniel A. Rivers. 2014. "Composing the Carpenter's Workshop." *O-Zone: A Journal of Object-Oriented Studies* 1 (1): 27–36.

Burgess, Sarah K., and Stuart J. Murray. 2006. "Review of *For More than One Voice: Toward a Philosophy of Vocal Expression* by Adriana Cavarero." *Philosophy & Rhetoric* 39 (2): 166–69. https://doi.org/10.1353/par.2006.0010.

Carlisle, Claire. 2014. *On Habit.* New York: Routledge.

Cavarero, Adriana. 2005. *For More than One Voice: Toward a Philosophy of Vocal Expression.* Translated by Paul A. Kottman. Stanford: Stanford University Press.

Cavarero, Adriana. 2011. *Horrorism: Naming Contemporary Violence.* New York: Columbia University Press.

Colton, Jared Sterling. 2016. "Revisiting Rhetorics of Digital Sampling with an Ethics of Care." *Computers and Composition* 40:19–31. https://doi.org/10.1016/j.compcom.2016.03.006.

Colton, Jared S., Steve Holmes, and Josephine Walwema. 2017. "From NoobGuides to #OpKKK: Ethics of Anonymous' Tactical Technical Communication." *Technical Communication Quarterly* 26 (1) : 59–75.

Crowley, Sharon. 1990. *The Methodical Memory: Invention in Current-Traditional Rhetoric.* Carbondale: Southern Illinois University Press.

Davidson, Jacob. 2014. "We Need to Do Better Than the Ice Bucket Challenge." *TIME.* http://time.com/3107510/ice-bucket-challenge-als-we-need-to-do-better/.

Davis, Diane. 2000. *Breaking Up (at) Totality: A Rhetoric of Laughter.* Carbondale: Southern Illinois University Press.

Davis, Diane. 2010. *Inessential Solidarity: Rhetoric and Foreigner Relations.* Pittsburgh, PA: University of Pittsburgh Press. https://doi.org/10.2307/j.ctt5vkfx1.

de Certeau, Michel. 1984. *The Practice of Everyday Life.* Translated by Steven F. Rendall. Berkeley: University of California Press.

Deleuze, Gilles. 1966. *Bergsonism.* Translated by Hugh Tomlinson and Barbara Habberjam. New York: Zone, 1991.

Deleuze, Gille, and Felix Guattari. 1987. *A Thousand Plateaus: Capitalism and Schizophrenia.* Minneapolis: University of Minnesota Press.

Depew, David. 2008. "Review of *Confronting Aristotle's Ethics* by Eugene Garver." *Philosophy and Rhetoric* 41 (2): 184–89.

Derrida, Jacques. 1978. *Writing and Difference.* Translated by Alan Bass. Chicago, IL: University of Chicago Press.

DeVoss, Danielle Nicole, and Sue Webb. n.d. "Grand Theft Audio." *Computers and Composition Online.* http://cconlinejournal.org/CConline_GTA/resources.html.

Dolmage, Jay T. 2014. *Disability Rhetoric.* Syracuse, NY: Syracuse University Press.

Dombrowski, Paul. 1999. *Ethics in Technical Communication.* New York: Allyn and Bacon.

Duffy, John. 2014. "Ethical Dispositions: A Discourse for Rhetoric and Composition." *JAC* 34 (1–2): 209–37.

Duffy, John. 2017. "The Good Writer: Virtue Ethics and the Teaching of Writing." *College English* 79 (3): 229–50.

Dunning, Brian. 2016. "Slacktivism: Raising Awareness." *Skeptoid* . Podcast audio, May 15. https://skeptoid.com/episodes/4419.

Edelman, Benjamin G., and Michael Luca. 2014. "Digital Discrimination: The Case of Airbnb.com." NOM Unit Working Paper 14-054, Harvard Business School. https://hbswk.hbs.edu/item/digital-discrimination-the-case-of-airbnb-com. https://doi.org/10.2139/ssrn.2377353.

Elbow, Peter. 1998. *Writing Without Teachers.* Oxford: Oxford University Press.

Ellis, Rehema. 2015. "Humans of New York Raises $1 Million for Brooklyn Schools." *NBC News.* https://www.nbcnews.com/nightly-news/humans-new-york-raises-1-million-brooklyn-school-n300296.

Eyman, Douglas. 2015. *Digital Rhetoric: Theory, Method, Practice.* Ann Arbor: University of Michigan Press. https://doi.org/10.3998/dh.13030181.0001.001.

Farenga, Vincent. 1979. "Periphrasis on the Origin of Rhetoric." *MLN* 94: 1033–55.

Farman, Jason. 2012. *Mobile Interface Theory: Embodied Space and Locative Media.* New York: Routledge. https://doi.org/10.1002/9781405165518.wbeosm155.

Federal Communications Commission. 2014. "FCC 14–12." Report released February 25, 2014. Accessed August 15, 2017. https://apps.fcc.gov/edocs_public/attachmatch/FCC-14-12A1.pdf.

Feenberg, Andrew, and Maria Bakardjieva. 2004. "Consumers or Citizens? The Online Community Debate." In *Community in the Digital Age: Philosophy and Practice,* edited by Andrew Feenberg and Darin Barney, 1–28. Lanham, MD: Rowman and Littlefield.

Felski, Rita. 2015. *The Limits of Critique.* Chicago, IL: University of Chicago Press. https://doi.org/10.7208/chicago/9780226294179.001.0001.

Fleckenstein, Kristie S. 2005. "Cybernetics, *Ethos,* and Ethics: The Plight of the Bread-and-Butter-Fly." *Journal of Advanced Composition* 25 (2): 323–46.

Fontaine, Sheryl I., and Susan M. Hunter. 1998. "Ethical Awareness: A Process of Inquiry." In *Foregrounding Ethical Awareness in Composition and English Studies,* edited by Sheryl I. Fontaine and Susan M. Hunter, 1–11. Portsmouth, NH: Heinemann.

Foot, Phillipa. 2001. *Natural Goodness.* Oxford: Oxford University Press. https://doi.org/10.1093/0198235089.001.0001.

Fountain, T. Kenny. 2014. *Rhetoric in the Flesh: Trained Vision, Technical Expertise, and the Gross Anatomy Lab.* ATTW Series in Technical and Professional Communication. New York: Routledge.

Foxton, Willard. 2014. "The Ice Bucket Challenge—A Middle-Class Wet-T-Shirt Contest for Armchair Activists." *The Telegraph.* http://blogs.telegraph.co.uk/technology/willardfoxton2/100014135/the-ice-bucket-challenge-a-middle-class-wet-t-shirt-contest-for-armchair-clicktivists.

Fraser, Nancy. 1997. *Justice Interruptus: Critical Reflections on the "Postsocialist" Condition.* New York: Routledge.

Freire, Paulo. 2000. *Pedagogy of the Oppressed.* Translated by Myra Bergman Ramos. New York: Bloomsbury.

Frey, Lawrence R., W. Barnett Pearce, Mark A. Pollock, Lee Artz, and Bren A. O. Murphy. 1996. "Looking for Justice in All the Wrong Places: On a Communication Approach to Social Justice." *Communication Studies* 47 (1–2): 110–27. https://doi.org/10.1080/10510979609368467.

Galloway, Alexander R. 2006. *Protocol: How Control Exists after Decentralization.* Cambridge, MA: MIT Press.

Garver, Eugene. 2006. *Confronting Aristotle's Ethics: Ancient and Modern Morality.* Chicago, IL: University of Chicago Press. https://doi.org/10.7208/chicago/978022628 4019.001.0001.

Gehrke, Pat. 2010. "Being for the Other-to-the-Other: Justice and Communication in Levinasian Ethics." *Review of Communication* 10 (1): 5–19. https://doi.org/10.1080/15 358590903248769.

Gilligan, Carol. 1982. *In A Different Voice.* Cambridge, MA: Harvard University Press.

Gilmore, Scott. 2014. "Why the Ice Bucket Challenge Is Bad for You." *MacLean's,* August 24. http://www.macleans.ca/society/health/why-the-ice-bucket-challenge-is-bad-for-you/.

Giroux, Henry A. 1983. *Theory and Resistance in Education: A Pedagogy for the Opposition.* South Hadley, MA: Bergin & Garvey.

Gladwell, Malcolm. 2010. "Small Change: Why the Revolution Will Not Be Tweeted." *New Yorker,* October 4. https://www.newyorker.com/magazine/2010/10/04/small-change-malcolm-gladwell.

Golumbia, David. 2013. "Cyberlibertarianism: The Extremist Foundations of 'Digital Freedom.'" Presentation at Clemson University, Clemson, SC, September 5. http://www.uncomputing.org/wp-content/uploads/2014/02/cyberlibertarianism-extremist-foundations-sep2013.pdf.

Goodling, Laurie B. 2015. "MOAR Activism, Please." *Kairos* 19 (3). http://kairos.technorhetoric.net/19.3/topoi/goodling/index.html.

Grabill, Jeffrey T., and W. Michele Simmons. 1998. "Toward a Critical Rhetoric of Risk Communication: Producing Citizens and the Role of Technical Communicators." *Technical Communication Quarterly* 7 (4): 415–41. https://doi.org/10.1080/105 72259809364640.

Green, Emma. 2016. "The Anger of the American People." *The Atlantic.* https://www.theatlantic.com/politics/archive/2016/05/martha-nussbaum-anger/481464/.

Gries, Laura. 2015. *Still Life with Rhetoric.* Logan: Utah State University Press.

Griswold, Charles. 2007. *Forgiveness: Philosophical Exploration.* Cambridge: Cambridge University Press.

Gross, Alan G., and Arthur E. Walzer, eds. 2008. *Rereading Aristotle's Rhetoric.* Carbondale: Southern Illinois University Press.

Grosz, Elizabeth A. 2013. "Habit Today: Ravaisson, Bergson, Deleuze, and US." *Body & Society* 19: 217–39.

Gurak, Laura J. 1997. "Technical Communication, Copyright, and the Shrinking Public Domain." *Computers and Composition* 14 (3): 329–42. https://doi.org/10.1016/S8755 -4615(97)90004-9.

Halbritter, Bump. 2012. *Mics, Camera, Symbolic Action.* Anderson, SC: Parlor.

Hall, Stuart. 1997. "The Work of Representation." In *Representation: Cultural Representations and Signifying Practices,* edited by Stuart Hall, 13–64. Thousand Oaks, CA: SAGE.

Harvey, David. 2007. *A Brief History of Neoliberalism.* New York: Oxford University Press.

Hawhee, Debra. 2004. *Bodily Arts: Rhetoric and Athletics in Ancient Greece.* Austin: University of Texas Press.

Hawk, Byron. 2007. *A Counter-History of Composition: Toward Methodologies of Complexity.* Pittsburgh. PA: University of Pittsburgh Press. https://doi.org/10.2307/j.ctt5hjqxd.

Hawk, Byron, ed. 2012. "Remixes and Revisions." Special issue, *enculturation: A Journal of Rhetoric, Writing, and Culture* 13. http://enculturation.net/13.

Hayles, N. Katherine. 1999. *How We Became Posthuman: Virtual Bodies in Cybernetics, Literature, and Informatics.* Chicago, IL: University of Chicago Press. https://doi.org/10.7208/chicago/9780226321394.001.0001.

Hayles, N. Katherine. 2010. "How We Read: Close, Hyper, Machine." *ADE Bulletin* 150:62–79. https://doi.org/10.1632/ade.150.62.

Heidegger, Martin. 1996. *Basic Concepts of Aristotelian Philosophy*. Translated by Robert D. Metcalf and Mark B. Turner. Bloomington: University of Indiana Press.

Held, Virginia. 2006. *The Ethics of Care*. New York: Oxford University Press.

Hesmondhalgh, David. 2006. "Digital Sampling and Cultural Inequality." *Social & Legal Studies* 15 (1): 53–75. https://doi.org/10.1177/0964663906060973.

Hess, Mickey. 2006. "Was Foucault a Plagiarist? Hip-hop Sampling and Academic Citation." *Computers and Composition* 23 (3): 280–95. https://doi.org/10.1016/j.compcom.2006.05.004.

Hilbert, Betsy. 1995. "Teaching Nature Writing at a Community College." In *Teaching Environmental Literature: Materials, Methods, Resources*, edited by Frederick O. Waage, 88–92. New York: MLA.

Hill, Jane H. 1998. "Language, Race, and White Public Space." *American Anthropologist* 100 (3): 680–89. https://doi.org/10.1525/aa.1998.100.3.680.

Holmes, Steve. 2014a. "Multiple Bodies, Actants, and a Composition Classroom: Actor-Network Theory in Practice." *Rhetoric Review* 33 (4): 421–38. https://doi.org/10.1080/07350198.2014.947232.

Holmes, Steve. 2014b. "Rhetorical Allegorithms in Bitcoin." *enculturation: A Journal of Rhetoric, Writing, and Culture* (18). http://enculturation.net/rhetoricalallegorithms.

Holmes, Steve. 2016. "*Ethos, Hexis*, and the Case for Persuasive Technologies." *enculturation: A Journal of Rhetoric, Writing, and Culture* (23). http://enculturation.net/ethos-hexis-and-the-case-for-persuasive-technologies.

Holmes, Steve. 2017. *The Rhetoric of Videogames as Embodied Practice: Procedural Habits*. New York: Routledge.

Holmevik, Jan. 2012. *Inter/vention: Free Play in the Age of Electracy*. Cambridge, MA: MIT Press.

Howard, Rebecca Moore. 2000. "Sexuality, Textuality: The Cultural Work of Plagiarism." *College English* 62 (4): 473–91. https://doi.org/10.2307/378866.

Hughes, James J. 2011. "After Happiness, Cyborg Virtue." *Free Inquiry* 32 (1): 1–7.

Hume, David. 1983. *An Enquiry Concerning the Principles of Morals*. Edited by Eric Steinberg. Indianapolis, IN: Hackett.

Hursthouse, Rosalind. 1999. *On Virtue Ethics*. Oxford: Oxford University Press.

Hyde, Michael J. 2004. Introduction to *The Ethos of Rhetoric*, edited by Michael J. Hyde, 1–19. Columbia: University of South Carolina Press.

Invisible Children. 2012a. "KONY 2012." YouTube video, 29:58. Posted May 5, 2012. https://www.youtube.com/watch?v=Y4MnpzG5Sqc.

Invisible Children. 2012b. "KONY 2012: Part II—Beyond Famous." YouTube video, 19:47. Published April 5, 2012. https://www.youtube.com/watch?v=c_Ue6REkeTA.

Jenkins, Henry. 2008. *Convergence Culture: Where Old and New Media Collide*. New York: New York University Press.

Johnson, Matthew S. S. 2008. "Public Writing in Gaming Spaces." *Computers & Composition* 25 (3): 270–83. https://doi.org/10.1016/j.compcom.2008.05.001.

Johnson-Eilola, Johndan. 2010. "Among Texts." In *Rhetorics and Technologies: New Directions in Writing and Communication*, edited by Stuart A. Selber, 33–55. Columbia: University of South Carolina Press.

Johnson-Eilola, Johndan, and Stuart Selber. 2007. "Plagiarism, Originality, Assemblage." *Computers and Composition* 24 (4): 375–403. https://doi.org/10.1016/j.compcom.2007.08.003.

Jones, Rebecca. 2009. "The Aesthetics of Protest." *enculturation: A Journal of Rhetoric, Writing, and Culture* 6 (2). http://enculturation.net/6.2/jones.

Judge, Mike, dir. *Office Space*. 1999. . Los Angeles, CA: Twentieth Century Film.

Juzwik, Mary. 2004. "Towards an Ethics of Answerability: Reconsidering Dialogism in Sociocultural Literacy Research." *College Composition and Communication* 55 (3): 536–67. https://doi.org/10.2307/4140698.

Kant, Immanuel. 1969. *Foundations of the Metaphysic of Morals.* Translated by Lewis White Beck. Indianapolis, IN: Bobbs-Merrill.

Katz, Steven B. 1992. "The Ethic of Expediency: Classical Rhetoric, Technology, and the Holocaust." *College English* 54 (3): 255–75. https://doi.org/10.2307/378062.

Kimball, Miles A. 2006. "Cars, Culture, and Tactical Technical Communication." *Technical Communication Quarterly* 15 (1): 67–86. https://doi.org/10.1207/s15427625tcq1501_6.

Kingma, Luke. 2015. "Fundraising in the Age of Facebook." Medium. https://medium.com /thoughts-on-media/fundraising-in-the-age-of-facebook-5c95a812f08e.

Kirsch, Gesa E. 1999. *Ethical Dilemmas in Feminist Research: The Politics of Location, Interpretation, and Publication.* Albany: SUNY Press.

Kirsch, Gesa E., and Joy Ritchie. 1995. "Beyond the Personal: Theorizing a Politics of Location in Composition Research." *College Composition and Communication* 46 (1): 7–29. https://doi.org/10.2307/358867.

Kosinski, Ben. 2016. "#IcebucketChallenge: Why You're Not Really Helping." HuffPost. https://www.huffingtonpost.com/ben-kosinski/icebucketchallenge-why -yo_b_5656649.html.

Kynard, Carmen. 2007. "Wanted: Some Black Long Distance [Writers]: Blackboard Flava Flavin and Other AfroDigital Experiences in the Classroom." *Computers and Composition* 24 (3): 329–45. https://doi.org/10.1016/j.compcom.2007.05.008.

Lacount, Amy. 2017. "Jay-Z and Azealia Banks Call Out Miley Cyrus on Cultural Appropriation." Bust. http://bust.com/general/10264-jay-z-and-azealia-banks-call-out -miley-cyrus-on-cultural-appropriation-she-doesnt-get-it.html.

Lanham, Richard. 1993. *The Electronic Word: Democracy, Technology, and the Arts.* Chicago, IL: University of Chicago Press. https://doi.org/10.7208/chicago/9780226469 126.001.0001.

Larrabee, Mary Jeane, ed. 1993. *An Ethic of Care: Feminist and Interdisciplinary Perspectives.* New York: Routledge.

Latour, Bruno. 1993. *We Have Never Been Modern.* Translated by Catherine Porter. Cambridge, MA: Harvard University Press.

Latour, Bruno. 1999. *Pandora's Hope: Essays on the Reality of Science Studies.* Cambridge, MA: Harvard University Press.

Latour, Bruno. 2002. "Morality and Technology: The End of the Means." Translated by Couze Venn. *Theory, Culture & Society* 19 (5–6): 247–60. https://doi.org/10.1177 /026327602761899246.

Latour, Bruno. 2004a. *Politics of Nature: How to Bring the Sciences into Democracy.* Translated by Catherine Porter. Cambridge, MA: Harvard University Press.

Latour, Bruno. 2004b. "Why Has Critique Run out of Steam? From Matters of Fact to Matters of Concern." *Critical Inquiry* 30 (2): 225–48. https://doi.org/10.1086/421123.

Lee, Yu-Hao, and Gary Hsieh. 2013. "Does Slacktivism Hurt Activism?" *Proceedings of the SIGCHI Conference on Human Factors in Computing Systems.* Paris, France, April 27–May 2. https://doi.org/10.1145/2470654.2470770.

Lewin, Tamar. 2015. "Harvard and M.I.T. Are Sued Over Lack of Closed Captions." *New York Times.* https://www.nytimes.com/2015/02/13/education/harvard-and-mit-sued -over-failing-to-caption-online-courses.html?rref=collection%2Fbyline%2Ftamar-lewin &action=click&contentCollection=undefined&region=stream&module=stream_unit& version=latest&contentPlacement=42&pgtype=collection.

Ling, Jonathan P., Olga Pletnikova, Juan C. Troncoso, and Philip C. Wong. 2015. "TDP-43 Repression of Nonconserved Cryptic Exons Is Compromised in ALS-FTD." *Science* 349 (6248): 650–55. https://doi.org/10.1126/science.aab0983.

Locke, John. 1988. *Locke: Two Treatises of Government.* Edited by Peter Laslett. New York: Cambridge University Press. https://doi.org/10.1017/CBO9780511810268.

Locke, John. 1996. *An Essay Concerning Human Understanding.* Edited by P. Kenneth. Cambridge, MA: Hackett.

Lockwood, Thornton C. 2013. "Habituation, Habit, and Character in Aristotle's *Nicomachean Ethics*." In *A History of Habit: From Aristotle to Bourdieu*, edited by Tom Sparrow and Adam Hutchinson, 19–37. New York: Lexington Books.

Lomax, Alan. 2011. *Sounds of the South*. Rhino Atlantic. Compact Disc.

Losh, Elizabeth M. 2009. *Virtualpolitik: An Electronic History of Government Media-Making in a Time of War, Scandal, Disaster, Miscommunication, and Mistakes*. Cambridge, MA: MIT Press.

Lynch, Paul, and Nathaniel A. Rivers, eds. 2015. *Thinking with Bruno Latour in Rhetoric and Composition*. Carbondale: Southern Illinois University Press.

Lyotard, Jean-Francois. 1984. *The Postmodern Condition: A Report on Knowledge*. Translated by Geoffrey Bennington and Brian Massumi. Minneapolis: University of Minnesota Press.

MacIntyre, Alasdair. 2007. *After Virtue: A Study in Moral Theory*. South Bend, IN: University of Notre Dame Press.

Marback, Richard. 1998. "Detroit and the Closed Fist: Toward a Theory of Material Rhetoric." *Rhetoric Review* 17 (1): 74–92. https://doi.org/10.1080/07350199809359232.

Markel, Mike. 2000. *Ethics in Technical Communication: A Critique and Synthesis*. Westport, CT: Ablex.

May, Todd. 2008. *The Political Thought of Jacques Rancière*. University Park: Pennsylvania State University Press. https://doi.org/10.3366/edinburgh/9780748635320.001.0001.

May, Todd. 2010. *Contemporary Political Movements and the Thought of Jacques Rancière: Equality in Action*. Edinburgh: Edinburgh University Press. https://doi.org/10.3366/edinburgh/9780748639823.001.0001.

McDaniel, Raymond. 2008. *Saltwater Empire*. Minneapolis, MN: Coffee House.

McFarlane, Nicole Ashanti. 2013. "Digital Memory and Narrative through 'African American Rhetoric(s) 2.0.'" *enculturation: A Journal of Rhetoric, Writing, and Culture*. http://enculturation.net/digital-memory.

McFarlane, Nicole Ashanti, and Nicole Elaine Snell. 2014. "Access Denied: Digital Jim Crow and Institutional Barriers to Open Access." Conference Presentation at the Conference on College Composition and Communication, Indianapolis, IN, March 19.

Meloncon, Lisa K., ed. 2013. *Rhetorical Accessibility: At the Intersection of Technical Communication and Disability Studies*. Amityville, NY: Baywood.

Micciche, Laura. 2005. "Emotion, Ethics, and Rhetorical Action." *JAC* 25:161–84.

Mill, John Stuart. 1998. *Utilitarianism*. Oxford: Oxford University Press.

Miller, Carolyn R. 2001. "Writing in a Culture of Simulation: *Ethos* Online." In *The Semiotics of Writing: Transdisciplinary Perspectives on the Technology of Writing*, edited by Patrick Coppock, 253–79. Turnhout, Belgium: Brepols.

Miller, Carolyn R. 2007. "What Can Automation Tell Us about Agency?" *Rhetoric Society Quarterly* 37 (2): 127–57.

Miller, Paul D. 2004. *Rhythm Science*. Cambridge: MIT Press.

Moon, Gretchen Flesher. 2003. "The Pathos of *Pathos*: The Treatment of Emotion in Contemporary Composition Textbooks." In *A Way to Move: Rhetorics of Emotion and Composition Studies*, edited by Dale Jacobs and Laura R. Micciche, 33–42. Portsmouth, NH: Boynton/Cook.

Morozov, Evgeny. 2012. *The Net Delusion: The Dark Side of Internet Freedom*. Philadelphia, PA: PublicAffairs.

Morton, Donald, and Mas'ud Zavarzadeh. 1991. *Theory/Pedagogy/Politics*. Urbana-Champaign: University of Illinois Press.

Nahon, Karine, and Jeff Hemsley. 2013. *Going Viral*. New York: Polity.

National Association of the Deaf (NAD). n.d.. "State and Local Colleges and Universities." Accessed August 15, 2017. https://www.nad.org/resources/education/higher-education/state-and-local-colleges-and-universities/.

Newcomb, Alyssa. 2015. "Hard of Hearing YouTube Star Campaigns for Better Closed Captioning." *ABC News*. http://abcnews.go.com/Technology/hard-hearing-youtube-star-campaigns-closed-captioning/story?id=28782531.

Nicotra, Jodie A. 2016. "Disgust, Distributed: Virtual Public Shaming as Epideictic Assemblage." *enculturation: A Journal of Rhetoric, Writing, and Culture* (22). http://enculturation.net/disgust-distributed.

Noddings, Nel. 1982. *Caring: A Feminine Approach to Ethics and Moral Education.* Berkeley: University of California Press.

Nozick, Robert. 1974. *Anarchy, State, and Utopia.* New York: Basic Books.

Nussbaum, Martha C. 1993. "Non-Relative Virtues: An Aristotelian Approach." In *The Quality of Life*, edited by Martha C. Nussbaum and Amartya Sen, 242–69. Oxford: Oxford University Press. https://doi.org/10.1093/0198287976.003.0019.

Nussbaum, Martha C. 2015. *Anger and Forgiveness: Resentment, Generosity, Justice.* Oxford: Oxford University Press.

O'Connell, Kit. 2014. "The 'Grinch' that Stole Water." Mint Press News. https://www.mintpressnews.com/nestle-the-grinch-illegally-bottles-68000-gallons-of-water-a-day-in-drought-stricken-california/211565/.

Olson, Gary A. 1999. "Encountering the Other: Postcolonial Theory and Composition Scholarship." In *Ethical Issues in College Writing*, edited by Fredric G. Gale, Phillip Sipiora, and James L. Kinneavy, 91–105. New York: Peter Lang.

Omizo, Ryan, and Bill Hart-Davidson. 2016. "Hedge-O-Matic. *enculturation: A Journal of Rhetoric, Writing, and Culture.*

O'Reilly, Tim. 2013. "Open Data and Algorithmic Regulation." In *Beyond Transparency*, edited by Brett Goldstein and Lauren Dyson, 289–300. New York: Code for America.

Owens, Derek. 2001. *Composition and Sustainability: Teaching for a Threatened Generation.* Urbana, IL: NCTE.

Palmeri, Jason. 2012. *Remixing Composition: A History of Multimodal Writing Pedagogy.* Carbondale: Southern Illinois University Press.

Pandey, Iswari P. 2007. "Researching (with) the Postnational 'Other': Ethics, Methodologies, and Qualitative Studies of Digital Literacy." In *Digital Writing Research: Technologies, Methodologies, and Ethical Issues*, edited by Heidi A. McKee and Dánielle Nicole DeVoss, 107–25. Cresskill, NJ: Hampton.

Pennycook, Alastair. 2007a. "Language, Localization and the Real: Hip-hop and the Global Spread of Authenticity." *Journal of Language, Identity, and Education* 6 (2): 101–16. https://doi.org/10.1080/15348450701341246.

Pennycook, Alastair. 2007b. "'The Rotation Gets Thick. The Constraints Get Thin': Creativity, Recontextualization, and Difference." *Applied Linguistics* 28 (4): 579–96. https://doi.org/10.1093/applin/amm043.

Pigg, Stacey. 2014. "Emplacing Mobile Composing Habits: A Study of Academic Writing in Networked Social Spaces." *College Composition and Communication* 66 (2): 250–75.

Plato. 1992. *The Republic.* Translated by G. M. A. Grube. Cambridge, MA: Hackett .

Porter, James. 1993. "Developing a Postmodern Ethics of Rhetoric and Composition." In *Defining the New Rhetorics*, edited by Theresa Enos and Stuart C. Brown, 207–26. Newbury Park, CA: SAGE.

Porter, James. 1998. *Rhetorical Ethics and Internetworked Writing.* Greenwich, CT: Ablex.

Powell, Katrina M., and Pamela Takayoshi. 2003. "Accepting Roles Created for Us: The Ethics of Reciprocity." *College Composition and Communication* 54 (3): 394–422. https://doi.org/10.2307/3594171.

Pratt, Mary Louise. 1992. *Imperial Eyes: Travel Writing and Transculturation.* New York: Routledge. https://doi.org/10.4324/9780203163672.

Pruchnic, Jeff. 2014. *Rhetoric and Ethics in the Cybernetic Age: The Transhuman Condition.* New York: Routledge.

Quandahl, Ellen. 2003. "A Feeling for Aristotle: Emotion in the Sphere of Ethics." In *A Way to Move: Rhetorics of Emotion and Composition Studies*, edited by Laura Micciche and Dale Jacobs, 11–22. Portsmouth, NH: Boynton/Cook.

Rancière, Jacques. 1992. "Politics, Identification, and Subjectivization." *October* 61:58–64. https://doi.org/10.2307/778785.

Rancière, Jacques. 1995. *On the Shores of Politics.* Translated by Liz Heron. New York: Verso.

Rancière, Jacques. 1999. *Disagreement: Politics and Philosophy.* Translated by Julie Rose. Minneapolis: University of Minnesota Press.

Raustiala, Kal, and Christopher Jon Sprigman. 2015. "Squelching Creativity: What the 'Blurred Lines' Team Copied Is Either Not Original or Not Relevant." *Slate*, March 12. http://www.slate.com/articles/news_and_politics/jurisprudence/2015/03/_blurred _lines_verdict_is_wrong_williams_and_thicke_did_not_infringe_on.html.

Rawls, John. 1971. *A Theory of Justice.* Cambridge, MA: Harvard University Press.

Reid, Alex. 2007. *The Two Virtuals.* West Lafayette: Parlor.

Rhett and Link. 2011. "CAPTION FAIL: Lady Gaga Putt-Putt Rally." YouTube video, 3:55. Posted January 31. https://www.youtube.com/watch?v=hVNrkXM3TTI&list=PLA220B A20D4D3DE46.

Rice, Jeff. 2003. "The 1963 Hip-Hop Machine: Hip-Hop Pedagogy as Composition." *College Composition and Communication* 54 (3): 453–71. https://doi.org/10.2307/3594173.

Rice, Jeff. 2007. *The Rhetoric of Cool: Composition Studies and New Media.* Carbondale: Southern Illinois University Press.

Rice, Jeff. 2015. "Digital Outragicity." Video of presentation at Indiana Digital Rhetoric Symposium, April 10. http://idrs.indiana.edu/program/presentations.shtml.

Rice, Jenny. 2014. *Distant Publics: Development Rhetoric and the Subject of Crisis.* Pittsburgh, PA: University of Pittsburgh Press.

Rickert, Thomas. 2013. *Ambient Rhetoric: The Attunements of Rhetorical Being.* Pittsburgh, PA: University of Pittsburgh Press. https://doi.org/10.2307/j.ctt5hjqwx.

Ricoeur, Paul. 1992. *Oneself as Another.* Translated by Kathleen Blamey. Chicago, IL: University of Chicago Press.

Rivers, Nathaniel A. 2014. "Tracing the Missing Masses." *enculturation: A Journal of Rhetoric, Writing, and Culture* (17). http://enculturation.net/missingmasses.

Roberts-Miller, Patricia. 2010. *Fanatical Schemes: Proslavery Rhetoric and the Power of Consensus.* Birmingham: University of Alabama Press.

Robertson, Christopher, and Aaron S. Kesselheim. 2016. Introduction to *Blinding as a Solution to Bias,* edited by Aaron S. Kesselheim and Christopher T. Robertson, 1–12. New York: Academic.

Ronell, Avital. 1991. *The Telephone Book: Technology, Schizophrenia, Electric Speech.* Lincoln: University of Nebraska Press.

Ronson, Jon. 2016. *So You've Been Publicly Shamed.* New York: Riverhead Books.

Roorda, Randall. 1997. "Nature/Writing: Literature, Ecology, and Composition." *JAC* 17 (3): 401–14.

Roth, Michael. 2014. *Beyond the University: Why Liberal Education Matters.* New Haven, CT: Yale University Press.

Royster, Jacqueline Jones. 1996. "When the First Voice You Hear is Not Your Own." *College Composition and Communication* 47 (1): 29–40. https://doi.org/10.2307/358272.

Royster, Jacqueline Jones, and Gesa E. Kirsch. 2012. *Feminist Rhetorical Practices: New Horizons for Rhetoric, Composition, and Literacy Studies.* Carbondale: Southern Illinois University Press.

Ruddick, Sara. 1989. *Material Thinking: Toward a Politics of Peace.* New York: Ballentine Books.

Rude, Carolyn D. 2004. "Toward an Expanded Concept of Rhetorical Delivery: The Uses of Reports in Public Policy Debates." *Technical Communication Quarterly* 13 (3): 271–88. https://doi.org/10.1207/s15427625tcq1303_3.

Sander-Staudt, Maureen. 2006. "The Unhappy Marriage of Care Ethics and Virtue Ethics." *Hypatia* 21 (4): 21–40.

Selfe, Cynthia L., and Richard J. Selfe Jr. 1994. "The Politics of the Interface: Power and Its Exercise in Electronic Contact Zones." *College Composition and Communication* 45 (4): 480–504. https://doi.org/10.2307/358761.

Sen, Amartya. 2004. "Disability and Justice." Keynote address, World Bank Conference on Disability, Washington, DC, November 30–December 1, 2004.

Sheridan, David, Jim Ridolfo, and Anthony J. Michel. 2012. *The Available Means of Persuasion: Mapping a Theory and Pedagogy of Multimodal Public Rhetoric.* Anderson, SC: Parlor.

Shirkey, Clay. 2009. *Here Comes Everybody: The Power of Organizing without Organizations.* New York: Penguin Books.

Sicart, Miguel. 2005. "Game, Player, Ethics: A Virtue Ethics Approach to Computer Games." *International Review of Information Ethics* 4 (12):14–18.

Simmons, W. Michele, and Jeffrey T. Grabill. 2007. "Toward a Civic Rhetoric for Technologically and Scientifically Complex Places: Invention, Performance, and Participation." *College Composition and Communication* 85 (3): 419–48.

Simon, David, creator/producer. *The Wire.* 2002. Home Box Office (HBO).

Singer, Peter. 2011. *Practical Ethics.* Cambridge: Cambridge University Press. https://doi.org/10.1017/CBO9780511975950.

Sirc, Geoffrey. 2002. *English Composition as a Happening.* Logan: Utah State University Press.

Sirc, Geoffrey. 2006. "Proust, Death, and Hip Hop in First-Year Composition." *Teaching English in the Two-Year College* 33 (4): 392–98.

Smitherman, Geneva. 1973. "'God Don't Never Change': Black English from a Black Perspective." *College English* 34 (6): 828–33.

Smitherman, Geneva. 1994. *Black Talk: Words and Phrases from the Hood to the Amen Corner.* Boston, MA: Houghton Mifflin.

Smyth, Melissa. 2015. "On Sentimentality: A Critique of Humans of New York." Warscapes. http://www.warscapes.com/opinion/sentimentality-critique-humans-new-york

Spigelman, Candace. 2001. "What Role Virtue?" *JAC* 21 (2): 321–48.

Squires, Judith. 2000. *Gender in Political Theory.* Maldon, MA: Polity.

Stoneman, Ethan. 2011. "Appropriate Indecorum Rhetoric and Aesthetics in the Political Theory of Jacques Rancière." *Philosophy & Rhetoric* 44 (2): 129–49. https://doi.org/10.1353/par.2011.0013.

Stotsky, Sandra. 1992. "Conceptualizing Writing as Moral and Civic Thinking." *College English* 54 (7): 794–808. https://doi.org/10.2307/378259.

Sullivan, Patricia, and James Porter. 1997. *Opening Spaces: Writing Technologies and Critical Research Practices.* Westport, CT: Ablex.

Sundararajan, Arun. 2016. *The Sharing Economy.* Cambridge: MIT Press.

Telofski, Richard. 2010. "Why Social Media Will Never Let BP Sleep." Triple Pundit. https://www.triplepundit.com/2010/07/rebrand-bp-logo-social-media-greenpeace/.

Thaler, Richard H., and Cass R. Sunstein. 2008. *Nudge: Improving Decisions about Health, Wealth, and Happiness.* New Haven, CT: Yale University Press.

Thomas, Zoe, and Tim Swift. 2015. "Who Is Martin Shkreli— 'The Most Hated Man in America'?" *BBC News.* http://www.bbc.com/news/world-us-canada-34331761.

3 Play Media. 2017. "Discovery Digital Networks: Video SEO Case Study." https://www.3playmedia.com/customers/case-studies/discovery-digital-networks/.

Ti, Andrew. 2013. "Closed Captioning." *Yo, Is This Racist?* Podcast audio, April 15. http://www.earwolf.com/episode/closed-captioning/.

Townley, Cynthia, and Mitch Parsell. 2004. "Technology and Academic Virtue: Student Plagiarism through the Looking Glass." *Ethics and Information Technology* 6 (4): 271–77. https://doi.org/10.1007/s10676-005-5606-8.

Townsend, Lucy. 2014. "How Much Has the Ice Bucket Challenge Achieved?" *BBC News Magazine.* http://www.bbc.com/news/magazine-29013707.

Tronto, Joan. 1987. "Beyond Gender Difference to a Theory of Care." *Signs* 12 (4): 644–63. https://doi.org/10.1086/494360.

Tronto, Joan. 2006. "Women and Caring: What Can Feminists Learn about Morality from Caring?" In *Justice and Care: Essential Readings in Feminist Ethics*, edited by Virginia Held and Carol W. Oberbrunner, 101–15. Boulder, CO: Westview.

Turkle, Sherry. 2011. *Alone Together: Why We Expect More from Technology and Less from Each Other*. New York: Basic Books.

UCB Comedy. 2010. "BP Spills Coffee." YouTube video, 2:48. Published June 9, 2010. https://www.youtube.com/watch?v=2AAa0gd7ClM.

Udo, John-Patrick, and Deborah I. Fels. 2010. "Universal Design on Stage: Live Audio Description for Theatrical Performances." *Studies in Translation Theory and Practice* 18 (3): 189–203.

Ulmer, Gregory. 1994. *Heuretics: The Logic of Invention*. Baltimore, MD: Johns Hopkins University Press.

Vallor, Shannon. 2010. "Social Networking Technology and the Virtues." *Ethics and Information Technology* 12 (2): 157–70. https://doi.org/10.1007/s10676-009-9202-1.

Vallor, Shannon. 2011. "Carebots and Caregivers: Sustaining the Ethical Ideal of Care in the Twenty-First Century." *Philosophy & Technology* 24 (3): 251–68. https://doi.org/10.1007/s13347-011-0015-x.

Vallor, Shannon. 2016. *Technology and the Virtues: A Philosophical Guide to a Future Worth Wanting*. Oxford: Oxford University Press. https://doi.org/10.1093/acprof:so/9780190498511.001.0001.

Vie, Stephanie. 2014. "In Defense of 'Slacktivism': The Human Rights Campaign Facebook Logo as Activism." *First Monday* 19 (4): n.p. http://firstmonday.org/article/view/4961/3868.

Viki. 2007. Social Media Platform. Founded by Razmig Hovaghimian, Changseong Ho, and Jiwon Moon. Accessed August 15, 2017. https://www.viki.com/?locale=en.

Vitanza, Victor J. 1990. "An Open Letter to My 'Colligs': On Paraethics, Pararhetorics, and the Hysterical Turn." *Pre/Text* 11 (3–4): 237–87.

Vitanza, Victor J. 1991. "Three Countertheses: A Critical In(ter)vention into Composition Theories and Pedagogies." In *Contending with Words: Composition and Rhetoric in a Postmodern Era*, edited by Patricia Harkin and John Schilb, 139–72. New York: Modern Language Association.

Vitanza, Victor J. 1997. *Negation, Subjectivity, and the History of Rhetoric*. Albany: SUNY Press.

Vivian, Bradford. 2000. "The Threshold of the Self." *Philosophy & Rhetoric* 33 (4): 303–18. https://doi.org/10.1353/par.2000.0029.

Walker, Jeffrey. 2000. *Rhetoric and Poetics in Antiquity*. Oxford: Oxford University Press.

Walters, Shannon. 2014. *Rhetorical Touch: Disability, Identification, Haptics*. Columbia: University of South Carolina Press.

Warner, Michael. 2005. *Publics and Counterpublics*. New York: Zone Books.

Warnick, Barbara. 2001. "Rhetorical Criticism in New Media Environments." *Rhetoric Review* 20 (1/2): 60–65.

Washeck, Angela. 2016. "A Push for Closed Captioning in the Digital Age." Mediashift. http://mediashift.org/2014/05/a-push-for-closed-captioning-in-the-digital-age/.

Weisser, Christian R., and Sidney I. Dobrin, eds. 2002. *Natural Discourse: Toward Ecocomposition*. New York: SUNY Press.

Welch, Kathleen E. 1999. *Electric Rhetoric: Classical Rhetoric, Oralism, and a New Literacy*. Cambridge: MIT Press.

Wharton University of Pennsylvania, Knowledge@Wharton. 2015. "Social Media Shaming: Can Outrage Be Effective?" http://knowledge.wharton.upenn.edu/article/social-media-shaming-can-outrage-be-effective/.

Whitford, Ben. 2013. "How Social Media Is Helping Galvanise the Greens." *Ecologist*. http://www.theecologist.org/node/1780506.

White, Eric Charles. 1987. *Kaironomia: On the Will-to-Invent*. Ithaca, NY: Cornell University Press.

Williams, Bernard. 1985. *Ethics and the Limits of Philosophy*. London: Fontana.

Williams, Bronwyn T. 2014. "From Screen to Screen: Students' Use of Popular Culture Genres in Multimodal Writing Assignments." *Computers and Composition* 34:110–21. https://doi.org/10.1016/j.compcom.2014.10.001.

Wilson, Elizabeth A. 2015. *Gut Feminism*. Durham, NC: Duke University Press. https://doi.org/10.1215/9780822375203.

Young, Abe Louise. 2010. "The Voices of Hurricane Katrina, Part I: What are the Ethics of Poetic Appropriation?" Poetry Foundation. https://www.poetryfoundation.org/article/239906.

Young, Iris Marion. 1990. *Justice and the Politics of Difference*. Princeton, NJ: Princeton University Press.

YouTube. 2016. "Use Automatic Captioning." https://support.google.com/youtube/answer/6373554?hl=en.

Zappen, James P. 2005. "Digital Rhetoric: Toward an Integrated Theory." *Technical Communication Quarterly* 14 (3): 319–25.

Zdenek, Sean. 2011. "Which Sounds Are Significant? Towards a Rhetoric of Closed Captioning." *Disability Studies Quarterly* 31 (3). https://doi.org/10.18061/dsq.v31i3.1667.

Zdenek, Sean. 2015. *Reading Sounds: Closed-captioned Media and Popular Culture*. Chicago, IL: University of Chicago Press. https://doi.org/10.7208/chicago/9780226312811.001.0001.

ABOUT THE AUTHORS

JARED S. COLTON is an assistant professor at Utah State University, where he teaches courses in rhetoric and technical communication. His research addresses the intersections of rhetorical theory, ethics, and politics, from concerns of pedagogy to social justice. His work has appeared in *Computers and Composition, Technical Communication Quarterly, Journal of Technical Writing and Communication, Rhetoric Review,* and other academic journals.

STEVE HOLMES is an assistant professor at George Mason University, where he teaches courses in digital rhetoric, rhetorical theory, and professional writing. He is the author of *Procedural Habits: The Rhetoric of Videogames as Embodied Practice* (Routledge 2017). Steve has previously published articles on videogames, contemporary political theory, trolling, augmented reality, software studies, tactical technical communication, and other related digital rhetoric topics.

INDEX